Praise for Ann Douglas'
Mother of All series:

Sleep Solutions for Your Baby, Toddler and Preschooler

"For sleep deprived Moms desperate to emerge from a bleary-eyed state of newborn or toddler exhaustion, help has arrived from parenting guru Ann Douglas."

—Stacy DeBroff, author of *The Mom Book: 4278 Tips from Moms for Moms* and the founder of MomCentral.com

"A one-stop, no-guilt answer book on sleep where *every* bleary-eyed parent can find wise, rational advice on any sleep issue from A to ZZZZZs."

—Paula Spencer, contributing editor to *Parenting* and *Baby Talk* magazines

The Mother of All Baby Books

"With humor, sensitivity, an easy, no jargon style, and a million 'extras' that the leading baby books on the shelves don't cover, Ann Douglas holds nothing back. Finally, a baby book written for women of my generation!"

—M. Sara Rosenthal, author of *The Breastfeeding Sourcebook* and founder of www.sarahealth.com

"*The Mother of All Baby Books* provides excellent advice for topics that are easily overlooked during the pregnancy/baby adventure. The real life examples do a superb job supporting these topics in addition to giving you creative ideas on how you can implement these helpful suggestions into your life."

—Sandra Gookin, co-author of *Parenting For Dummies* and *Parenting For Dummies, 2nd Edition*

The Mother of All Parenting Books

"This book has *all* the answers that are missing from other parenting books! It's honest, complete, well researched . . . and not preachy. Finally, a book I can hand to parents with confidence that they will not end up feeling guilty."

—Dr. Cathryn Tobin, author of *The Parent's Problem Solver*

"*The Mother of All Parenting Books* is a comprehensive guidebook designed to help moms and dads cope with the day-to-day demands of parenting. Because this very practical book is written in an easy-to-read, parent-friendly style, it is the kind of book parents can turn to again and again."

—Nancy Samalin, best-selling *Loving Your Child is*

D1506621

Medical Disclaimer

This book is designed to provide you with general information about some of the general food, nutrition, and mealtime behavior problems that babies, toddlers, and preschoolers may experience as well as some general health and medical conditions that may contribute to those problems. It does not contain medical advice. Rather, it is intended to provide information so that you can be a more informed health consumer and parent.

This book is not intended to provide a complete or exhaustive treatment of this subject, nor is it a substitute for advice from your physician, who knows you and your child best. Seek medical attention promptly for any specific medical condition or problem that your child may have and do not administer medication to your child without obtaining medical advice.

All efforts were made to ensure the accuracy of the information contained in this publication as of the date of writing. The author and the publisher expressly disclaim any responsibility for any adverse effects arising from the use or application of the information contained herein. While the parties believe that the contents of this publication are accurate, a licensed medical practitioner should be consulted in the event that medical advice is desired.

The information contained in this book does not constitute a recommendation or endorsement with respect to any company or product.

mealtime
solutions

The Ultimate No-Worry Approach™
for Each Age and Stage

for your
baby, toddler
and preschooler

ANN DOUGLAS

Author of The Mother of All® Pregnancy Books

WILEY

John Wiley & Sons Canada, Ltd.

CHAPTER 4:

Your Top Toddler Mealtime Mysteries Solved 99

CHAPTER 5

The Discriminating Diner: Feeding
Your Preschooler 126

food; (2) casserole is just a fancy word for disgusting. And, do you also remember swearing that there was no way you would ever let any kid of yours pull *that kind of stuff* once you became a grownup?

Who knows? Maybe you even managed to carry those "my kid will never be like that" fantasies well into adulthood, smiling smugly to yourself as you dined with other parents and their equally picky offspring, or when you spotted people who clearly should never have been allowed to be parents as they inflicted their unruly brats on other restaurant patrons. And then you became a parent yourself and your children refused to follow your blueprint for mealtime perfection. The baby became high-chair phobic, the toddler thought it was a big joke to try to eat your dinner instead of his own, and the preschooler decided she wanted to eat only those foods that she had seen advertised on TV. How could your visions of doing this food thing right have gone so terribly wrong?

Another Book about Feeding Babies, Toddlers, and Preschoolers?

YOU'RE PROBABLY WONDERING why I decided to chime in with my two cents on the subject of feeding kids. It's not as if there's a book shortage in this particular subject. Pretty much every parenting expert, cookbook author, nutritionist, and pediatrician on the planet has ventured into this turf, and if they haven't written a book on this subject yet, they're probably being chased down right this second by some publisher waving a book contract. The reason is obvious: parents are hungry for information on what it takes to get kids off to a healthy start nutrition-wise. And given that today's generation of kids are more overweight and less fit than ever before, the stakes have never been greater. But, still, that's no excuse for writing another book unless you think you have something unique to add to the discussion, so I had to think long and hard before I agreed to write this book. What would a book in this series bring to the table that would be of unique benefit to parents and their children? What did I have to say that would help other parents grapple with this big-stakes issue? Here's what I came up with as my reasons for tackling this project long before I ever sat down to write the first chapter of this book.

- **The Mom factor.** What has been missing from the bookstore shelves is a book that takes a truly mother-centered approach to the issue of feeding a young child—a book that taps into the considerable mother wisdom on this subject (after all, who knows more about feeding babies, toddlers, and preschoolers than moms) and that factors in all the worry and "mother guilt" that is so much a part of this issue for mothers. Just as previous generations of pregnancy books were guilty of overlooking the fact that pregnancy actually had something to do with the mom (e.g., it wasn't all about "the fetus"), food books have been guilty of being so focused on solving the child's feeding problem that they've forgotten to consider how breast-feeding problems, food refusal issues, and other feeding concerns affect a mother when feeding is so much a part of how mothers nurture their children. This, of course, ties into the entire childhood obesity issue, which can have its roots in the early years, and that mothers tend to feel particularly guilty about. These are important issues that deserve to be examined through the lens of motherhood.

- **No one-size-fits-all solution:** Rather than pretend that a one-size-fits-all mealtime solution—or variations on that same theme—will meet the needs of all parents and all children without taking into account the sometimes complex and messy variables that go into any parenting equation, this book:

  - provides you with a crash course in the basics of nutrition and eating during the baby, toddler, and preschooler stages so that you can understand what is happening to your child developmentally and ensure that your food expectations of your child are both age appropriate and realistic.

- ensures that menu ideas and suggestions reflect the day-to-day realities of busy parents as well as the typical preschool palate.

- gives you the low-down on specific strategies to increase the odds that a particular child will develop a healthy relationship with food.

- summarizes the best and most accurate nutrition information that was available as this book was going to print.

- includes a smorgasbord of checklists, charts, and other tools, including a handy food log, to help you troubleshoot your child's eating problems in a low-stress and parent-friendly way.

- provides you with an exhaustive list of suggested food and nutrition resources so you can stay on top of new developments in the exciting and ever-evolving world of food and nutrition.

- **The no-worry approach:** I can't eliminate all of the worry of being a parent (especially since food-related worries tend to be particularly insidious), but I can reassure you that other parents have experienced many of the same "normal" (but crazy-making) eating behaviors in their kids. And because this book contains ideas, tips, strategies, and stories from the more than 240 parents who agreed to be interviewed, it won't be me talking away throughout this entire book. Not only would that be boring, you'd only be getting my point of view as opposed to the collective wisdom of many parents of babies, toddlers, and preschoolers. (More about that in a minute.)

- **And as a bonus—no guilt:** I wish there was an official "guilt-free zone" sticker on the cover that would alert you that I'm not going to do a guilt number on you in this book. No bashing you because you let your child have a piece of chocolate cake on his first birthday—or because you didn't. Your parenting choices are your choices. Enough said. It's my job to provide you with the most accurate, unbiased information I can and to present it in a non-bossy way. That's the approach that made The Mother of All Books series a highly trusted information source for parents, so I'm going to stick with it in The Mother of All Solutions series as well.

So What Is This New Series about Anyway?

THE MOTHER OF All Solutions is the sister series to The Mother of All Books series. Like all siblings, they've got some things in common, but there are also some key differences. While the books in The Mother of All Books series are designed to follow each age and stage—*The Mother of All Pregnancy Books, The Mother of All Baby Books, The Mother of All Toddler Books,* and *The Mother of All Parenting Books* are each devoted to a particular chapter in your life as a mom or a mom-to-be—the books in The Mother of All Solutions series zero in on a key parenting problem that you may be facing at a particular stage of motherhood. The two kickoff titles in the series—*Mealtime Solutions for Your Baby, Toddler and Preschooler* and *Sleep Solutions for Your Baby, Toddler and Preschooler*—focus on two perennial challenges for parents with children under the age of three: encouraging healthy eating habits in young children right from day one and helping your child to become a great sleeper.

If you've read The Mother of All Books series, you know how central "mother wisdom" was to the success of that series. We're carrying on that tradition with The Mother of All Solutions. You can expect that same "real-world" tone and feel to these books: practical tips, ideas, and solutions that can only come from another mom or dad who is being worn down by a toddler who is into the third day of a macaroni-and-cheese food jag.

Caught the "dad"? We've got a growing number of dads providing input, too, because their perspective is truly invaluable. When your toddler's food whims are flip-flopping or your baby has been crying for three hours straight and no one is getting any sleep, it's easy for moms and dads to lose sight of the fact that they are playing for the same team. This series tries to bridge that gap by having both moms and dads actively engaged in the dialogue.

Want More Experts? We've Got Experts!

OF COURSE, THIS book wasn't based on the input from parents alone, although they really were the true experts driving the Mealtime Solutions mothership from start to finish. Not only did I conduct exhaustive research by pouring through all the leading nutrition and pediatric journals and reading thousands of food-related articles from science, parenting, and other magazines and newspapers published over the past 15 years or so (to say nothing of dropping an obscene amount of money in the food books aisle of my favorite bookstore), I also had the manuscript vetted by a panel of experts who were handpicked by me, not only because of their outstanding credentials and real-world experience, but also because they each brought a unique perspective to the technical review panel. You can "meet" the expert reviewers who offered equal measures of encouragement and great technical advice by flipping to the acknowledgments page of this book.

The Slightly Harried Parent's Quick Guide to This Book

IF YOU'RE TRYING to whip up dinner while reading this book, you probably want the low-down on how this book works and where you can find the information you need—and fast. Here's a quick overview. (You can find more details in the Table of Contents as well as a keyword guide in the Index.)

	This Section of the Book Focuses on ...	You'll Want to Read This If You Have a		
		Baby (Birth to Age One)	Toddler (Ages One and Two)	Preschooler (Ages Three and Four)
Chapter 1: What's on Tap?: In Praise of the Liquid Breakfast, Lunch, and Dinner	Reasons to breast-feed, getting breast-feeding off to a reasonably stress-free start, and more.	✓	✓	
Chapter 2: That Lovin' Spoonful: Introducing Solids	Introducing solid foods—the when and the how; also a guide to making your own baby food.	✓		
Chapter 3: Mr. Spaghetti Head: Added Tastes and Textures for Baby	Introducing your baby to added tastes and textures.	✓		
Chapter 4: Your Top Toddler Mealtime Mysteries Solved	Toddler mealtime strategies, snack tips, and more.		✓	
Chapter 5: The Discriminating Diner: Feeding Your Preschooler	Your top preschooler mealtime worries and concerns.			✓
Chapter 6: Dining in and Dining out	Timesaving mealtime tips and the secrets to dining out with young children.	✓	✓	✓

continued on p. 8

This Section of the Book Focuses on ...	You'll Want to Read This If You Have a		
	Baby (Birth to Age One)	Toddler (Ages One and Two)	Preschooler (Ages Three and Four)
Chapter 7: No More Food Fights — Strategies for parenting a "picky eater."		✓	✓
Chapter 8: When Your Child Is Sick — Nutrition and health concerns.	✓	✓	✓
Food and Nutrition Tools — In this section you'll find recipes for basic baby food purées; tips on combining purées; a baby food texture guide; meal and snack ideas for babies, toddlers, and preschoolers; moms' favorite online recipes (plus a few mom-invented recipes, too); a convenience food label decoder; a list of food staples for babies, toddlers, and preschoolers; and tips on adapting favorite family recipes to make them healthier.	✓	✓	✓
Reference Tools — A directory of organizations, on-line resources, and books about food and nutrition.			
• Appendix A: Directory of Organizations	✓	✓	✓
• Appendix B: Directory of On-line Resources	✓	✓	✓
• Appendix C: Further Reading	✓	✓	✓
Index	✓	✓	✓

Same Old, Same Old ...

IF YOU'VE READ the other books in this series, the look and feel of the book will be familiar. You'll even recognize a few of the ever-popular icons that alert you to noteworthy facts, figures, or the much-loved mom quotes.

 MOM'S THE WORD: Insights and advice from other parents.

 MOTHER WISDOM: Bright ideas, practical tips, pop culture tidbits, and more.

 FOOD FOR THOUGHT: Facts and figures related to the always fascinating subject of feeding young children.

 FRIDGE NOTES: Leads on food and nutrition resources that are definitely worth checking out.

So, as you can see, *Mealtime Solutions for Your Baby, Toddler and Preschooler* is quite unlike any other book about feeding children you may have read. It's comprehensive, thoroughly researched, fun to read, and based on real-world advice from other moms and dads who've done their time at the family dinner table, and who want to pass their best mealtime solution tips along to you. Now, that's something to raise a glass to, even if that "glass" happens to be a sippy cup that has been dragged through a plate of spaghetti a dozen times. Bon appetit!

Ann Douglas

P.S.

When you reach the final page of the last chapter of this book (go ahead, flip to the back—I won't tell anyone), you'll see that I am big on the idea of parents swapping ideas with other parents. I hope you'll pass along to some other slightly desperate parent some of the mealtime solutions that were helpful to you. I also hope that you'll write to me to pass along some of those tips so that I can ensure that

Table 1.1 (Continued)

How Breast-feeding Is Beneficial for Babies

Emotional health benefits for babies	Breast-feeding provides regular opportunities for skin-to-skin contact between mother and baby, encouraging emotional security and mother-child bonding.
Developmental benefits for babies	• Breast-feeding is the natural way to ease a baby's transition from life inside the womb to life outside the womb, and to encourage that baby's optimal development. • Breast-feeding promotes healthy cognitive development. School-age children who were breast-fed during infancy score higher on cognitive and intelligence tests than their formula-fed counterparts. • Breast-feeding encourages healthy eating habits. Breast-fed babies have greater control over the amount of food consumed at each serving, so breast-feeding may lay the groundwork for healthy eating habits.

How Breast-feeding Is Beneficial for Mothers

Physical health benefits for mothers	• Breast-feeding boosts oxytocin levels, thereby reducing the amount of postpartum bleeding and encouraging the mother's uterus to return to its pre-pregnancy size more rapidly. • Exclusive breast-feeding reduces the risk of anemia by delaying the return of the first post-pregnancy menstrual cycle by 20–30 weeks. • Breast-feeding reduces the rate of maternal obesity. Breast-feeding moms are more likely to return to their pre-pregnancy weight than mothers who are not breast-feeding. They are also less likely to become obese. • Breast-feeding delivers significant health benefits later in life. Women who breast-fed their babies are less susceptible to ovarian cancer, pre-menopausal breast cancer, and osteoporosis.
Emotional health benefits for mothers	• Breast-feeding can help to ease the transition to motherhood by making motherhood easier. Not only is it a more convenient method of feeding a baby, it's also a highly valuable mothering tool.

How Breast-feeding Is Beneficial for Mothers	
	• The hormones associated with breast-feeding (prolactin, oxytocin, and others) reduce anxiety and promote a sense of well-being (the much talked about breast-feeding high), an instinct to reach out to other mothers for support (the "tend and befriend" stress response), and a powerful bond with your baby.
Family planning benefits for mothers	Mothers who breast-feed their babies exclusively may also experience a delayed resumption of ovulation, which may allow for an increased gap between children.
How Breast-feeding Is Beneficial for Society	
Environmental benefits	Breast-feeding doesn't require packaging, electricity, or fuel. It's the ultimate just-in-time method of product delivery, with supply being perfectly timed to meet demand, and the product being manufactured right on site.
Economic benefits	• Breast-feeding reduces health costs to society because breast-fed babies are healthier than formula-fed infants. • Parents with breast-fed babies don't miss as many days of work because their babies are healthier. • Breast-feeding is less expensive. Formula-feeding costs four times as much when you factor in the cost of purchasing formula vs. the cost of the food a breast-feeding mother needs to eat in order to generate the additional calories needed to make milk for her baby.

Mothers soon start to appreciate other benefits of breast-feeding as well, which they might not have anticipated before they started.

Sharlene, 34, the mother of eight-month-old Makenna, focused on the immunological protections offered by breast-feeding when she was making her decision, but she doesn't think that's what she'll carry with her from her breast-feeding experiences. She explains: "Now that we have been nursing for a while, I think I will remember the bonding and quiet times the most. I love nursing because it gives me time with Makenna and allows me to give something to her that no one else can give."

FOOD FOR THOUGHT

While breast-feeding is the ideal feeding method for the majority of babies, there are some situations when breast-feeding is *not* recommended. Your health care provider is likely to advise against breast-feeding if:

- your baby is diagnosed with galactosemia (a rare genetic disorder in which babies are born without the liver enzyme required to process the simple sugar galactose, which is found in all kinds of milk, including breast milk)

- you are an illegal drug user

- you have untreated, active tuberculosis

- you have been infected with human immunodeficiency virus (HIV)

- you are using a medication that is not considered safe for use by breast-feeding mothers (e.g., radioactive isotopes, anti-metabolites, cancer chemotherapy agents) (If it is necessary for you to take medication while you are breast-feeding, your health care provider will weigh the benefits of breast-feeding against any known risks to the baby. In cases where a particular medication is not recommended for use by a breast-feeding mother, your health care provider may suggest an alternative medication that is less harmful.)

Jennifer, a 30-year-old mother of two, has discovered some far-reaching benefits to breast-feeding, noting that, for her, breast-feeding has become a powerful mothering tool: "Breast-feeding goes far beyond nutrition. I have used breast-feeding to help lull my babies to sleep when they were overtired and fussy, to keep them quiet when I needed to pay close attention to something (e.g., at medical appointments or on the phone) or out of courtesy to others (e.g., on airplanes), to relieve pain from vaccinations and other bumps, to soothe fears.... Countless times and for countless reasons, I have nursed my babies when they were not hungry. I think the convenience of having this amazing one-stop solution always at hand cannot be overestimated. I also love being able to go out with my baby and change my plans on a whim, staying out hours longer than expected, and not having to worry about having enough food for my baby."

MOM'S THE WORD

"My son was nine months old and on Christmas Eve developed a horrible fever. Christmas morning found us in the ER, and in our panic to get out of the house and to the hospital, we hadn't packed anything for my son to eat. Thankfully, I was still nursing him once a day at that point, and I was able to nurse him every hour or so while we waited the entire day in the ER for various tests to be performed. Not only was it comforting for him in a scary time, but it managed to keep his little tummy full—it isn't as if I could have pulled something out of the vending machines for him. And even though I had only been nursing once a day, my supply ramped right up to the amount needed to keep him hydrated and satisfied during a very long day."

—*Dani, 36, mother of two*

The convenience factor also scores heavily with many moms. "Breast-feeding is so much less time consuming than bottle-feeding (washing and sterilizing bottles, mixing formula, warming bottles, etc.)," says Erin, 30, mother of one. "It was so much better when baby was starving to just pop the boob in her mouth than to go through the process of getting a bottle ready."

Getting Off to a Reasonably Stress-Free Start

IN THEIR BOOK *Breastfeeding Made Simple: Seven Natural Laws for Nursing Mothers*, Nancy Mohrbacher, IBCLC, and Kathleen Kendall-Tackett, PhD, IBCLC, make the point that breast-feeding is an emotional, right-brain activity, not a totally rational left-brain activity that someone can master by studying a series of one-size-fits-all breast-feeding "rules": "The heavily left-brained, instructionally oriented way that many mothers learn to breastfeed ... can encourage [mothers and babies] to tune out their natural responses or to violate their instincts.... [This] can leave some others feeling incompetent, because it feels as if there is a list of ten thousand things they need to remember."

MOTHER WISDOM

Have your baby room in with you in order to maximize opportunities for breast-feeding in the night. The American Academy of Pediatrics' 2005 policy on breast-feeding recommends that "mothers and babies sleep in proximity to each other to facilitate breastfeeding." According to both the AAP and the Canadian Paediatric Society, it's safer to have your baby share your room rather than your bed.

This left-brained approach to learning how to breast-feed—hold your baby at a certain angle while trying not to poke your left nipple into baby's right eye—doesn't work particularly well for mothers. It irritates the baby, who resents being treated like a crash test breast-feeding dummy, and it leaves the mother feeling like an incompetent boob. Literally.

Here are some other strategies that can make the early weeks of breast-feeding a lot less stressful for you and your baby.

- **Take a moment to breathe before you pick up your baby.** If you relax and calm yourself before you start breast-feeding your baby, you'll be less likely to transmit stress vibes to your baby, who reacts very strongly to your mood and body language. You'll also find that the very physiology of breast-feeding works better when you're calm, cool, and reasonably collected. Your milk has a hard time letting down when your stress-o-meter is in overdrive.

- **Offer the breast when your baby is likely to be responsive.** That means learning to read the feeding cues that newborns make (e.g., rooting, which means turning her head whenever something touches her cheek, lip-smacking, or putting her hand in her mouth) and trying to feed her when she's calm and awake (as opposed to overly hungry and unhappy or so sleepy that she keeps dozing off at the breast).

- **Help your baby to achieve a good latch.** Find a nursing position that's comfortable for you and your baby. (Your baby's body should not be twisted and her feet should not be pressing against anything, or she'll be inclined to push off. If you apply too much pressure to her head, her chin may be pushed down against her chest, which makes swallowing difficult, or her nose may get pressed into your breast, which makes breathing a lot tougher for your baby.) Stimulate her to open her mouth wide by lightly stroking your breast against her chin and lips. Then pull her toward the breast and make sure that your nipple and areola find their way deep into your baby's mouth. You don't want her chomping down on your nipple. Not only is this painful for you, it also doesn't work well from your baby's point of view. Aim for what Mohrbacher and Kendall-Tackett refer to as "the comfort zone,"—a deep latch that allows for comfortable nursing for you and easy breast-feeding with a good milk flow for your baby.

- **Tune into the natural rhythms of life in the mom-and-baby zone.** There's a rise and fall of "the milk tide." Your milk supply is much more abundant in the morning than it is at night. And there are peaks and valleys in your energy levels that are tied to your sleep-wake cycle, the time you last ate, and your baby's sleep-wake-feeding cycles. You'll find it a lot easier to cope with the unpredictability of the early weeks of breast-feeding and motherhood if you learn to go with the flow.

- **Let the mommy marsupials teach you a trick or two about baby soothing.** It's hard to breast-feed a baby who is crying inconsolably (your baby's tongue will get in the way when you try to offer the breast!), so make like a mama kangaroo and use skin-to-skin time to soothe your baby. If you strip your baby down to her diaper and put her against your bare chest (either take your shirt off or slip her inside a loose-fitting shirt that's loose enough to cover yourself and your baby to keep the two of you warm), you can slip your baby between your breasts and allow her the comforting feel of being skin to skin against your chest. She'll feel your heartbeat, breathe your scent, and may even try to find her way to the breast on her own.

The Truth about Breast-feeding

SOME PEOPLE are reluctant to be totally frank with new moms about the potential challenges of breast-feeding, fearing that if they tell it like it is, a would-be breast-feeding mother might be inclined

Table 1.2 (*Continued*)

Problem	Type of Problem	Possible Solutions
		• Has breast-feeding been difficult for your baby? Is it possible he's so frustrated he's waving the white flag? Could he be struggling with a breast-feeding problem that you're not aware of—a poor latch, milk supply problems, etc.?
		• Is your baby responding to stress in the family? Babies are very tuned into the feelings of people they love.
		Provide reassurance to your baby and encourage him to warm up to the idea of breast-feeding again by having plenty of skin-to-skin contact.
		Offer the breast when your baby is sleepy or half asleep. He may be less inclined to refuse the breast. Don't get stressed or upset if he refuses the breast. Continue to offer and pump your breast milk in the meantime. You can feed it to him by an alternative means (ideally avoiding a bottle). You might want to try using a lactation aid taped to your breast (to provide your newborn with an immediate payoff for continuing to breast-feed) or to feed your baby breast milk from a medicine dropper or tiny shot glass-style baby cup. Your lactation consultant will discuss the pros and cons of these and other feeding options with you.

Breast engorgement	Your breast becomes overly firm as a result of increased circulation, your increased milk supply, and retained tissue fluid. Because your areola is overly firm, it makes it difficult for your baby to extract milk from your breast, which leaves you susceptible to developing sore nipples.	Apply warm compresses to your breasts right before breast-feeding in order to encourage milk flow. Use cold compresses in between feeding to reduce the amount of swelling in your breasts. Nurse frequently in order to reduce the amount of engorgement. Ideally, nurse your baby at least eight to 12 times each day. If your baby is not nursing often enough or draining your breasts at each feeding, use a breast pump to drain your breasts frequently and often. Watch for signs of a breast infection, including a fever or redness and breast soreness. Get in touch with your health care provider if your symptoms persist.
Inadequate milk supply	Most women who breast-feed their babies produce enough milk. If you're worried that you may or may not be producing enough milk for your baby, look for the following clues: • Day one: One wet diaper • Day two: Two wet diapers • Day three: Three wet diapers • Day four: Four wet diapers • After that point: Five to six wet diapers per day and at least three to four yellowish stools	If you need to build up your milk supply because your baby has been losing weight or not gaining weight adequately, your health care provider will likely recommend that you: • breast-feed your baby at least eight times per day and that you offer each breast at least once at each feeding and express milk after your baby has finished feeding in order to stimulate your breasts to produce more milk • focus on improving your baby's latch in case he's not getting very much milk for all the effort he's putting into nursing • keep your baby awake until he has nursed actively for at least 10 minutes at each breast

continued on p. 26

Table 1.2 (*Continued*)

Problem	Type of Problem	Possible Solutions
	If you are concerned that your baby may not be getting enough milk, talk to your health care provider. She may suggest bringing your baby in for a checkup so that baby's latch can be monitored, his weight can be checked, and he can be assessed for overall signs of health and well-being.	• talk to your health care provider about prescription and herbal products that can be used to boost your milk supply
Overabundant milk supply	You'll know that your baby is struggling to deal with your overabundant milk supply if he gulps, chokes, or pulls away as he is trying to nurse. Some babies become so frustrated in trying to deal with the huge volume of milk that they actually refuse to nurse.	Stick to one breast per feeding so that your baby receives more of the calorie-rich (and baby-satisfying) hind-milk that comes as your baby finishes nursing on each side. Pump to comfort on that side. If your baby is still struggling with your oversupply, start with that same breast at the next few feedings. Hand-express or pump some milk before you put your baby to the breast so your milk flow will be a little less powerful by the time your baby starts nursing. Nurse in the side-lying breast-feeding position so that your baby can let any excess milk dribble out of his mouth. He'll be less inclined to choke.

Flat or inverted nipples	Approximately 10 percent of women have flat or inverted nipples—a situation that can make breast-feeding more challenging for two reasons: (1) it is more difficult for the baby to latch on to the breast and (2) the nipple is more susceptible to injury.	Using a breast pump immediately prior to each nursing session can encourage inverted nipples to protrude long enough for babies to get a good latch.
Positioning problems	Shallow infant latch (baby is latching on to the nipple itself rather than on to the areola, the flat, pinkish area surrounding the nipple). This sets up a truly vicious circle: the baby has to work longer and harder to get milk out; baby is getting less milk from the breast, which causes milk production to drop; and mom's nipples are getting more sore, which may actually inhibit her letdown.	Make sure that you are breast-feeding your baby in a position that is effective for her and comfortable for you (seek help from a lactation consultant or other breast-feeding expert right away if you suspect a positioning problem).
Nipple trauma	If you don't use your breast pump as directed (e.g., it's set on too high a setting or you're using it for an extended period of time in the hope of extracting more milk from your breast), you could end up with sore nipples. You can also end up with this problem if you attempt to remove your baby from the breast while he's still actively nursing and you don't insert your baby finger to break the suction first.	Use your breast pump as directed and pay attention to your body's signals when you are pumping. If your breast pump is causing you pain or discomfort, it's time to stop pumping. You may need to reread the instructions or you may have a poorly designed pump. Not all breast pumps were created equal. Break the suction in your baby's mouth before you remove your baby from the breast.

continued on p. 28

Table 1.2 (Continued)

Problem	Type of Problem	Possible Solutions
Breast infection	If your nipples become cracked, bacteria or yeast can lead to a breast infection.	See your health care provider. You will require oral antibiotics to treat a bacterial breast infection or some sort of anti-fungal medication to treat a yeast-based breast infection. See also sore nipple tips above.
Mastitis	Mastitis is any inflammation of the breast, whether or not there is a fever involved. It typically starts out as a plugged milk duct, which feels like a tender spot or lump in your breast. If that plugged milk duct becomes infected, you'll start feeling very sick. You may develop a fever that is accompanied by symptoms of a breast infection (e.g., red streaks on your breast, a cracked nipple with pus, pus or blood in your milk). You'll also feel exhausted as if you've been hit by a huge body-blow to the system, which you have.	The best way to deal with a plugged milk duct is to keep the milk flowing, either via a nursing baby or via a breast pump. If your breast becomes engorged, your symptoms will only get worse. Having a warm bath or shower or soaking your breasts in a warm basin before you nurse can encourage the milk in your plugged milk duct to let down. You may also want to try massaging your breast in a circular motion, moving from your armpit to your nipple. And don't forget to experiment with different nursing positions. You may find that a nursing position that's a little out of the ordinary for you works wonders at extracting milk from that plugged milk duct. Cabbage leaves compresses work wonders, too. If your baby refuses to nurse on the affected side, pump on that side instead and continue to nurse from the unaffected breast. If nursing becomes too painful, you may find it helpful to take a pain medication. Avoid tight or restrictive clothing, particularly overly tight bras. Get plenty of rest so that your body can focus on fighting off the infection. This may mean taking your baby to bed and letting other people take care of you. Don't be afraid to ask for the help you need.

Thrush/yeast infections (*Candida albicans*)	This type of infection can sometimes be tricky to diagnose because the symptoms aren't always the same. Sometimes you'll notice some telltale white patches inside your baby's mouth, a white tongue (thrush), or a fiery-red yeast-based diaper rash. Your baby may also seem to be experiencing some pain or discomfort when he's nursing—like his mouth is sore. And if the yeast infection has spread to you as well, you're likely experiencing burning, shooting nipple pain. The skin of the areola may be red and shiny, scaly and flaky, or it may look perfectly normal. Your nipples may suddenly become irritatingly itchy, particularly after a nighttime feeding. And it's possible for you to experience nipple pain even if you can't see any symptoms of thrush in your baby's mouth, contrary to what many people believe.	Seek medical treatment for yourself, your baby, and your partner. (Yeast infections can be transmitted to your partner during sex.) Yeast can be a pain to get rid of, so talk to your health care provider about your various treatment options (nystatin cream or ointment, gentian violet, or anti-fungal creams).

continued on p. 30

Table 1.2 (*Continued*)

Problem	Type of Problem	Possible Solutions
		Special Circumstances: Issues Related to Mom
Raynaud's phenomenon	A sudden constriction of the arteries that causes particular body parts—typically the hands or feet, but it can occur in the nipple as well—to turn red, white, or blue. When you finish breast-feeding your baby, you'll experience a sudden, searing pain. You'll also notice that your nipple has lost its color. (Both the pain and the color change are temporary.)	Talk to your health care provider about the problems you have been experiencing. She may suggest that you take nifedipine, a medication that is helpful in managing this condition and that is compatible with breast-feeding.
Structural problems with the breasts	Structural breast problems that have been linked with possible milk production problems include *significantly* asymmetrical breasts (one breast is *significantly* smaller than the other and doesn't enlarge much during pregnancy or when your milk comes in), tubular breast deformity (the breasts are long and tubular, shaped like a cucumber rather than a cone) and hypoplastic breasts (an underdeveloped breast that does not have much glandular breast tissue).	Talk to your health care provider about your plans to breast-feed your baby so that you can obtain the necessary support to provide your baby with a full or partial breast milk supply.

Breast-augmentations reduction surgery	Certain types of breast-augmentation or reduction procedures can damage nerves in the breasts and cut the milk ducts, reducing the milk supply.	If you've had surgery on your breasts, find out the specifics of that surgery. Recent surgical advances have led to better outcomes for women who have gone on to breast-feed their babies. Your health care provider should be able to provide you with information about your odds of providing your baby with a full or partial milk supply. If you can't provide enough milk on your own, a lactation aid (basically a tube taped to your breast) can allow your baby to receive additional nutrition while breast-feeding.

Special Circumstances: Issues Related to the Baby

Exaggerated newborn jaundice	Exaggerated newborn jaundice is an extreme form of the normal newborn jaundice that occurs in about half of all newborns. In most babies, the jaundice appears on days two to five and takes care of itself, particularly if the baby is breast-feeding well because colostrum (the first milk a baby receives) acts as a laxative. This can help the baby to get rid of some of the bilirubin in his system. (Bilirubin is a byproduct of the break-down of the extra red blood cells that babies are born with.) If babies aren't feeding well (often because they are extra sleepy), babies can become severely jaundiced and even more sleepy, which can lead to even more feeding problems.	Breast-feed your baby often. Your health care provider will monitor your baby's bilirubin levels. Some babies need to be treated with pho-totherapy to help break down the bilirubin. This doesn't need to inter-fere with breast-feeding. Talk to your health care provider about how you can continue breast-feeding your baby while he is being treated.

continued on p. 32

Table 1.2 (*Continued*)

Problem	Type of Problem	Possible Solutions
		Special Circumstances: Issues Related to the Baby
Baby with reflux	Gastroesophageal reflux disease (GERD) occurs when stomach acids back up into the esophagus, damaging the delicate tissues. This can lead to extreme distress in babies, both during and after feedings. Your baby may cry during and after feedings and may experience bouts of extreme crying after he has fallen asleep because he is so uncomfortable when he is lying down.	Experiment with breast-feeding positions until you find one that works well for your baby. Generally, positions that keep the baby's head elevated higher than his bottom work best. Keep him in an upright position for at least half an hour following each feeding. Talk to your health care provider about whether she recommends a modified sleeping position for babies with GERD.
Premature baby	Premature babies may not all be capable of nursing at the breast or staying awake for a full feeding at the breast, which can make the early weeks or months of breast-feeding a little more challenging.	Start pumping as soon as possible so that your baby can benefit from your breast milk, even if he can't breast-feed right away. Your milk is uniquely designed to meet your premature baby's needs. It is higher in substances designed to protect your baby from infection and to give your baby's immune and digestive systems an added boost. It even varies in its chemical composition because Mother Nature knows that premature infants require a breast milk recipe that's higher in nitrogen, protein nitrogen, sodium, chloride, iron, and fatty acids than the milk that is manufactured for their full-term counterparts. Learn about the benefits of kangaroo care (skin-to-skin contact). Connect with other parents of premature babies.

Baby who is tongue-tied	If your baby makes clicking sounds while he is nursing, has trouble staying on the breast, has poor weight gain, or you experience a great deal of nipple pain even though your baby's latch appears to be good, it's possible that your baby is tongue-tied. This means that his frenulum (the stringy piece of membrane under his tongue) is unusually short.	Your baby's pediatrician or a specialist (typically an oral surgeon or an ear, nose, and throat specialist) will clip your baby's frenulum to treat this problem, which sounds much worse than it is. Because there aren't many nerves and blood vessels in the frenulum, it's a fairly simple, painless, and relatively blood-free procedure.
Baby with a physical condition or structural problem that makes breast-feeding more difficult (e.g., Down syndrome, cleft lip, or cleft palate)	A baby with Down syndrome may have difficulty with tongue thrusting, so he may have a little more difficulty establishing an initial latch. He may also tend to have low muscle tone in his facial muscles, which you can help compensate for by providing some chin support while your baby is breast-feeding. (Your lactation consultant can demonstrate some effective techniques.) A baby with a cleft lip is generally capable of breast-feeding if you use your thumb to plug the opening in the lip so that your baby can maintain suction while breast-feeding. A baby with a cleft palate (an opening in the palate) will likely require surgery before the baby is able to nurse at the breast and even then, partial breast-feeding may be a more realistic goal.	Seek help from a lactation consultant so that you can learn how to make breast pumping and breast-feeding work for you and your baby. Breast-feeding encourages the development of healthy facial muscles, which is important for all babies, but particularly those with low muscle tone in their facial muscles or structural abnormalities. If your baby has a cleft palate, talk to your lactation consultant about whether it might be helpful to have a palatal obturator (a mouth appliance that provides a firm surface at the roof of the mouth) made for your baby, or whether your baby would benefit from using a Haberman feeder (a bottle that can be adjusted for slower or faster flow and that is compression rather than sucking driven). In the latter case, you would pump breast milk and feed it to your baby via the Haberman feeder.

It Takes Time to Hit Your Breast-feeding Stride

Breast-feeding may be the most natural and convenient way of feeding a baby, but many moms need time to figure out what they are doing. Like any new dance partners, you and your baby need the chance to learn to read one another's cues and to respond to one another's rhythms while trying to figure out the basic dance steps at the same time.

During those early weeks—a period of round-the-clock marathon feeding sessions when you're flipping your baby from breast to breast, changing your baby's diaper, and getting little sleep before you start the whole cycle again—you may wonder if breast-feeding will always be this demanding and if your life will always be this chaotic. Fortunately, it won't. At around the six-week mark, the tide suddenly turns and things are looking up big-time.

"The first six weeks can be challenging, but after that something happens and it's amazing," says Bonnie, 36, the mother of one.

"I read somewhere that you should give breast-feeding 40 days before deciding if it was for you," adds Naomi, 36, the mother of one. "This was a fabulous piece of advice because it took about that long for me to be comfortable with breast-feeding, and reading the cues of my son."

Some of the lessons that breast-feeding teaches you—patience, persistence, and the ability to read your baby's cues—will serve you well during any stage of motherhood. Breast-feeding can even boost your confidence in your mothering abilities: "The process of learning to breast-feed my baby was very transformative for me as a mother," says Chelsea, 32, the mother of 15-month-old Rossignel. "I feel like it taught me how to take care of myself so I could provide for my child. The demands of nursing were something I never would have known I could meet until I just did it. I have a lot of confidence in my mothering thanks to nursing my baby."

MOM'S THE WORD

"I was surprised at how difficult and painful the initial learning-to-latch phase was. She was enthusiastic and fierce, earning her first nickname 'barracuda.' Some advice might be that breast-feeding is difficult at first, but much easier in the long run, while formula-feeding might seem easier at first, but gets more annoying."

—*Pam, 28, mother of one*

Having a Breast-feeding Goal Can Help You Stay the Course

Setting a breast-feeding goal for yourself can help to get you over the rough patches. That goal might be to breast-feed for six weeks or six months or for a year or until your baby weans herself, or it might simply be to try breast-feeding for today, and to see what happens next. All those breast-feeding goals are wonderful and worthy.

Ali, a 31-year-old mother of one, explains how her breast-feeding goal played out for her. "Some moms have a fixed goal in mind ('I'm going to breast-feed for an entire year') other moms decide to take a wait-and-see approach. My mother and grandmother couldn't breast-feed, but I decided to give it my best shot, but not put unnecessary pressure on myself. I had no fixed idea of how long I would breast-feed for as I didn't even know if I would be able to breast-feed. Once it was successful, I was too cheap and lazy to switch to formula and decided to breast-feed until he was able to drink whole milk from a cup."

Michelle, a 30-year-old mother of two, was motivated by a picture in her head: "I saw the picture of the babies nestled at the breast and wanted that. With Ava we had a very rocky start and I spent a lot of my time at the local baby clinic (who also helped breast-feeding mothers) and I seem to need their support to tell me that I was doing a good job and Ava was thriving and to go home and do it for another couple days and come back. Before I knew it, it was six weeks and it got easier, and I ended up letting her wean herself at 23 months. Now I share the same wonderful bond with Elise, who is now eight months."

The Pressure to Breast-feed Can Be Very Overwhelming

The tide has definitely turned in the breast-feeding vs. formula-feeding debate. While a decade or two ago, you could find plenty of allies in the room if you "went public" with your decision to formula-feed your baby, today it's a lot more difficult to find a like-minded mom in your prenatal class, or at least a like-minded mom who's willing to admit to anyone other than her best friend (and perhaps not even her best friend) that she is intending to formula-feed her baby.

Kelly, a 29-year-old mother of two, definitely felt that she was swimming against the tide by making a conscious decision to bottle-feed her children, and that she'd been stamped with the "bad mother" label as a result of her decision. "I was not comfortable with the idea of breast-feeding and it caused me a great amount of anxiety, so I researched some formulas and felt that they would be a better choice than forcing myself to do something that I didn't really want to. I agree with the benefits of breast-feeding, but I also think someone should also promote the fact that there is nothing wrong with you as a mother if you choose to bottle-feed."

Mary Lynn, a 35-year-old mother of one, also feels that mothers are judged—often severely—by whether or not they breast-feed their babies, a decision that is sometimes entirely out of their hands. "I do not judge moms who decide that formula-feeding is the route they need to take. At the same time, I don't think I was capable of cutting myself slack in quite the same way. One of the things that kept me pumping and bottle-feeding all those weeks was that I felt that I would be a failure if I switched to formula. So in a way the pressure that I felt to breast-feed helped me stick with it till baby took to the breast herself. However, it also caused me a great deal of anxiety when I thought that baby would never take to the breast and I would have to switch to formula-feeding. I cried a lot in those first few weeks after my daughter was born, thinking I was a failure."

Lisa, 29, mother of one, puts it in even starker terms: "The shame that surrounds bottle-feeding can make you go crazy. If breast-feeding works, fantastic. If you have trouble, give it your best shot and move on. Your sanity and your child's health are more important than your need to be the perfect, breast-feeding mom. Sometimes it just doesn't work out."

What makes the rush to judge all the more frustrating is that sometimes the practical advice and hands-on help you need to make breast-feeding work for you isn't always there when you need it most: "No one covered the trauma of waiting for one's milk to come in, the panic of babies that are starving for the first time in their lives, and how lactation consultants don't work weekends where I'm from," recalls Laura, a 29-year-old first-time mother.

So what do you do if you're forced to make some hard choices about how to feed your baby? You come up with the best solution given the realities of your situation.

Karen, a 34-year-old mother of two, explains how she made the decision to start supplementing with formula, which wasn't in her original breast-feeding plans. "I had to let go of the idea of solely breast-feeding early on. My son was colicky, and I had postpartum depression, and being so sleep-deprived and worried about how much Jake was eating was just too much. I finally made the decision

---

📢 **MOM'S THE WORD**

"We tried breast-feeding for the first three months and we were both miserable. Because I felt so much pressure to nurse, I put off switching. When I did switch, it was like I had a different child. I felt a lot of guilt over this switch and didn't read anything anywhere that supported this decision. I agree that breast-feeding is best for the baby, but there needs to be support out there for the mothers who can't, or just don't want to, breast-feed."

—*Emily, 29, mother of one*

to supplement with bottles when he was three months old. I just couldn't keep breast-feeding exclusively. I needed to sleep at night (my nice hubby offered to give the baby bottles so I could sleep through the night some nights and that was such a boost to my sanity), and I needed to know that Jake had eaten and wasn't screaming because he was hungry (because he screamed for hours). I think you need to do what makes you feel sane as a parent, and try not to feel too guilty if you are unable to solely breast-feed. There are plenty of people out there who will make you feel like a less-than-perfect mother for supplementing with bottles, but rest assured there are plenty of babies out there who grow into vibrant, healthy adults who were bottle-fed from birth. It is much more important that you take care of yourself, and if breast-feeding feels too difficult for whatever reason, supplement with bottles of breast milk or formula."

Top Breast-feeding Questions

HERE ARE SOME REASSURING answers to the breast-feeding questions that may be keeping you up at night.

How Can I Tell Whether or Not Breast-feeding Is Actually Working?

Lactating moms have to use sensible methods of measuring babies' milk intake. Here's what to look for:

- You can hear your baby making swallowing sounds while she is nursing.

- Your baby is breast-feeding eight to 12 times every 24 hours.

- Your baby is producing six wet diapers and a couple of very full bowel movements every 24 hours (bowel movements can vary quite a lot from baby to baby, so don't panic about this particular wellness sign if your baby is otherwise thriving; discuss her patterns with her health care provider).

- Your baby is gaining weight. (It's normal to lose weight during the first few days after the birth, but this initial weight loss should turn around quickly as breast-feeding becomes established.)

Do I Need to Introduce a Bottle to My Breast-fed Baby?

It depends. If you expect to be away from your baby for extended periods of time (e.g., long enough that your baby may miss a feeding), you may want to consider introducing a bottle. While there are other methods of feeding a breast-fed baby when mom is unavailable, they aren't as convenient as bottle-feeding. These methods include feeding your baby from:

- a miniature cup that is designed for this purpose (Medela sells such a cup)
- a spoon
- a dropper
- a sippy cup with a soft spout
- a lactation aid (a tube that can be taped to your breast or someone else's finger)

There are other ways to work around the bottle issue: "I would take my husband with me where I needed to go and nurse there just before we got separated and have him bring my baby back about when I was done," recalls Chelsea, 32, mother of one. "That way I saved the travel time and didn't have to factor it in to how long I was gone. Also, my baby usually went longer stretches between feedings in the morning and cluster-fed in the afternoons, so it was always easier to schedule separations in the morning."

If you plan to introduce a bottle to your breast-fed baby, you may find that your baby is most willing to accept the bottle if you introduce the bottle around age three to four weeks. (You don't

---

FOOD FOR THOUGHT

Approximately 70 percent of breast-fed babies will willingly take to the bottle with great gusto. Another 26 percent of babies will accept a bottle eventually after much hard work and coaxing on your part. And 4 percent are absolute bottle refusniks. You can empty your bank account buying every brand of bottle and nipples on the market, but your baby has already established her feeding preference: Brand Mom.

want to introduce the bottle any earlier than this, however, in case your baby finds it confusing to switch back and forth from breast to bottle, nor do you want your baby to develop a preference for the bottle, which can happen because it's easier for a baby to get milk out of a bottle than to nurse at the breast.)

You shouldn't feel pressured to introduce a bottle around this age, however. Many lactation consultants and moms insist that it's possible to introduce a bottle later on or to avoid introducing a bottle altogether.

"I had done enough research to know that a baby might never actually need to drink out of a bottle, even when very young," notes Stephanie, 30, mother of a seven-month-old. "So I decided a long time ago that the cup would be the route I'd take and I had the luxury of being able to avoid the bottle altogether. Plus, I've had a fair number of breast-feeding difficulties and I decided that I didn't want to jeopardize our breast-feeding relationship any further by introducing a bottle."

Of course, that's simply not an option for some families, particularly dual-income families who will be leaving baby with a caregiver at a fairly young age. If you are looking for some practical tips for encouraging your breast-fed baby to accept a bottle, you may find some of these suggestions helpful.

Give some thought to the time and place and who will be offering the bottle. Some babies will protest heavily:

- if mom offers the bottle
- if mom is anywhere in the building when the bottle is being offered
- if they are too hungry by the time the bottle is offered
- if they are held in their usual nursing position
- if they are being fed in the usual nursing chair
- if they hate the particular style of bottle or nipple you are using; borrow different types of bottle and/or nipple styles from friends with bottle-fed babies if your baby is rejecting the bottle outright; your baby may not be objecting to the bottle as much as the style of bottle or nipple you are offering

≥🔊 **MOM'S THE WORD**

"We tried a few nipples that seemed hard for her to manage, but then I had a brain wave and ended up using the bottle nipple that was most similar to her familiar soother."

—*Pam, 28, mother of one*

- if you are offering something other than breast milk in the bottle; you might as well stick with a beverage you know your baby likes when you're trying to introduce a new feeding method

Of course, for every rule there's a baby willing to prove the rule-maker wrong: "I tried all the literature suggestions of leaving the house and having my daughter fed by my husband, mother-in-law, and mother and none worked. She took the bottle from me. Word of advice for other parents—try what you know and feel to be best for your child," says Lolita, 25, mother of one.

Realize That There Can Be Some Fallout from the Bottle-Breast Transition

"Kaitlyn took to the bottle somewhat," recalls Karyn, a 34-year-old mother of two. "The problem I had was every time we gave her a bottle, the next breast-feeding session, my sweet daughter turned into a little vampire! She would bite me very hard. Thankfully, she didn't have teeth. Her latch was not quite right either. After conferring with a lactation consultant, and after having endured my daughter's biting more than anyone should have to endure that kind of pain, I gave up on the bottle. It just wasn't worth the effort to retrain her after every bottle feed."

Watch your baby for cues. "If you want to breast-feed, but you find that your baby is getting too comfortable with the bottle because it is less work for him or her to get the milk, then stick to the breast alone or offer bottles only occasionally," suggests Judy, a 32-year-old mom of one.

When Is the Best Time to Pump?

If you plan to pump and store milk for your baby (as opposed to offering your baby formula), the best time to pump is in the morning when your milk supply is most abundant. (You can pump throughout the day if you need to collect a lot of milk, but if you only need to stockpile the occasional extra serving of milk, then morning is the time to do it.) Try to time your pumping session for 30–60 minutes after your baby finishes nursing. With any luck, this will be about an hour before she wants to nurse again.

You can store your expressed breast milk (EBM) in the refrigerator for up to eight days, in the freezer compartment of your refrigerator for three to four months, or in the deep freeze for six to 12 months. See familydoctoring/828.xml for more about breast milk storage.

I Heard That the AAP Is Recommending That All Babies Be Put to Bed with a Pacifier, But I've Also Heard That Pacifiers Interfere with Breast-feeding. Can You Explain This?

In late 2005, the American Academy of Pediatrics updated its existing policy on sudden infant death syndrome. One of the most controversial recommendations stated that infants should be offered a pacifier when they go to sleep at bedtime and naptime. The AAP qualified this recommendation by noting that breast-fed babies should not be offered the pacifier until age one month, in order to give breast-feeding an opportunity to become well established. Pacifiers are believed to help protect infants against SIDS by preventing babies from drifting into an overly deep sleep. Breast-feeding advocates who are opposed to this recommendation have argued that breast-fed babies do not need pacifiers to receive this type of stimulation because they already receive the protective effect that comes from suckling during the night. The Academy of Breastfeeding Medicine responded to the AAP recommendation by noting that, "Pacifiers would only be of possible benefit to infants lacking in the natural opportunity of night-time suckling (breast-feeding)."

Can Foods That I Eat Make My Baby Fussy?

In some cases, yes. Babies can have pretty discriminating tastes. Some of the foods that can make babies edgy, cranky, or downright colicky include caffeine (but you have to overdo it with most babies to get a reaction, so don't give up your Starbucks habit yet); citrus fruits (look for a runny nose, diarrhea, a skin rash, hives, or excessive spitting up, fussiness); dairy products (gas, rashes, a runny nose, congestion, fussiness); eggs, gluten (wheat, rye, oats), corn, fish, nuts, soy (diarrhea, rashes, hives, runny nose, spitting up); gassy vegetables (onions, garlic, broccoli, cauliflower); spicy foods (which can change the flavor of your milk). Don't go crazy trying to eliminate all of these foods from your diet or you'll be on the "Grumpy Mom Diet" before you know it. Try to figure out what might have caused the problem and then eliminate that food or food group for two weeks. Then gradually reintroduce it and see if you notice a change in your baby's symptoms.

Do I Have to Give Up All of My Vices While I'm Breast-feeding?

It depends on what those vices are.

While most health authorities don't have a problem with a nursing mother using alcohol in moderation (most recommend that you limit yourself to one drink per day and that you have that drink right after a feeding), drinking excessive amounts of alcohol while you are breast-feeding can be harmful to your baby, who can be affected by alcohol through your breast milk. Alcohol can make your baby extra sleepy, which can interfere with breast-feeding; and drinking excessively can increase the risk of SIDS if you are bed-sharing. (See Appendices A and B.)

And smoking is definitely a vice that's worth giving up. Not only does second-hand smoke increase your baby's risk of SIDS, it lowers your milk production, interferes with your milk ejection, brings down your prolactin levels (your feel-good mother hormones), and increases the incidence of infant colic. The verdict? Very bad news all around.

How Long Should I Breast-feed My Baby?

Both the American Academy of Pediatrics and the Canadian Paediatric Society recommend that babies be exclusively breast-fed for six months, and breast-fed even after solid foods have been introduced, for as long as mother and baby are willing (see Table 1.3). While your baby is mastering the mechanics of eating solids and getting used to all those new tastes and textures, breast milk will continue to be the mainstay of her diet.

Do Breast-fed Babies Need to Drink Water?

You don't need to worry about giving your baby water until she's eating a variety of solid foods. At that point, you can give her a bit of water in a sippy cup so that she can practise drinking from it. Even then, this is more about sippy cup skill building than about her needing water per se. She'll still be getting plenty of liquids from her diet—from breast milk as well as from the puréed "solid" foods she'll be noshing on by this time.

Should You Wean from Breast to Formula or Straight to Cow's Milk?

Infants who stop breast-feeding before age 12 months need to switch to iron-fortified infant formula rather than cow's milk. A baby's system isn't mature enough to digest all the minerals and proteins in cow's milk, plus there's an increased risk that your baby will become sensitized (hypersensitive) to the milk protein in cow's milk if you switch to cow's milk too soon.

What Works Best When It Comes to Breast-feeding Twins? Breast-feeding Them Both at Once or One after Another?

"I decided long before the birth that I would always feed the twins at the same time—tandem in the football hold. Always," recalls Nancy, 38, the mother of three-year-old twins Trevor and Ben. "I can say I did that 99 percent of the time. Why? My intentions were to (1) get them on the same/similar schedule and (2) open up some

Table 1.3

Key Breast-feeding Recommendations from the American Academy of Pediatrics and the Canadian Paediatric Society

	American Academy of Pediatrics (AAP)	Canadian Paediatric Society (CPS)
Basic philosophy regarding breast-feeding	"Human milk is the preferred feeding for all infants, including premature and sick newborns, with rare exceptions."	Recommends exclusive breast-feeding for "healthy, term infants."
How long to breast-feed your baby exclusively (no supplements other than necessary vitamins, minerals, and medications)	For the first six months	For the first six months
How long to breast-feed your baby (both exclusive breast-feeding and non-exclusive breast-feeding, after solid foods have been introduced)	The AAP recommends that breast-feeding continue for "at least 12 months, and thereafter for as long as mutually desired."	According to the CPS, "breast milk is the optimal food for infants, and breast-feeding may continue for up to two years and beyond."
When to introduce solid foods	Solid foods should be introduced during the second six months, at which point they are treated as complementary foods, not foods that are meant to replace breast milk: "Gradual introduction of iron-enriched solid foods in the second half of the first year should complement the breast milk diet."	Solid foods should be introduced during the second six months, at which point they are treated as complementary foods, not foods that are meant to replace breast milk: "Nutrient-rich complementary foods, should be introduced at six months."

continued on p. 46

Table 1.3 (*Continued*)

	American Academy of Pediatrics (AAP)	Canadian Pediatric Society (CPS)
Vitamin D and iron	Vitamin D and iron supplements may be required by select groups of infants. Babies whose mothers are vitamin D-deficient or who aren't exposed to adequate sunlight may require vitamin D supplements. The AAP recommends 200 IU of vitamin D for all breast-fed babies, starting at two months of age. Formula-fed infants receive vitamin D through infant formula. Babies who have low iron stores or who are anemic may require iron supplements.	"Breast-fed babies should receive a daily vitamin D supplement until their diet provides a reliable source or until they reach one year of age." It's important to include iron-rich foods (e.g., iron-fortified infant cereals) when you're introducing solids to your baby's diet.

Sources: American Academy of Pediatrics—Work Group on Breastfeeding: Breastfeeding and the Use of Human Milk. AAP Policy, Revised February 1, 2005; Margaret Boland, MD, FRCPC Chair, Nutrition Committee, Canadian Paediatric Society, "Exclusive Breastfeeding Should Continue to Six Months," *Pediatrics & Child Health* 10(3) (2005):148.

time so I could eat, shower, sleep. (Ha!) I started on Day 2 that way and stuck with it and it worked well for us. They still always eat at the same time. I just was not prepared to go back and forth and back and forth between babies and never get a break."

If you find it's difficult to get your babies to eat at the same time—e.g., you'd have to work hard at rousing the second twin while the first twin was screaming to be fed!—you may need to feed the babies one after the other. Either way, you may find it helpful to keep track of who ate when. Some moms of twins draw a line down the center of a piece of paper and assign each half of the page to each twin. You note who nursed when and on which breast. Since they are likely to have their own individual nursing patterns, you'll likely switch babies and breasts from feeding to feeding.

Guilt Marketing: The Formula for Breast-feeding Success?

EVEN THOUGH SCIENTISTS have discovered all kinds of amazing ingredients in breast milk in recent years and formula company product development engineers have done their best to replicate those same ingredients in their products, no one has or ever will crack the recipe for breast milk. Breast milk is, after all, a custom-tailored product that is uniquely manufactured to meet the needs of each individual baby at any given time.

Health authorities are no longer positioning formula-feeding as the second-choice method to putting an infant to the breast. They're encouraging mothers who haven't had success with breast-feeding (as in "baby-at-the-breast" breast-feeding) to consider other options to ensure that their babies benefit from breast milk, if not direct mom-and-baby breast-feeding. "Many parents believe that if breast-feeding isn't working, formula is the next choice," explains Bonnie, a 30-year-old mother of two. "Not true. Expressed breast milk is second choice, milk from a milk bank is third choice, and formula is fourth on the list of healthiest ways to feed your baby."

Di, 28, who is currently expecting her second child, isn't so sure that all parents are getting that message clearly enough—that saying "breast is best" doesn't tell parents what they really need to know. "I think new parents definitely need to understand that not only is breast better, but formula is inferior. I don't think the breast-feeding advocates can often say that for fear of making formula-feeding parents (especially mothers) feel guilty. Unfortunately, implying that something is just better doesn't always get the message across. People don't always want to do what is best because that requires more effort. If they can settle with okay, they'll do it. Parents also need to realize that breast-feeding is not always easy and doesn't always come naturally, at least initially. They really need to do their research and build a support network in order to ensure success."

Doris, a 50-year-old mother who recently adopted a 19-month-old toddler from China, points out that there's a serious downside to taking that approach—trampling on one set of mothers in order to reassure another set of mothers that they made the right choice. "I realize the great benefits to breast-feeding, but for those of us whose children never had a choice, I think you want to tread carefully to avoid scaring us into thinking our children will never measure up or be as healthy because they were unable to have the best start."

Cheri, a 29-year-old mother of two, also prefers less black-and-white thinking when it comes to infant feeding methods. She's found a way to combine both breast-feeding and formula-feeding with her youngest child, who is now seven months old. "I think the decision to breast-feed or bottle-feed is a very personal one and one where the whole family needs to be taken into consideration, not just the new baby. With Kalissa, I really wanted to try, but I was scared of becoming depressed again. So, in conjunction with my psychiatrist, I decided to try and breast-feed, but bottle-feed at night as well to allow my husband to get up with her so I could get enough sleep, as sleep deprivation can be a causal factor in post-partum depression. She takes both the bottle and breast like a pro: no nipple confusion here."

It's a solution that's familiar to Jennifer, 25, mother of two. "I breast-feed my second, but use formula once a day. Moms need to know it doesn't have to be all or none: you can successfully do both."

MOM'S THE WORD

"I knew that breast-feeding was the number-one choice for feeding infants so I never even considered formula. Parents need to know that formula-feeding is not as good as breast-feeding. Yes, it's an option, but it is one that may have consequences for your baby and child. It really needs to be fully researched by parents. I don't think many parents make an informed choice."

—*Bonnie, 30, mother of two*

The Not-So-Secret Formula: What's on the Infant Formula Menu?

YOU'VE MADE the decision to offer your baby formula, so how do you choose a formula?

While the number of choices may seem overwhelming, your formula options basically amount to the following.

- **Milk-based formulas:** Milk-based formulas are recommended for full-term and pre-term infants who don't have any special nutritional needs. They are made from regular cow's milk, but much of the protein found in cow's milk has to be removed so that babies' livers and kidneys can digest the formula. There is also a new generation of hydrolyzed cow's milk formulas available for babies who have had difficulty digesting the protein in cow's milk. (The protein is predigested.)

- **Soy protein formulas:** Soy formulas are recommended for infants who are lactose intolerant, who have a milk-protein allergy, or who cannot drink standard cow's milk-based formula for other (religious or cultural) reasons. These formulas are derived from soy protein rather than cow's milk protein. Soy protein is not a suitable choice for all infants, however, as some babies are allergic to soy and some animal studies have indicated that exposure to soy may have long-term effects on the fertility and sexual development of rats. (No such effects have been found in humans, but these kinds of studies tend to make people, especially parents, understandably nervous, so some parents have decided to steer clear of soy for now.)

- **Formula for premature infants:** These types of formulas are designed to encourage rapid growth in premature babies.

- **Specialized formulas:** There are a variety of specialized formulas designed to meet the needs of infants with metabolism problems, heart disease, and other medical conditions.

Some of the more specialized formulas are available only by doctor's prescription.

Most formulas are fortified with iron (critical for infant development) and some manufacturers are now adding DHA (docosahexaenoic acid) and ARA (arachidonic acid), also known as omega 3 and 6 fatty acids. These fatty acids are known to contribute to brain and eye development; DHA and ARA naturally occur in breast milk.

Shaken and Stirred

Some babies have become seriously ill because their parents didn't understand how to mix, store, and heat infant formula. If you intend to give your baby infant formula, review the instructions below and carefully research the formula preparation instructions for each brand of formula. Here are the key points to remember:

- **Read the formula preparation instructions carefully.** If you over-dilute your baby's formula, she won't be getting enough calories per serving. If her formula is under-diluted, your baby's biochemistry could be thrown seriously out of whack, leading to dehydration and kidney problems.

- **Pay careful attention to hygiene when you're preparing and storing infant formula.** Sterilize all feeding equipment until your baby is at least five months old. Boil your formula-making supplies for about five minutes. Then tightly seal and refrigerate the prepared bottles of formula in the refrigerator. Use all formula within 24 hours. Discard any unfinished formula from your baby's bottle.

- **Don't change from one formula to another, just because a particular brand is on sale.** If you find a brand that agrees with your baby, stick with that brand. It's worth paying a little extra to give your baby some gastrointestinal stability.

MOTHER WISDOM

While baby-care experts used to tell mothers to feed formula-fed babies on a schedule, that way of thinking went out of vogue a long time ago, so don't watch the clock. Watch your newborn for signs of hunger: lip-smacking, rooting behaviors (turning her face from side to side in search of a food source), and trying to shove her thumb or fist into her mouth. If you miss those cues, your baby will give you a slightly less-subtle sign, a full-fledged wail that says, "Feed me now!"

Bottle-Feeding Basics

- **Don't heat your baby's bottle in the microwave.** As tempting as it may be to opt for the speedy route, the safest way to heat a bottle is in a pan of hot water. If you heat a bottle in a microwave oven, your baby's mouth could be scalded by a "hot spot" of liquid.

- **Use a baby-friendly feeding position.** When it's time to feed your baby, hold her in the cradle position (neck cradled in the crook of your arm with her head tilted back slightly). Hold her bottle up so that the nipple is full of liquid, which will minimize the amount of air that your baby swallows during a feeding. Burp your baby frequently during the early weeks to get rid of any air that your baby swallows during a feeding.

- **Never prop a bottle.** Not only does it pose a choking hazard, it deprives you and your baby of time that might otherwise be spent cuddling and getting to know one another.

FOOD FOR THOUGHT

Some babies have become seriously ill—and a few have even died—due to outbreaks caused by a bacterium known as *e. sakazakii* in powdered infant formula. The outbreaks led Health Canada to recommend that infants with compromised immune systems or those in intensive care be fed only liquid infant formula. (See Appendix B.)

FRIDGE NOTES

Want to dig a little deeper into infant nutrition? The information at the back of the book will help you make informed feeding decisions for your baby. The food tools provide you with basic recipes and meal ideas geared to your baby's feeding stage, and the appendices list useful organizations, websites, and books.

Is Your Baby Ready for Solids?

THE AMERICAN PEDIATRICS Association and the Canadian Paediatric Society both recommend introducing solids at age six months. Does this mean that every baby in North America wakes up on his half-year birthday craving a hefty bowl of infant cereal? Of course not. Babies achieve feeding-related milestones when they are ready, not when someone else thinks they should be ready. This means that some babies will be ready for cereal ahead of schedule, while others will be pushing the cereal bowl away for a few extra weeks. Of course, you don't want to overshoot or undershoot the mark by too far. Here's why.

Starting too early. Introducing solids too early (perhaps in the mistaken belief that doing so will help your baby to sleep through the night sooner):

- increases the risk of choking because your baby isn't developmentally ready to chew and swallow food
- increases the odds of your baby developing food allergies, particularly if you have a family history of food allergies
- reduces the amount of breast milk or formula that your baby is receiving during a period when these are the preferred forms of nutrition for infants
- may cause your baby to experience gastrointestinal discomfort if she isn't ready for solids quite yet
- increases her life-long risk of becoming overweight or obese (research has shown that large infants or infants who grow rapidly during the first two years of life face an increased risk of becoming obese children and adults).

FRIDGE NOTES

While most dietitians and pediatricians continue to recommend single-grain iron-fortified infant cereals as baby's first foods (particularly if there are a history of allergies in your family), some pediatric health authorities argue that babies over age six months can eat a wider variety of foods than most parents feel comfortable offering to their babies. The Start Healthy Feeding Guidelines for Infants and Toddlers recommend meat as a possible alternative first food, for example, because it also provides an excellent source of iron. See "Some Advice from the Start Healthy Feeding Guidelines" ww.kidsnutrition.org/consumer/nyc/vol_2004_3/StartHealthyGuidelines2.html and "Experts Seek to Debunk Baby Food Myths" for more on the first foods debate www.msnbc.msn.com/id/9646449/.

Waiting too long. If you wait too long to introduce solid foods:

- Your baby may become resistant to trying solid foods and have difficulty learning to chew. There's a specific window of opportunity when it comes to starting babies on solids. If you don't start offering solid foods to a baby before age nine months, it's a lot more difficult to get that baby to learn how to eat solid foods.

- Your baby needs an external source of iron now that the stores of iron that he was born with have been depleted. This is why infant cereals are fortified with iron.

FOOD FOR THOUGHT

It's normal for newborns to go through growth spurts during which time they want to eat more frequently than usual because they are growing at an extra-rapid rate. When babies are breast-feeding, their extra-frequent nursing helps to build up the mother's milk supply. After a few days, the baby's feeding schedule settles back down again, but while the growth spurt is at its peak and baby is nursing around the clock, parents may wonder if their six-week-old or three-month-old needs to start solids. The baby doesn't, of course. He just needs temporary round-the-clock access to mom's milk buffet.

Spotting the Signs of Readiness

So you've got a rough indication of the timing. You're probably wondering when to start offering solids to your baby. Here are the key signs to watch for.

Your baby

- can sit up well, so you know he's ready to sit in a high chair or other feeding chair
- controls his head and neck muscles well when he's in a seated position, which is important so that he can turn his head away to indicate whether or not he wants to eat or to signal that he's finished eating
- can move her tongue well (she needs to be able to move food from the front of her mouth to the back of her mouth in order to swallow)
- is interested in food and the process of eating (he may carefully track the path of your spoon)
- opens her mouth when she sees food coming her way on a spoon—proof positive that she's making the connection between food and eating.

Of course, some babies go for the more direct approach. Kris, 34, mother of two, knew her baby was ready for solids when her baby started "air chewing" along with the rest of the family while they were eating at the dinner table. Karyn's baby was a little less subtle: "She intercepted my fork and put it right into her mouth!" the 34-year-old mother of two recalls.

FOOD FOR THOUGHT

If your baby was born at or before 36 weeks gestation (4 weeks early) your health care provider will advise you to use her corrected age (her chronological age in weeks less the number of weeks she was born premature) rather than her chronological age when you try to predict the age at which she will be ready for solid foods.

No-Stress Feeding Tips for Parents and Babies

MEALTIMES ARE SUPPOSED to be fun, but it's easy to forget that if you get stressed about what your baby is or isn't eating. You may feel better if you remind yourself that this stage is more about giving your baby a chance to get comfortable with eating solid foods, to practise her chewing and swallowing skills, and to develop a taste for something other than breast milk or formula. Sure, you eventually want her to start eating different nutrient-rich foods so she'll get enough of "the good stuff" in her diet, but, for now, as long as she nursing well or eating an adequate amount of infant formula (your health care provider will define what is "adequate"), then she's likely getting the nutrients she needs to thrive. Breast milk or formula is, after all, the first-year front-line of nutritional defense for babies.

Why Do They Have to Make Things So Complicated?

I think one reason that parents find starting solids so stressful is that everyone makes it so complicated. Every baby food manufacturer has its own set of "rules" and steps and stages, and none of them match up exactly. Also, the major health authorities don't agree on fairly big issues like how many days you should allow before introducing the next new food (I came across definitions ranging from "three to five days" to "one week" while researching this book and noted that at least one baby food manufacturer wants to speed that up to "two to four days," maybe so that you can expose your baby to a few more varieties of puréed foods before your baby moves on to table foods); when it's okay to introduce cow's milk to your baby; and how many tablespoons of a particular food a baby should have at a particular age/stage. So I've pulled together the best wisdom from a variety of sources, cross-checking it against a number of different sources, and running it past my panel of experts to see it if my summary of "the baby food rules" rings true for them, too. Inevitably, you'll read other sources that contradict some of the material in this chapter. That's just the nature of the beast when you're writing on this topic. There's no single, unified consensus on all things related to feeding babies. I think the most you can hope for is to find some sensible middle ground that makes sense for you and your baby. That's what I've attempted to offer here.

What Mothers Want Taken Off the Menu— Crazy-Making Baby Food Rules!

One final point before we plunge into the main discussion: there's been much talk in the media recently about how mothers should trust their instincts in feeding their babies—how mothers should not becomes slaves to the often crazy-making baby food charts that tell you which foods to introduce in what order. That's why I've kept things deliberately flexible here, stressing only points that the nutrition experts emphasize—for example, that iron-fortified rice infant cereal is recommended as a first food for babies (although there is even some debate on that point!)—rather than providing you with dictatorial food lists of what your baby should be eating from which food group in which month. That's not helpful to you or your baby at all. It becomes yet another case of some outside expert who has never met you or your baby presuming to know all about your baby's tastes, appetite, and eating patterns—and of assuming that one menu plan will work for all babies of a particular age. *As if!*

I think it makes much more sense to recognize a mother's ability to master a few basic principles of infant feeding (what I'm presenting in this chapter and the next) and to apply those principles to her family's situation, given what she knows about her baby, her family's nutritional history (allergies, food intolerances, food preferences, etc.), what she's learned by watching friends feed their babies and by talking to other mothers, her own research into infant nutrition, and so on. I'll be talking more about this in upcoming chapters, so stay tuned!

Baby's First Feeding: What You Need to Know

You want your baby's first feeding to be fun for both of you. Here are some tips to help eliminate the worry and the stress.

Gather up your gear. That means a baby spoon (ideally an all-plastic spoon or a metal spoon with a rubber or plastic tip); a bowl (the bowl is staying in your hands for now, so don't waste money on one of those suction-cup water-filled bowls: besides, most babies quickly learn how to peel them off and dump them); a bib (baby's comfort is more important than wear-and-tear, wipeability, and clothing coverage); and either an infant seat or high chair, whichever works best for feeding baby right now.

Decide what to serve your baby. The nutritional consensus these days is that iron-fortified rice cereal makes an ideal first solid food for babies, although not everyone agrees.

Time baby's first experiment with solids to coincide with baby's happiest time of the day—typically morning or midday rather than evening. You might as well take advantage of the natural ebb and flow in baby's mood and energy cycles rather than work against them.

Offer your baby solid food after you've breast-fed or formula-fed him. Not only does your baby still need the nutrients in breast milk or formula, your baby will be more receptive to experimenting with solids if she's in a less-than-famished state. So treat solids as the second course of baby's meals for the foreseeable future—the après breast or bottle food course—and you may find that baby sees them as a novel delight rather than something getting in the way of what she really wants to be eating. (See Table 2.1.)

MOM'S THE WORD

"We put our daughter in a high chair with one of those snap-off dishwasher safe trays. I wish the designers would be forced to spend a week cleaning hardened baby food off these things—even though ours was the easiest to clean model we could find, there are still crevasses that catch food! Luckily we can wash the straps and cover in the washing machine."

—*Chelsea, 32, mother of one*

Table 2.2

First Foods: A Step-by-Step Guide to Feeding Your Baby

What to Add to Baby's Diet at This Stage	Quantity	How Many Times Per Day	Notes	How Long to Stick with This Feeding Stage before Moving on
			First Foods Step 1	
First single-grain cereal, iron-fortified One of • rice • oatmeal • barley	1 tablespoon mixed with 4 tablespoons of breast milk or formula (to add both flavor and nutrition to the cereal). Aim for the consistency of thin gravy.	Once a day (lunch)	Rice infant cereal is generally offered first because it has a sweet taste, very few babies are allergic to it, and it is easy for babies to chew and digest. However, there's nothing wrong with offering a different single-grain cereal as baby's first food. Most nutritionists feel that parents should start with infant cereals, however, because they are fortified with iron and, by age six months, a baby has pretty much run through the iron stores that he was born with.	You should wait three to five days (some say one week) each time you introduce your baby to a new food, in order to check for signs of any food sensitivities or intolerances, so this stage lasts for up to one week.
			First Foods Step 2	
Introduce your baby to the other two single-grain infant cereals	Gradually increase the quantity of cereal your baby is eating. Don't offer your baby any more food than she wants, however. A typical serving for a baby age six to nine months is about 4–6 tablespoons.	Once a day (lunch)	During this stage, you introduce your baby to the remaining two single-grain cereals, one at a time. As before, introduce the first cereal and then allow three to five days each to check for any signs of a food sensitivity or intolerance.	Two weeks

First Foods Step 3

Mixed-grain cereals	4–6 tablespoons (see note above)	Twice a day (breakfast and dinner)	Mixed-grain cereal includes wheat, so allow another three to five days for your baby to adjust to this cereal, too, unless you were able to find a single-grain iron-fortified wheat cereal for infants and you introduced it separately.	One week

First Foods Step 4

Fruits and vegetables (puréed)	Start with 1–2 tablespoons (one to two frozen baby food cubes) of the new fruit or vegetable you are offering. Gradually increase the total amount of fruit and vegetables that your baby is consuming to 4–8 tablespoons daily.	Twice a day (breakfast and dinner)	Since keeping track of what foods your baby has tried gets a little more complicated from this point forward, start keeping a record now, if you haven't already. It can be as simple as jotting each new food tried on the calendar in your kitchen or use the Baby Food Diary available for download from Motherofallsolutions.com. You don't need to introduce your baby to every fruit and vegetable before moving on to the chart in Chapter 3; but you want your baby to have well-developed biting, chewing, and swallowing skills so that she'll be able to handle more complex textures.	One month (The timing will vary. You move on to Table 3.2 in Chapter 3 when your baby is ready for more complex textures.)

Note: The Food and Agricultural Organization of the United Nations operates a web site that allows you to search for global information on food. This is an excellent source of baby food recipes and feeding guidelines from other parts of the world, in case you are interested in taking a multicultural approach to feeding your baby. See www.fao.org/waicent/

FOOD FOR THOUGHT

Let your baby decide whether or not he's hungry. Babies are born with a well-functioning eating "on-off" switch that tells them when they've had enough to eat. If the grownups in their life try to coax them to "try another bite" when they're not hungry, they learn to disregard their natural signals of fullness, which encourages unhealthy eating habits and can lead to weight or eating problems down the road. So pay close attention to your baby's signals when you're feeding him. If your baby turns his head away or closes his mouth, that's your cue that he's had enough to eat.

- Sometimes babies deliberately push food back out with their tongues because they don't want to eat it.

- Sometimes they push it back out with their tongues because there's a powerful tongue-thrust reflex at work. (If this is the case, your baby may not be ready for solids quite yet. Wait a week or two before reintroducing solids. A short period of time can make a huge difference developmentally in the life of a baby. If she continues to have difficulty with the mechanics of feeding, talk to your pediatrition to see if there may be an underlying feeding problem.)

- Sometimes they don't know that they have to keep their mouths closed if they want to keep food from oozing out.

- And, of course, some babies see the spoon coming and they decide they don't want anything to do with it. If your baby starts out as a spoon hater, try offering her a small amount of cereal on your fingertip. Once she's decided that food is yummy, she may decide that the spoon is no big deal.

FOOD FOR THOUGHT

Babies need to be carefully supervised when they're eating. If baby has a mouthful of cereal, don't dash out of the room to answer the doorbell. Take him with you or let the doorbell ring until he's had the chance to swallow that food.

MOTHER WISDOM

You'll notice a change in the color, consistency, and odor of your baby's stools once he starts on solid foods. Your baby's stools will become darker, firmer, and stinkier. The change will be particularly noticeable if your baby is breast-fed. Solid foods make for much more fragrant diapers, as you're about to discover.

If your baby's stools become extremely hard or infrequent, or he seems to have extreme difficulty passing a stool, contact your health care provider. It's possible that your baby may be constipated. In many cases, increasing your baby's fluid or fruit intake will take care of the problem.

If at first you don't succeed.... If baby isn't interested in trying solid foods because he's just had the breast or bottle equivalent of a nine-course meal, give him a partial feeding the next time around and then pop him in his high chair. Then once he's had a chance to sample some solids, you can top him up with some breast milk or formula.

Your baby will be exclusively breast-fed or formula-fed when you first start using this chart. To progress from stage to stage, you add each new type of food while continuing to offer your baby the existing foods in his diet. For example, in Step 1, you will continue to breast-feed or bottle-feed your baby after you introduce iron-fortified infant cereal to your baby's diet. Once you have completed each of the steps outlined in this chart, you decide whether your baby is ready to progress to more textured foods. When he is, you start reading Chapter 3 and continue with Table 3.2.

On Solid Ground: More Baby Feeding Success Tips

So you've got your baby's first solid meal behind you. Congratulations! So while you're on a roll, let's run through a few more strategies that may save you major angst and worry on the baby-feeding front. Here goes.

Expect the unexpected. Don't get freaked out if your baby's appetite fluctuates wildly from day to day and she may not necessarily like the same foods from one day to the next. This is perfectly normal for babies.

Don't be a fuddy-duddy when it comes to food exploration. If your baby wants to dip her finger in a new food before trying it, let her. It's all part of learning about food.

Assume that your baby will like a new food until proven otherwise. Your attitude toward that food transmits a lot of powerful information to your baby. If you assume she's going to hate it, she may very well live up to your expectations.

Play it cool. Try not to tip off your baby to any negative reactions you may have toward particular foods.

If your baby isn't keen on a new food initially, try again in another couple of days. Try offering it 10–20 times, in fact. (That's how many times you may have to offer a new food to your child in order to see whether or not she actually likes it.) If your baby likes the food, serve it again soon so that it will be come a familiar part of her nutritional repertoire. And remember that offering means just that—not shoving a spoonful of food in your baby's mouth, whether or not she wants it or expects it.

Don't add salt or sugar to your baby's food to make it more appealing to your baby. Salt is hard on a baby's kidneys and there's no point in introducing your baby to refined sugar before you have to. That day will come soon enough.

Walk the menu-planning tightrope. Strike a balance between repetition (serving your baby the same foods on a regular basis so that he can become familiar with these foods and learn to like them) and variety (constantly introducing new foods to your baby's food repertoire to keep eating interesting and to encourage him to try new foods). This will help your baby's eating habits to develop in a natural and age-appropriate way (see Table 2.3).

Table 2.3

Menu Snapshot: What Might Show Up on Baby's Menu at the Start and End of the "First Foods" Stage

	Beginning of the "First Foods" Stage (Baby Starts Solid Foods)		End of the "First Foods" Stage (Baby Is Ready to Move on to More Tastes and Textures)	
Breast milk or infant formula	Breast milk or infant formula will continue to be the key source of nutrition for baby while she makes the transition to eating solid foods.	Baby is breast-feeding or formula-feeding five to six times each day.	Breast milk and infant formula continue to provide key nutrients to baby, but she is relying on other foods to get the nutrients her body needs.	Baby is still breast-feeding or formula-feeding five to six times each day (if baby doesn't drink at least 24 ounces of formula per day or want to breast-feed at least three times per day, she may be consuming too much solid food).
Iron-fortified infant cereal	Baby starts out with rice cereal and then moves on to barley and oats.	1 tablespoon of infant cereal combined with 4 tablespoons of breast milk or infant formula.	Baby has tried all the single-grain cereals (rice, barley, oats) and mixed-grain cereals.	12 tablespoons total for the day, served at breakfast and dinner.
Fruits and vegetables	None yet	None yet	Baby is eating a wide variety of fruits and vegetables, such as Fruit: avocados, apples, bananas, mangoes, melons, peaches, pears Vegetables: carrots, parsnips, rutabagas, potatoes, sweet potatoes	A total of 4–8 tablespoons daily, served at breakfast, lunch, and dinner.

Wheat is still marketed as single-grain cereal in Canada, but none of the major infant cereal manufacturers are producing such a product for the U.S. market.
* Remember that your baby's appetite will fluctuate from day to day and that one baby's eating habits can be very different from another's, so don't worry if your baby's eating habits are slightly different than this chart indicates. That's to be expected.

Think your food strategies through carefully. Team up an unfamiliar food with a familiar food to increase the odds that it will be accepted, but weigh the pros and cons before you start mixing foods together. You could end up convincing your baby that the unfamiliar food is a winner, or you might convince her to hate a food that she's loved until now.

Make mealtimes relaxed and enjoyable. Keep the mood light and relaxed by making the experience pleasant for yourself, too. Put on some music you enjoy and talk to your baby.

Food Allergies and Intolerances

NOW THAT YOUR baby has been introduced to the world of solid foods, the world must seem like a giant buffet to her. And while many of the foods are safe for babies (or will be, once she makes the transition to solid foods), there are some that she needs to steer clear of for health and safety reasons either because the foods in question pose a serious choking or food poisoning risk, or because they could trigger an allergic reaction.

Food Intolerances

Food intolerances are the most common food reaction in babies. A food intolerance is when the body has trouble tolerating a particular food or food additive such as an artificial flavor or color. Typical symptoms include wheezing, diarrhea, rashes, itching, and headaches.

Only 8 percent of babies have full-blown food allergies (a.k.a. "food hypersensitivities") and half of them will outgrow these allergies when they reach three years of age.

Here are some important facts that every parent should know about food allergies, whether or not their own child is affected.

- Eight foods are responsible for 90 percent of food allergies in children: peanuts, tree nuts (e.g., hazelnuts, walnuts, almonds, cashews), wheat, cow's milk, strawberries, fish, and eggs.

- A child can experience an allergic reaction to a food within minutes or the reaction may occur up to 72 hours later.

- Symptoms of a food allergy may range from a runny nose, itchy eyes, and a skin rash to full-blown anaphylactic shock (when a child's mouth or throat swells, the child has difficult breathing, and, should medical assistance not be administered, the child goes into shock). Anaphylactic shock can be life threatening, even fatal, if help is not received in time. This is why children with known food allergies to peanuts—the prime cause of anaphylactic shock reactions—should be fitted with a MedicAlert bracelet listing food allergies and should carry a dose of epinephrine in a pen-style injector that caregivers can be taught to use in the event of an emergency.

- Even being exposed to these foods (as opposed to eating these foods) can trigger a reaction in children who are severely allergic (e.g., being kissed by a playmate who has just eaten a peanut butter sandwich or being massaged with a nut-based oil).

- Certain types of food allergies tend to run in families. If there's a history of food allergies in your family, your health care provider may have recommended that you avoid certain types of products—like peanuts and peanut butter, for example— while you were pregnant or breast-feeding. Likewise, your health care provider may recommend that you avoid introducing any cow's milk products to your baby's diet (e.g., no yogurt or cheese) during baby's first year, just to play it safe. Just realize that what people tend to broadly describe as "food allergies" are more accurately described as "food intolerances." Your health care provider can help you to put these issues in perspective when you're making dietary decisions for yourself and your baby. For additional resources related to food allergies, see Appendices A, B, and C.

If you suspect that your baby is allergic to a particular food, have your suspicions confirmed by your health care provider. She will likely recommend avoiding the problem food for a couple of years and then bringing your child back for a challenge test, in which your child is re-exposed to the food in a medically supervised environment. That test will determine whether your child has outgrown the allergy (in which case your child will be able to eat the food again) or whether your child will need to continue to avoid that food.

Table 2.4

What's *Not* on the Menu: Foods That Are Unsafe for Babies

Foods That Should Be Avoided for Food Allergy Reasons	
Nuts and nut products	Avoid peanuts and tree nuts (e.g., hazelnuts, walnuts, almonds, cashews) as well as nut products (e.g., peanut butter) and any products that may have come into contact with these products.
Egg whites	Egg whites are the problem. You can give your baby well-cooked scrambled egg yolks starting at age nine months, however. If there's a history of egg allergies in your family, talk to your doctor before introducing eggs to your baby's diet. Also avoid egg substitutes as well as foods containing albumin, globulin, ovomucin, or vitellin. *Note:* Flu shots contain egg products.
Shellfish	Avoid until age 18 months.
Foods That Pose a Choking Risk for Babies	
Celery	Choking hazard can't be eliminated. Avoid.
Grapes	Cut into tiny strips or wedges. Don't give any pieces that are penny- or marble-shaped.
Candies, hard as well as soft and jellied	Choking hazard can't be eliminated. Avoid.
Carrots, raw	Puréed carrots make a good first food for babies. Then move on to mashed or finely chopped cooked carrots and then finely shredded raw carrots. Wait until the late toddler years before introducing very finely cut carrot sticks and even then, don't give your toddler any carrot pieces that are thicker than her index finger.

Gum	Choking hazard can't be eliminated. Avoid.
Nuts	Choking hazard can't be eliminated. Avoid.
Olives	Remove pit and slice into tiny pieces.
Popcorn	Choking hazard can't be eliminated. Avoid.
Raisins	Choking hazard can't be eliminated. Avoid.
Tomatoes, cherry	Cut into tiny strips or wedges. Don't give any pieces that are penny- or marble-shaped.
Sausages	Slice into thin strips lengthwise and then chop into bite-sized pieces crosswise. Do not cut into penny-shaped pieces. Not recommended until baby is older and should be served only in limited amounts due to high salt content.
Weiners	Slice into thin strips lengthwise and then chop into bite-sized pieces crosswise. Do not cut into penny-shaped pieces. Not recommended until baby is older and should only be served in limited amounts due to high salt content.
Foods That Should Be Avoided for Other Reasons	
Honey	Honey can contain botulism spores. An adult's gastrointestinal system is hardy enough to deal with the problem, but a baby's isn't, so babies shouldn't eat honey until after their first birthday.
Cow's milk	Cow's milk is difficult for a baby's gastrointestinal system to process because cow's milk is biologically different from breast milk or infant formula, which has

continued on p. 72

Table 2.4 (Continued)

Foods That Should Be Avoided for Other Reasons	
	been formulated to resemble the components of breast milk. Babies aren't ready to start drinking cow's milk until 12 months of age, according to the American Academy of Pediatrics (nine to 12 months, according to the Canadian Paediatric Society). You can, however, introduce moderate amounts of dairy products into your baby's diet once your baby makes the transition to more textures and table foods (e.g., cottage cheese, grated cheese, yogurt, etc.). Babies and young toddlers should receive only whole milk products because they need the higher fat content. Don't switch to lower fat dairy products until your child is at least age two and, even at this age, make sure that your child's growth is on track before making such a change.
Rare ground beef, uncooked hot dogs, and luncheon meat; lox (cold smoked fish); raw milk and raw milk cheese (such as quesco fresco); soft cheeses (such as feta, brie, camembert, roquefort); unpasteurized apple juice; bean sprouts; alfalfa sprouts	These foods are at risk of being contaminated with harmful bacteria and should be avoided by babies, toddlers, and preschoolers as well as pregnant and breast-feeding women.

MOTHER WISDOM

Don't forget to continue to educate friends and family members about important health and safety issues. Show them the relevant sections of this book or give them a gift certificate for infant and child CPR classes as a gift. You could end up saving your own child's life.

MOM'S THE WORD

"Our kids are considered to be at elevated risk for developing food allergies due to severe food allergies in the family. So far, neither child has shown any signs of allergies, but we're not taking any chances. We took our time introducing new foods, and delayed introducing potentially allergenic foods. Isaac was the only child we knew who still had not had wheat or dairy by his first birthday. It was kind of a pain avoiding easily obtainable, toddler-friendly foods, but we did manage to find some substitutes and I tried to remind myself that if short-term avoidance could possibly help prevent a lifetime of necessary avoidance, it would be worth it. If either child does develop food allergies, at least I'll know we did all we could to reduce the risk."

—Jennifer, 30, mother of two

Baby Food Making: The Basics

YOU'VE DECIDED to make your own baby food. You may be in it for the money, love, or desire to give your baby a fresher, better-tasting product than what's available in a jar. Whatever motivated you to make your own baby food, here are the simple facts on making nutritious and good-tasting baby food, and possibly saving yourself a bit of cash along the way.

Equipment

Here's what you'll need to steam, process, and freeze your baby's food. The advantage to steaming fruits and vegetables—as opposed to zapping everything in the microwave—is that steaming preserves nutrients, color, and flavor.

- a steamer basket that fits in a double boiler
- measuring cups
- spoons
- a method for puréeing your baby's food. For example, a blender, a food processor, a baby food grinder, a ricer, a sieve.
- ice cube trays
- muffin tins (small cup size)
- freezer bags

Decide what type of equipment you'll use to purée your baby's food. Food processors can handle large quantities of food at once and do a better job with some foods than your blender. A case in point: a food processor can do a much better job of processing meats to a smooth, consistent purée. Blenders do a great job with fruits and vegetables, but process meat into something that looks stringy and pre-chewed. This can be a pretty big deal to a baby who's sizing up a particular food based on how that food feels in her mouth. If it feels repulsive, she probably won't get around to judging it on the basis of taste.

A blender will meet your needs just fine during round one of baby food making—the cereals, vegetables, and fruits stages. (You won't be working with meat right away.) If you already own a blender, look for some of the small-sized blender containers that are designed for making baby food. You'll be working with small quantities of food.

There are also cheaper alternatives if you don't think you'll have enough other uses for a food processor to justify the cost: A baby food grinder (or baby food mill) typically costs about $20. You simply put baby's food into the grinder, turn the manual handle, and everything is processed into a fine purée. These units are compact and portable. Some even come with their own carrying cases, which makes it easy to take to a restaurant or to grandma's house. You may want to add a little liquid—formula or breast milk rather than water for added nutrition—to moisten baby's food when you're running it through the grinder.

If you want the ultimate budget-friendly solution, you can use a sieve and a decent-quality wooden spoon (one that will stand up to the beating you're about to give it). Just be forewarned: this method is much more work unless you're working with naturally soft foods, like really ripe bananas (which, by the way, should be served right away rather than frozen, since they become really sticky and gummy in texture). If you're working with a food that needs to be cooked first (like carrots), cook the food, cut it into little pieces, mash it with a fork or a potato masher (the kind with a fine-meshed grill), mix in some liquid (again, breast milk or formula for added nutrition—whatever you decided to add), and push the mashed food through the sieve, using the wooden spoon. *Note:* See Food Tool 1 for some Baby Food Purée recipes and Food Tool 2 for some tips on mixing and matching purées.

Kitchen Hygiene

You can't be too careful about getting your kitchen spic and span before preparing food for a baby.

- Wash your hands in warm, soapy water before handling and food or equipment.

- Clean your work area and your equipment before you begin any food preparation.

- Make sure there aren't any food particles trapped in your food strainer.

- To wash your food strainer, run it through a dishwasher. Or wash it thoroughly in a sink of hot soapy water, rinse well in hot tap water, and let it air dry.

- Sterilize your ice cube trays, cookie sheets, or muffin tins by running them through the dishwasher or by placing them in a pan of boiling water. (Make sure the plastic in the ice cube trays won't melt.)

- Wash the outer surface of fruits and vegetables prior to food preparation.

Note: See Appendices A and B and Chapter 6 for more important kitchen hygiene tips.

The Best Baby Food Your Baby Ever Tasted

If you follow these basic techniques and try the no-fail recipes at the back of this book, you'll be well on your way to baby food bliss.

FOOD FOR THOUGHT

Here are some important safety tips to keep in mind if you are using commercial baby food products.

- Check for best-before dates and popped vacuum seal buttons on the jars of commercial baby food jars before you purchase the baby food. If the vacuum seal button has popped, the vacuum seal has been broken and the food may be spoiled or otherwise contaminated. Don't take a chance.

- Store unopened jars of baby food in a cool location and place the jars in the refrigerator as soon as they have been opened.

- Never feed your baby directly from a baby food jar (unless you're giving your baby the last serving in the jar or feeding the entire jar at one sitting). Otherwise, you'll contaminate the remaining food by introducing bacteria from your baby's saliva into the jar, making the remaining baby food unsafe for feeding to your baby.

- Start with the freshest ingredients you can find. Scout out the produce aisles in area supermarkets and produce specialty stores to see what you can find. Don't forget your local farmers' market for fresh options.

- Cut the produce into small, similarly sized pieces, which will reduce the blending or processing after the produce has been steamed and help you to achieve a more consistent purée.

- Steam the produce using the smallest quantity of water possible. This will help to preserve the nutrients in the fruit or vegetables you are preparing.

- If you're using a blender, work with no more than $3/4$ cup of food and a small amount of liquid at a time. If you're using a food processor, you can work with larger quantities of food.

FOOD FOR THOUGHT

Organic foods are grown free of synthetic chemicals like pesticides. Some parents feel that buying organic foods is the responsible choice to make for their babies. Others feel that washing produce thoroughly provides adequate protection for their babies. See Appendix B for links to some organic baby food websites.

(Follow the instructions that came with your food processor when gauging the amount of food to process at one time. See also the "Tools" section at the back of this book for some basic instructions for baby food purées.)

• Test the consistency of the baby food by rubbing a small amount of the purée between two fingers to feel for lumps. If necessary, blend or process for a few seconds longer. Remember, you're not trying to totally liquefy your baby's food by eliminating all pulp and texture; just eliminate any large lumps that could cause your baby to gag or choke while she is eating.

The Big Chill

So you've made your first batch of baby food. You've got ice cube trays filled with orange, green, and yellow baby food purées. Here's what you need to know to store your batch of baby food safely and protect it from freezer burn.

• Baby food can't sit at room temperature once it's been cooked and processed. You need to refrigerate or freeze it right away (as opposed to leaving it to cool at room temperature, which gives bacteria the opportunity to start breeding).

• If you're planning to store baby food in the refrigerator, it should be used up within one to two days. To keep baby food from losing its nutrients, drying out, or absorbing odors from other foods in the refrigerator, store it in a tightly sealed container. Mark the container with the date the baby food was made and when it should be discarded.

MOTHER WISDOM

Keep a rough inventory of how much baby food you have in your freezer. This can prevent "orange mystery vegetable" syndrome—when you pull out a bag of orange frozen something out of the freezer, and you can't remember whether it's the batch of squash baby food you made in October or the carrot baby food you made in September.

≥⟅⟆   **Mom's the word**
    "My sister also make lots of her own baby food and since we had
children at nearly the same time, we just shared."
—*Jodi, 33, mother of two*

• If you're planning to store baby food in the freezer, it should be
  used up within one month. While you might be tempted to fill
  your entire freezer with baby food, remember that your baby
  will probably eat only two cubes worth of puréed food at each
  of her meals when she is eating puréed baby food (roughly a
  two-month period). After that, she'll move on to meals with
  added texture (see Chapter 3).

• To package baby food for the freezer, place approximately 2
  tablespoons of puréed baby food into each cube of an ice cube
  container or place spoonfuls of roughly the same quantity of
  baby food on a cookie sheet. (Divide the baby food into individual servings. Baby food is more likely to spoil if it is thawed
  and refrozen or if it is reheated several times.) Cover and freeze.
  When the baby food is frozen solid, store the ice cubes in a freezer
  bag. Label and date the bag before adding the food cubes and
  then remove as much air as possible to minimize nutrient loss.
  When your baby starts eating larger portions of a particular food,
  you can switch from ice cube trays to muffin tins.

Thawing and Reheating Baby Food

• Thaw frozen baby food in the refrigerator, in a small bowl
  inside a larger bowl of hot water, or over a double-boiler. Don't
  leave baby food out to defrost at room temperature because the
  part that thaws first can form bacteria while the other part is
  still frozen.

• Remember that babies are used to foods that are heated no
  warmer than body temperature—the temperature of breast
  milk—so if you make her baby food too warm, she'll be unpleas-
  antly surprised. And there's nothing wrong with serving a baby
  room-temperature or even refrigerator-temperature baby food,

by the way. Contrary to what your grandma might have told you, she won't end up with a stomachache. So aim for thawed (as in defrosted) and slightly warmed up, not steaming hot.

- If you decide to heat baby food in a microwave oven (which most experts don't recommend because it's so easy to get the baby food too hot and because of the increased potential for nutrient loss), choose a shallow, microwave-safe bowl; stir the baby food thoroughly to eliminate any "hot spots" in the food (do this well away from your baby in order to avoid any possible splashes and burns); and remember to check the temperature right before you serve the food to your baby. Food continues to cook for a while after it comes out of a microwave oven.

- Never reheat food inside a small-necked jar in the microwave. Steam can build up inside the jar, causing it to shatter.

And now that you've got that baby food thawed:

- Never refreeze baby food once it has been thawed.

- If you're storing your baby's food in the refrigerator, don't heat up the entire contents of the original baby food storage container when you're making your baby's meal: just heat up an individual serving.

- Don't save any partially eaten servings of food. Bacteria from your baby's mouth can be transmitted to the food, causing the food to spoil. If you were to offer your baby this food again at a subsequent feeding, your baby could become seriously ill.

MOTHER WISDOM

"Carrots and sweet potato stain worse than anything! I have tried four different types of stain removers, hanging clothes in the sun, using bleach, and the stains are still showing up pale yellow in my baby's bibs and diaper shirts. Anytime you're feeding your baby these foods, use the darkest bib you have and immediately soak any garment that gets carrot or sweet potato on it. Otherwise these stains will be permanent!"

—*Kris, 35, mother of two*

Solutions Central—The Last Word

WHEN YOUR BABY starts on solids, you can feel overwhelmed by the amount of information on feeding your baby—much of it confusing and conflicting. This chapter focused on the need-to-know information for the first foods stage when baby is introduced to infant cereals and fruits and vegetables. Once baby has mastered those early tastes and textures, he's ready to move on to more sophisticated textures and table foods, the subject of Chapter 3.

Mr. Spaghetti Head: Added Tastes and Textures for Baby

When Reece showed an interest in feeding himself, we let him.
Floors, walls, and babies can be cleaned.

—SHANNON, 27, MOTHER OF ONE

AFTER A MONTH or two of dining on purées, your baby will likely be ready to expand his culinary repertoire. After all, as delicious as sweet potato and rice cereal and other such foods may be, they can get a little ho-hum after a while. First your baby will progress to mashed foods, and then to finely chopped versions of the very same things that you're eating, like spaghetti! Your mission at this stage of the baby-feeding game? To introduce your child to a variety of tastes and textures. If baby sticks with puréed foods for too long, he'll find it more difficult to chew more complex foods later on.

Your baby's burgeoning self-feeding skills will also influence the types of foods that she eats. When she first starts feeding herself, she'll rely on foods that she can scoop up or that stick to her hand. As her fine motor skills improve and she develops a pincer grasp, she'll be able to pick up smaller bits of food like Cheerios or tiny pieces of cheese.

Mealtime Milestones

MEALTIMES WILL BECOME more exciting at your house—crazier in some ways, but also a lot more fun. You'll have this really engaging and funny dining companion at your dinner table from now on—someone who will make you laugh with his blunt reactions to menu items that didn't quite measure up to his expectations and his other mealtime antics. Because your baby is achieving developmental breakthroughs so quickly, you'll see some major changes at the dinner table. Here's the scoop on some of the exciting mealtime and feeding breakthroughs and behaviors that you're either seeing now or will likely encounter soon.

The Age of Independence

Self-feeding is just around the corner. (Or maybe it's already here!) What you know about your baby's temperament should give you some clues about whether she'll be a take-charge kind of baby who doesn't want you to have anything to do with feeding her anymore, whether she'll be very cautious about learning to feed herself, or whether she's so laid back about everything—including learning to feed herself—that she may need some gentle encouragement to learn to use that spoon! You know your baby best. Here's how to ensure that your baby is getting enough to eat if she decides to go solo before she's fully mastered her spoon-feeding skills.

- Offer a variety of finger foods. Choose ones that she's able to chew and swallow right now. (See Tables 3.1 and 3.2 for ideas about what babies are eating right now.)
  - Cheerios (they dissolve easily in baby's mouth)
  - soda crackers (salt-free), toast, rice cakes, tiny pieces of toast
  - fresh fruit, cut into small pieces
  - cooked vegetables, cut into small pieces
  - well-cooked pasta, cut into small pieces
  - hard cheese, cut into small pieces or shredded

- For those foods that have to be eaten with a spoon, try to feed her while she's feeding herself. Have plenty of spoons on hand: a spoon for her (maybe two—she may want one for each hand), a spoon for you (so that you can get spoonfuls of food into her mouth if she'll let you), and a few spares (in case a few of the spoons fall on the floor).

- Let her work through some of the frustration of learning to use a spoon. Realize that there will be times when she'll get frustrated when that blob of cereal almost makes it to her mouth, but splats on her tray at the very last second. While you don't want her to become too frustrated, it's important to provide her with the chance to learn to navigate that spoon. If we eliminate all the frustration by always doing everything for our children, we eliminate a lot of the learning. And sometimes we rush in to eliminate the frustration because *we're* the ones who can't stand the fussing or the other signs of frustration that may accompany a learning breakthrough. Are we helping or hindering our kids by trying to eliminate all frustration from their lives? That's something we all have to decide for ourselves.

Table 3.1

Added Tastes and Textures and Table Foods: What's on the Menu?

| Milk | Breast milk or infant formula will continue to be your baby's nutritional mainstay throughout his first year of life. Your baby will still be having three to five feedings by breast or bottle at this stage. The Canadian Paediatric Society says that babies may be weaned to cow's milk at nine to 12 months of age, but the American Academy of Pediatrics does not advise this before age 12 months. Other milk products: Hard cheese (grated or cubed), cottage cheese, or yogurt. Use milk products that have been made from whole milk. Your baby won't be ready for low-fat cheeses for quite some time. Her body and brain need the higher fat content.

Also, if your baby has been on a soy-based formula because she was not able to drink milk-based infant formula, consult with your health care provider or a pediatric dietitian about alternatives to cow's milk products. |
|------|------|

continued on p. 84

Table 3.1 (Continued)

Grain Products	Iron-fortified infant cereal still has a lot to offer your baby, particularly if she's not eating a lot of iron-rich foods quite yet, so continue to start her day with infant cereal. If your baby has difficulty tolerating infant cereals containing wheat, barley, rye, or oats, she may be gluten-intolerant, in which case you'll want to avoid products that include these ingredients as she heads into the solid-foods stage. A dietitian can suggest interesting menu alternatives for a baby on a gluten-free diet. Contact organizations such as The American Academy of Allergy, Asthma, and Immunology or your local allergy association for information about deciphering food labels and choosing safe alternatives to wheat. (See Appendix A.) Infant cereals with added fruit are higher in sugar than plain infant cereals. That's why many nutritionists advise that you stick with plain infant cereals instead. Some infant cereals contain formula or milk; others require that you add your own formula or breast milk. Make sure that you know which type of infant cereal you are purchasing and that you are purchasing one that is suitable for your baby.
Fruit and Vegetables	You can buy off-the-shelf baby food fruit and vegetables (regular or organic) or you can make your using fresh, frozen, or canned produce. Now that your baby is handling more tastes and textures, you don't have to make such a smooth texture in your baby food purées. You can also start running new types of foods through the food processor—stews, casseroles, and other table foods that might be difficult for your baby to eat as is,

but that she would enjoy the taste of. Try not to over-process or over-blend these foods. You want her to learn how to deal with more complex textures. Eventually, you'll mash, chop, or serve these table foods as is—likely sooner than you think!

Fruit: Watch out for fruits with peel. While peel on fruits like pears and apples can be easy for adults to chew, they can cause a baby to choke. Also, make sure that fruit is very ripe and soft so that your baby can chew it or else serve your baby an unsweetened canned or cooked version of the fruit. Remember that berries pose a choking hazard for babies and that it's best to introduce citrus fruits after age one.

Vegetables: Don't serve corn to your baby until after age one. Some babies have difficulty digesting corn; others have had problems choking on it; and some babies are allergic to corn. It's not a great choice for babies.

Meat and Beans	Beans, lentils, legumes, tofu, egg yolks (no whites), boneless fish (e.g., soft, flaked white fish), chicken, turkey, beef, pork. Avoid highly salted deli meats. (See Table 2.4 in Chapter 2.)
	Certain types of fish (mainly the larger predatory fish that survive in the water the longest) have high levels of toxins and are therefore not recommended for pregnant or breast-feeding women or very young children. See www.cfsan.fda.gov/~dms/admehg3.html.

Note: See also Table 2.4: *What's Not on the Menu* for a list of foods that are not suitable for babies.

Table 3.2

More Textures and Tastes: A Step-by-Step Guide to Feeding Your Baby

What You're Adding to or Changing about Your Baby's Diet at This Stage	Notes	How Long to Stick with This Feeding Stage before Moving on
Step 1		
Until now, your baby has been eating liquid or puréed foods. Now you'll change the texture of a couple of her favorite foods by adding less liquid to her infant cereal or one of her fruit or vegetable purées.	The rationale for varying the texture of a couple of your baby's familiar foods first (as opposed to introducing brand new foods with challenging textures) is that if your baby were to reject the new food entirely or to have trouble chewing, swallowing, or digesting it, you would have a hard time figuring out whether it was the texture or the new food itself she was struggling with.	Move on to the next stage when your baby accepts and is comfortable with handling familiar foods with increased texture. See Food Tool 3 for more about textures.
Step 2		
Add new types of thick puréed foods (or foods of a similar texture) to your baby's diet: for example, puréed meats, tofu, cottage cheese, yogurt.	Keep track of the new foods so that you'll know which foods you introduced and when. Continue to wait three to five days before introducing each subsequent new food so that you will know which food is responsible for any reaction.	Move on to the next stage when your baby accepts and comfortably handles new types of foods of a fairly thick consistency.

Step 3

Introduce foods with even more complex textures, like mashed or chopped foods (mashed potatoes, mashed bananas) and some basic finger foods (Cheerios, finely chopped cooked carrots, finely chopped meat).

Keep track of the new foods so that you'll know which foods you introduced and when.

Continue to wait three to five days before introducing each subsequent new food so you will know which food is responsible for any reaction.

Move on to the next stage when your baby accepts and comfortably handles new types of foods of a fairly thick consistency.

Step 4

Introduce table foods to your baby's diet. Give her the opportunity to practise with added tastes and textures and to become accustomed to the types of foods that your family eats.

Keep track of the new foods so that you'll know which foods you introduced and when.

Continue to wait three to five days before introducing each subsequent new food so that you will know which food is responsible for any reaction.

Move on to the next stage when your baby accepts and comfortably handles new types of foods of a fairly thick consistency.

Note: This chart picks up where Table 2.2 left off in Chapter 2. At that point, your baby was exclusively eating puréed foods. To progress from stage to stage, you add new tastes and textures while continuing to offer your baby many of the existing foods in his diet. Some of the foods will be unchanged (e.g., breast milk or infant formula). In some cases, you'll be altering the texture—for example, making his puréed sweet potatoes a little less soup-like and a lot more potato-like. And in other cases, you'll be making significant changes, e.g., offering foods like chopped pasta or grated cheese. This chart ends when your child enters the toddler years, but learning about tastes and textures will continue throughout those years.

The Age of Unpredictability

This is a stage when your baby's appetite and food preferences may vary from day to day and meal to meal. You won't know exactly how much your baby will eat at any given time or on any given day, so follow your baby's lead. Offer baby-sized portions: a quarter-cup of foods like fruit, vegetables, yogurt, finely diced meat or cheese, and other foods that can be measured; a quarter to a half slice of bread, and so on. (See Table 3.3 for some guidelines on portion sizes.) But don't start fixating on portion sizes and the number of servings your baby should be consuming in a day. Measure something once to get a rough idea of what a baby-sized portion looks like and follow your baby's lead in determining how much she needs to eat. She'll tell you when she's full by closing her mouth, turning her head, or pushing the spoon away. (She may be even more direct and throw all the contents of her meal on the floor.) Feeding your baby should be fun for both of you. If it starts feeling like you're trying to make your baby follow a rigid meal plan, you're being too intense and stressed about food, which will make eating stressful for your baby.

The Age of Impatience

It wasn't that long ago that your baby was taking his first tentative slurps of infant cereals off the baby spoon. Now he protests vigorously and loudly if you're too slow in moving the spoon between the bowl and his mouth, and he considers it a major insult if you momentarily put the spoon down. *Is this the same baby?*

The Age of Exploration

This is the age of exploration, and your baby will want to learn everything about food—how it tastes, looks, smells, and feels. You can't really claim to know all about spaghetti, after all, until you understand what happens when you squish it between your fingers.

The Age of Communication

Your baby's ever-increasing understanding of language will make it easier for her to understand what you're trying to teach her about food and eating. And if you've been teaching her some basic signs to communicate when she's hungry or thirsty, either official sign-language signs or gestures that mean something only to the two of you, you'll find it easier to figure out when she's hungry or thirsty, when she wants more food or to get down from the high chair, and so on.

- Remember that your baby's appetite will fluctuate from day to day and that one baby's eating habits can be very different from another's, so don't worry if your baby's eating habits are slightly different than this chart indicates. That's to be expected.

- Don't add salt and sugar to your baby's foods.

- Your baby's diet will also expand to include oils and some discretionary calories. Think about the types of foods you want your child to develop a preference for over the long term. You may want to limit fast foods and sweets so that your child doesn't start to think of these as everyday foods. See MyPyramid.gov for more about these food groups.

MOM'S THE WORD

"Sometimes it is exhausting to feed the baby at the table (i.e., dealing with the baby who screams at the top of her lungs with her mouth closed until her face turns beet red because you can't get the spoonfuls of food to her mouth fast enough)."

—Sharlene, 34, mother of one

Table 3.3

Menu Snapshot: What Might Show Up on Baby's Menu at the Start and End of the More Tastes and Textures Stage

	Start of the More Tastes and Textures Stage (Baby Starts More Tastes and Textures Stage)	End of the More Tastes and Textures Stage (Baby Is Ready to Head into the Toddler Eating Stage)		
Milk	Breast milk and infant formula continue to provide key nutrients to baby, but she is relying on other foods to get the nutrients her body needs.	Baby is still breast-feeding or formula-feeding five or six times each day (if baby doesn't drink at least 24 ounces of formula per day or want to breast-feed at least three times per day, she may be consuming too much solid food).	Breast milk, infant formula, and, for some Canadian babies, cow's milk are still important, but your baby is now relying on a variety of other foods to meet her nutritional requirements.	Baby is still breast-feeding or formula-feeding three or more times each day. (Some Canadian babies may be drinking whole milk by this age. The Canadian Paediatric Society says it's okay to introduce whole milk at age nine to 12 months.)
Grains	Start adding less breast milk or infant formula to her cereal to thicken the consistency.	12 tablespoons total for the day, served at breakfast and dinner.	Iron-fortified infant cereal, dry cereal, toast, other servings from cereals.	Four daily servings. Each serving is equivalent to 2–4 tablespoons or more of iron-fortified infant cereal or half a slice of bread or 2 tablespoons of rice or other foods from the grains group.

Vegetables and Fruits	Thicken vegetable and fruit purées by reducing the amount of liquid in them.	A total of 4–8 tablespoons daily, served at breakfast, lunch, and dinner.	Your baby is eating both puréed vegetables and fruits and slightly more textured foods from this group.	Four daily servings. A serving is equivalent to 2–4 tablespoons of fruits and vegetables cut into bite-sized pieces.
Meat and Beans	All foods from this group are highly soft and smooth: e.g., yogurt, puréed meat, beans, and lentils, etc.	Your baby is eating small servings of 1–2 tablespoons of various foods in this food group.	Your baby can eat foods from this group that have a lot more texture: grated hard cheese, mashed cottage cheese, finely chopped meat or fish, etc. Your baby is also eating a lot of table foods that include foods from this group.	Two or three daily servings. A serving is equivalent to 2–4 tablespoons of foods from this group.

Note: See Food Tool 3 for more about textures.

MOM'S THE WORD

"I found that the grandparents were very eager for Kaylei to eat things like peanut butter, so I would have to educate them by telling them about some of the things we do now that might have been different from when they were raising their kids."

—Michelle, 36, mother of one

he's ready for pieces of steak and large pieces of crusty bread. My husband and I have to constantly remind her of our wishes for feeding him. And then she gives *me* attitude." Melanie, 29, ran into problems with her son Erik's grandparents wanting to offer her child sweets and other foods that weren't age-appropriate. The solution for her was to tell the grandparents that the doctor said Erik couldn't have them: "It was easier to put my foot down when I had a source to back me up and it wasn't just my own crazy idea." If you want your child to follow a specific diet or to eat certain foods, you may find it works well to be very clear about your expectations, says Brandy, 32, mother of two. "Make sure that everyone in the family and all your friends know that they need to consult with you about feeding your children anything. Especially now that we are vegan, this is so important. People can't be aware of every detail, so it is up to us, as parents, to pack foods for play dates and to cook when we are visiting relatives. It is up to us to make easy lists of okay and not okay stuff, and to provide lists of favorite foods, restaurants, etc., if we aren't available. Mistakes will be made, but given enough notice, people will understand better what the special needs are."

"How Can I Deal with Other People's Advice about What I Should and Shouldn't Be Feeding My Baby?"

Top-notch research skills (so that you feel confident that you know what you're talking about) and diplomacy skills are key. If you're on solid ground about solid foods, you won't get all huffy whenever someone offers an opinion, no matter how crazy or ill-informed that advice may be. Naomi, 36, has received her fair share of advice on what her son, Aiden, should be eating: "Although we don't intend for our son to be a vegetarian forever, he is currently on a vegetarian diet. We are very careful to include protein in all his meals. We serve him chickpeas, lentils, and kidney beans, as well as cottage cheese. I intend to include other types of beans as well and tofu. The main piece of advice I have to offer is to be sure you are confident in choosing this type of diet. You will get a lot of comments from people who think meat is important, and that your baby should be having meat. I am very happy giving him a completely vegetarian diet, and he is thriving!"

"My Baby Doesn't Seem to Like Table Foods at All. She Just Wants Baby Food."

Making the transition can be tough for some babies, given the difference in both texture and taste. Make the change one step at a time, perhaps giving your baby a chance to adjust to the taste first and the texture later on. Serve your baby a puréed version of what everyone else is eating. And if your baby is giving a thumbs-down to textures period, you may have to take a baby-steps approach to tastes and textures, like Karyn, a 34-year-old mother of two, did: "I tried to be patient. I would go back to the smooth foods and very, very gradually add texture to the same dish. This was easy for me since I made my daughter's food. It's a little trickier if you buy pre-made baby foods."

MOTHER WISDOM

If the food that the rest of the family is having for dinner isn't baby-friendly in taste or texture, or if it contains some ingredients that are off-limits to babies (see Table 2.4 in Chapter 2), you may need an alternative meal for your baby. If you keep bags of pre-cooked and pre-diced foods in the freezer (e.g., chicken, carrots, peaches, and some of baby's other favorites), you won't have to play short-order cook in order to meet the nutritional needs of various family members.

"My First Baby Had No Trouble Adjusting to Foods with Texture, But My Second Baby Has Been Gagging on *Everything*."

This can be a really hair-raising experience for parents. "The twins would gag on anything for months, which often resulted in a full-blown vomit of anything previously ingested," recalls Nancy, 38, the mother of twins. "It was so frustrating. We just kept trying and trying and finally, somewhere very close to 12 months, we finally seemed in the clear. It was also embarrassing when it would happen when we were eating at a friend's house or a play date. What a mess. I was always so jealous of friends who had children the same age or younger who could eat things with no problem, and meanwhile all my guys would do is puke." The best way to deal with the problem is to accept that your child is taking a little longer to deal with textures than some of his age-mates. Continue to give him opportunities to practise with textures and realize that there will be occasional upchucking episodes as he copes with and practises those all-important chewing and swallowing skills. And try to stay as relaxed as possible. Like every other frustrating stage of parenting that preceded it and has yet to come, it's a time-limited offer. (Some children do develop feeding disorders that are more long term. See Appendices A and B for pediatric health resources if you suspect that your child could be experiencing such a problem.)

MOM'S THE WORD

"To make it easier for baby to understand the cup, we took out the spill-proof stopper so the milk or water would flow easily into my son's mouth. Once he got the idea of what the cup was for and how to suck the liquid out, we reintroduced the stopper to prevent spills."

—*Dani, 36, mother of two*

BE SAFETY SAVVY

Only a wiggly eight-month-old baby can turn sitting in a high chair and eating a bowl of pasta into an adventure. Here's what you need to know to keep baby safe.

- Your baby may try to make like Houdini once he decides it's time to get down from his high chair. To prevent that great escape from turning into a tumble, make sure he's always belted in well. (Age seven to nine months is the peak age for these types of accidents.)

- Don't overestimate your baby's feeding abilities just because he's dining on table food. Your baby may be getting more teeth all the time, but this doesn't mean he's ready to chow down on a piece of steak or bite into a piece of corn on the cob. Your baby's chewing motions are more about gumming his food and letting the saliva in his mouth do its work, so offer food that will dissolve in his mouth quickly and easily.

- Don't let your baby dine alone. It takes young children two or three years to master chewing and swallowing foods safely, so supervise your baby while he's eating. You need to react quickly if your baby starts to choke and gag on food. Almost all babies experience at least one such episode, the result of shoving too much food in the mouth at once, not chewing food enough, or otherwise miscalculating the mechanics involved in processing food. You can reduce your baby's risk of choking by letting him eat only while sitting down, by cutting his food into small pieces, by teaching him to eat slowly, and by keeping the dinner atmosphere relaxed and calm so he can concentrate on eating.

- Don't leave any half-eaten food in the tray of your baby's high chair for him to graze on at his next meal. Food breaks down quickly once it has come into contact with saliva, and finding a half-chewed treasure a few hours after the fact could make your baby sick. And don't forget to give your baby's high chair a thorough cleaning after each meal. Remember, his high chair tray is the equivalent of his dinner plate.

"My Baby Doesn't Have a Clue What to Do with Her Cup. She Just Plays with It."

Playing with a cup is the first step. If you keep showing her how the cup works—both by using a cup yourself and by showing her how the cup goes into her mouth—she'll quickly get the idea of what cups are for and why she might want to use one. (If your baby has been relying on a breast or bottle to get her liquids until now, there can be a bit of learning curve involved!) Here are some tips on helping her to make the cup connection.

- Give your baby water in a sippy cup to practise with. Remove any no-spill flow valve initially until she figures out how the cup works. If your baby finds it hard to figure out how the sippy cup works, try a plastic cup with a built-in straw instead.

- Stick with water as much as possible. You don't want your baby to develop a juice habit. Not only can too much juice cause diarrhea and diaper rash, it can lead to dental health problems if baby gets in the habit of sipping from a cup of juice all day long. It's fine to serve your baby some fruit juice. Just make sure that it's unsweetened and limit her total daily juice consumption to 4–6 ounces.

Solutions Central—The Last Word

INTRODUCING ADDED tastes and textures and starting your baby on table foods is building on the nutritional foundation that you so carefully put in place during the first foods stage. And now that baby is ready to blow out the candles on her birthday cake, both of you are ready to face the nutritional joys and challenges of the toddler years together.

CHAPTER 4

Your Top Toddler Mealtime Mysteries Solved

Take a look at the big picture. What did he eat this week?
Or even this month. As long as that balances out in the end,
that's all that's important.

—ANDREA, 33, MOTHER OF ONE

A TODDLER-IMPOSTER IS sitting in your child's high chair, doing a darned good impression of the toddler who should be sitting there. This other toddler *looks* and *acts* like your toddler, but *can't* be your child because he is refusing to eat sweet potatoes, your toddler's favorite food on the planet. Someone has swapped your toddler for a veggie-phobe lookalike.

Peeved? Puzzled? Perplexed? Join the club! The on-again, off-again (but mostly off-again) eating patterns of toddlers have frustrated and baffled countless parents before you. This chapter talks about how the rules of the mealtime game have changed and what's on and off the menu for your child at the toddler stage (you'll also want to check out Food Tools 4 and 5 for a comprehensive list of toddler-friendly meal and snack ideas), and how to handle some common feeding-related problems during the toddler years. I've devoted Chapter 7 to the subject of picky eaters, so while I briefly touch upon that topic in this chapter, you'll find a more thorough discussion in that part of the book.

The Rules of the Toddler Mealtime Game

THE RULES of the mealtime game have certainly changed since you and your baby first ventured into the World of Solid Foods. Here's an updated copy of the mealtime playbook, something that should come in handy now.

1. Your Toddler's New Theme Song Is "My Way"

Your toddler's newfound independence is expressing itself in all areas of her life, even in her eating behaviors and food choices. She wants to feed herself as much as possible (which can lead to endless frustration if she can't quite get that spoon or cup to do what she wants it to do) and she's becoming increasingly clear about what she likes and doesn't like. You'll need much patience and a working knowledge of what makes toddlers do what they do. See Table 4.1 for a summary of the key feeding-related milestones and behaviors for one- and two-year-olds.

It really helps to have friends with slightly older toddlers—ideally toddlers who also gave their moms the gears when they were this age. So make that call, fire off that e-mail, or check one of the on-line message boards for moms: do whatever it takes to find out what other moms have been through with their little ones and to get the support you need.

MOTHER WISDOM

A strategically placed shower curtain makes a great drop cloth for a toddler who takes the term "mess hall" to a whole new dimension. Shower curtains are cheap, they're durable, and the better-made ones wash well. (You just chuck 'em in the washing machine.)

Table 4.1

Feeding-Related Milestones and Behaviors for One- and Two-Year-Olds

	Typical Feeding-Related Milestones and Behaviors for One-Year-Olds
Your One-Year-Old Will ...	**What You Can Do**
... become even more skilled at feeding herself with a spoon.	Give her plenty of opportunities to work on those skills and don't fret about the resulting mess. It's okay to help your toddler to feed herself (if she'll let you!), but you don't want to take over the feeding entirely. It's a matter of assessing your baby's skills and frustration level and letting your mother's intuition cue you as to when it might be time to offer a little more hands-on help.
... start eating with a toddler fork (at around 18 months).	Purchase a decent-quality toddler fork that actually picks up food, but that won't hurt your child if she accidentally jams the fork in her eye. Don't purchase a child-sized knife for your toddler just yet. She won't have the skills to manage a knife until she's four.
... continue to enjoy eating with her hands.	This is still very age-appropriate behavior. Her hands will still be her preferred eating "utensils" for some time. Encourage spoon use, when appropriate, but don't try to discourage her from eating with her hands in an effort to prevent her from making a mess. That's part of the learning process.
... be an old pro in getting her sippy cup to her mouth, but may have difficulty putting the sippy cup back down.	Give her opportunities to practise so she can conquer that cup one day soon.

continued on p. 102

Table 4.1 (Continued)

Your One-Year-Old Will ...	Typical Feeding-Related Milestones and Behaviors for One-Year-Olds
	What You Can Do
... continue to experiment with new tastes and textures.	Introduce her to new foods and not just foods of a single type of taste or texture. Some she'll like, others she'll tolerate, and others she'll reject outright—at least for now—but by constantly exposing her to new tastes and textures, you'll expand her food repertoire. Your toddler will be most receptive to trying new foods when she's at her hungriest, so offer new foods at the start rather than the end of a meal and—to maximize the odds of acceptance—serve them alongside a food you know your child likes (e.g., honeydew melon with cantaloupe). Don't introduce new foods if your toddler is sick, teething, or otherwise out of sorts. She's more likely to gravitate toward familiar tastes and textures when she's not quite herself, assuming she has much of an appetite at all. See Chapter 7 for tips on dealing with a toddler who is a picky eater.
... show increased interest in eating the same foods as you are.	Take advantage of this opportunity to expand her culinary repertoire. Give her a chance to experiment with new cuisines and slightly more adventurous dining choices by giving her small servings of what's on your plate. Just don't overdo it with the spices (her taste buds are much more sensitive than yours) and make sure that everything you're sharing with her is safe for toddlers. (See Table 4.4.)
... find routines comforting and reassuring.	Serve your toddler's meals and snacks at a predictable time. Her body will get used to eating at particular times of day. And because eating is one of the biological cues that our bodies use to regulate our sleep/wake cycles, feeding your toddler at predictable times helps to regulate her sleep patterns, too.

... experiment with different behaviors to see how you're going to react.	Set limits for your toddler and don't be afraid to set appropriate consequences for wacky dinnertime behaviors. For example, if you throw your dinner in the air, mom or dad will keep your spaghetti bowl for the rest of the meal. If you say "All done," and you get down from your high chair, dinner's over and you have to wait until your bedtime snack if you want something else to eat.
... spit out food that she doesn't like.	When she spits out a hunk of meat that she finds completely repulsive, she's simply trying to get rid of it as quickly as she can. Over time, you can start to teach her to get rid of the offending piece of meat via a napkin. (Note: She should know it's okay to do whatever it takes to get the meat out if she's choking!)

Typical Feeding-Related Milestones and Behaviors for Two-Year-Olds

Your Two-Year-Old Will ...	What You Can Do
... make her food likes and dislikes more apparent than ever before.	Your toddler's growing vocabulary and her increased sense of who she is as a person are fuelling her desire to offer her opinion on everything, including food. You may want to start teaching her to say "No thank you" (or equivalent words and gestures) as opposed to "Yuck!" See Chapter 7 for some tips on working with your toddler's food likes and dislikes—within reason.
... have a strong preference for simple foods that she can recognize easily (e.g., she may not be a big fan of casseroles).	Realize that this is standard practice for most toddlers: they like to know what it is they're eating *before* they put it in their mouths.

continued on p. 104

Table 4.1 (Continued)

Your Two-Year-Old Will ...	Typical Feeding-Related Milestones and Behaviors for Two-Year-Olds What You Can Do
... have other strong opinions about food, like what shape toast should be cut in, what bananas are supposed to look like (yellow, never brown), and how food should be positioned on the plate (nothing can touch another food, ever).	Make an effort to accommodate your toddler's requests when those requests are reasonable. (You may also want to start teaching your toddler that she has to make her food requests before you start making her food. It's hard to change the shape of toast after it's been cut or to unmash a banana.) You'll find life is easier for you and your child if you limit the food choices to two rather than offering to make your toddler anything she'd like at each meal. Parents can't be short order cooks!
... become positively fixated on rituals and routines and hooked on favorites.	Having some things in her world stay the same gives her a sense of security at a time when she's learning so much so quickly. That's why she freaks out if her favorite blue cup is in the dishwasher. She absolutely *has* to have it *right now.*
... add a new catch phrase to her vocabulary (alongside "no"): "Me do it."	Realize that your toddler's declaration of independence is a good thing, even at the dinner table. That drive to do things for herself will fuel the next round of feeding-related developmental breakthroughs.
... want to help you by doing jobs.	Ask her to help you to pick out the fruits and veggies at the grocery store (maybe she'll be more willing to try some new ones, given that they were her own handpicked choices). Or not.
... make the transition from a high chair to a booster seat.	Help her start to make the transition so that she can join the rest of the family at the dinner table. You'll find it easier to tote her booster seat when you're dining at other people's homes, and there's a lot less surface area to clean on the average booster seat than the typical high chair.

2. Your Toddler Has You under Surveillance

You are your toddler's number one food role model, the one she's looking to for guidance as she starts to formulate her attitudes toward eating and food. Here are the key points to keep in mind.

- Understand that you're not in charge of what or how much your toddler eats. That's a difficult concept for most parents to grasp. Today, dietitians and pediatricians are encouraging parents to take a much more laid-back approach to kids and eating. While you decide what type of food to serve, only your toddler can decide whether or not she's hungry.

- Try not to be too outspoken about your own food likes and dislikes, at least in front of your toddler. Let her make up her own mind about different foods.

- Resist the temptation to use food as a bribe, punishment, or reward. Now that your child is a toddler, you'll spend more of your time setting limits for her and finding all kinds of creative discipline methods that work for her and for you. Bribing toddlers with food gives them mixed messages about food. You should reward yourself when you do something good. Eat food when you're happy. That kind of thing.

MOTHER WISDOM

Continue to establish some age-appropriate mealtime rules. You may want to decide, for example, whether to allow toys at the dinner table. Do these toys help to keep your toddler happy and entertained (and possibly in her high chair a little longer) or do they distract her so much that she forgets to eat?

You may also want to have a rule that your toddler eats only when she's in her high chair or booster seat, not when she's sitting on someone's lap. It's not only inconvenient for you to try to eat your meal with a toddler on your lap, there's a safety concern as well. You may miss the early warning signs that your toddler is starting to choke if she's sitting on your lap, facing away from you.

See Chapter 3 for more on the issue of mealtime rules.

- Give your child messages that will help her to become body confident. Instead of just commenting on how she looks, encourage her to focus on what her body can do. (We'll return to this topic in Chapter 5, but it's worth mulling over now. Body confidence is another piece of the healthy living puzzle, along with physical activity, good nutrition, and having a healthy attitude toward food.)

3. Your Toddler Has This Amateur Food Critic Thing Down to an Art

We're all individuals when it comes to food, and it's important that you respect that fact when you're feeding your toddler. But there's a world of difference between *respecting* your toddler's food preferences and letting a two-year-old dictate what's on the family menu. The sooner you figure out where to draw that line in your family, the easier mealtime parenting will become.

Toddler food likes and dislikes tend to be most pronounced at approximately 18 months old, but—as with anything else toddler-related—the exact timing can vary from child to child. Here are some basic coping strategies when your toddler passes through this challenging stage.

- Encourage your toddler to try new foods by serving a small portion of a favorite food alongside an unfamiliar food. While you might be tempted to hide the new food by blending it with an old favorite, this strategy can backfire by causing your child to refuse to have anything to do with the old favorite food from that point forward. Suddenly spaghetti sauce, a once-loved favorite, is ruined by a puréed tofu experiment gone terribly wrong.

- Realize that toddlers may have to be reintroduced to a new food repeatedly before they eventually decide that they like it—as many as 10 to 20 times. Serving the vegetable your toddler has decided she hates 20 days in a row is a sure-fire way to get her to dig in her heels. A better strategy is to offer that vegetable every few days in slightly different forms (steamed? baked? au gratin? with lemon?) in a very matter-of-fact way. It may take months for her to finally decide that broccoli is not the enemy.

MOM'S THE WORD

"Hana has a few foods she always likes (cheese, pasta, egg, cucumber, sweet potato, watermelon) and a few foods she always dislikes (peas, pear). I find there are some foods that she tends not to like unless they are mixed in with other things. For instance, she rarely will eat chicken or beef, but if we give either of them to her in a stew or a meat pie, she will eat them. Her palate keeps expanding so that she eats many more foods now than she did a couple of months ago."

—*Mary Lynn, 35, mother of one*

You have to be pretty patient and prepared to eat a lot of broccoli castoffs yourself.

- Have an idea about what's reasonable and what's not when making food accommodations for your toddler. You don't want to end up playing short-order cook or making five separate dinners in the hope that one of them will be pleasing to a two-and-a-half-foot-tall dictator who changes his food whims even more frequently than you change his diaper. Nor do *you* want to be the one who's being autocratic and nasty. You want to find some sensible middle ground. Just don't lose sight of the fact that it's the parents' job to make the final menu call. Most toddlers lack the nutritional know-how to plan a balanced meal. (See Chapter 7 for more on this issue.)

4. Your Toddler Has Better Things to Do Than Come to the Dinner Table

By now, some of the novelty of sitting in a high chair and feeding herself has started to wear off. She may have a limited attention span when it comes to being in her high chair and when something distracts her from eating, mealtime is over as far as she's concerned. Here are some mealtime solutions that have worked well for other moms.

- Give your toddler a few minutes of warning before each meal so she can make the mental shift from playtime to mealtime. She'll be less resistant to coming to the table and will find it easier to relax and enjoy her meal.

- If your toddler finds it really difficult to make the shift from playtime to mealtime, no matter how much notice you give her, work a logical break into her routine when it's time to get ready for dinner (e.g., washing her hands) or involving her in mealtime preparations, either watching you wash and chop vegetables (if she's still quite young) or helping you put the cutlery on the kitchen table (if she's a little older).

- Minimize mealtime distractions. It's hard to focus on eating if there's a lot of chaos and background noise at the table. If you're in the habit of eating dinner in front of the TV, that's a habit you'll want to ditch anyway. You can't really enjoy or focus on the food you're eating if you're paying more attention to the tube than what's happening at the table.

- Don't let your toddler get up and down from her high chair or booster seat so she can play for a couple of minutes, have a few more bites to eat, and then run off to play again. That's not what mealtimes are all about, and your toddler needs to learn that lesson now. Getting down from the table means that mealtime is done. The food is put away and you have to wait until the next snack or mealtime for food to be offered again. Of course, to make this advice work in the real world, you'll have to come up with a gameplan for entertaining your toddler while the adults finish eating. (Unless, of course, you intend to eat a toddler-sized entrée.) You may want to use some of the strategies that work well when you're dining out: having some "dinner toys" or table activities, or having one parent actively engage the toddler in conversation while the other parent eats. (See Chapter 6 for more tips.)

5. Your Toddler's Appetite May Have Gone AWOL

This is because she is no longer growing at the same extraordinary rate as she was when she was younger (most babies almost triple their weight during the first year of life) and she simply doesn't need as much food to sustain her current rate of growth. Here are some important points to remember when your toddler is passing through this often worrisome stage.

- Your toddler's appetite will vary from one day to the next. It's more important to pay attention to what your toddler is eating over a period of days than to zero in on what your toddler has eaten on any given day.

- Let your toddler be the judge of how much food she needs. Children know when they are hungry and when they've had enough to eat. If we consistently force them to take a few more bites because we think they should be eating more, over the long run that can result in overeating and weight problems.

- Give your toddler a reasonable amount of time to eat her dinner and then remove her plate. Twenty to 30 minutes should be enough time for most toddlers to get through their meal. Of course, if your toddler is still happily dining away at that point, do not take her dinner away from her. That's not the idea at all. But at some point, you have to declare dinner over if your child is clearly not interested in dinner, and a guideline of 20–30 minutes works well for most parents and toddlers.

- Keep the mealtime atmosphere calm and relaxed. Your toddler will have an even more difficult time focusing on eating her meal if she senses that you're obsessing about what she is or isn't eating. Besides, you want mealtimes to be a pleasant experience for her, not a source of stress for the two of you.

- Realize that dinnertime tends to be the most challenging meal of the day for toddlers and their parents. You're tired, your toddler is tired, and your toddler's appetite is likely to be at its low point for the day. Nutrition experts have different theories about why toddlers are less hungry later in the day. They've been eating on and off all day and they may finally be full. Or they may have reached the point in the day where getting some sleep—rather than having something else to eat—is becoming their overriding biological focus. And along with the ebb in appetite comes a lack of interest in trying any foods other than the old favorites (and even some of *them* may have found their way on to the Least Wanted List), it can make dinner a challenging time, so take a deep breath and repeat one more time: "My toddler is not acting this way just to drive me crazy." Saying it—and believing it—makes motherhood easier.

Table: 4.2
What's on the Menu?: The Toddler Food Pyramid

Food Group	Total Daily Amount from This Food Group	Important Notes: $^1/_4$ cup is roughly an egg-sized portion of food, $^1/_2$ cup is roughly an ice cream scoop portion of food, 1 cup is roughly a baseball-sized portion of food
Grains	3 ounces	Make half of your toddler's servings from this group whole grains. You can increase your toddler's intake of whole grains by choosing foods with one of the following ingredients as the first ingredient on the label: brown rice, bulgur, graham flour, oatmeal, whole-grain corn, whole oats, whole rye, whole wheat, wild rice. Foods that are labeled multi-grain, stone-ground, 100 percent wheat, cracked wheat, seven-grain, or bran are usually not whole-grain products. They still have lots of other redeeming qualities (they're rich in other important nutrients) but they're not your best source of whole grains. One ounce of grains equals one slice of bread, 1 cup of ready-to-eat cereal, or $^1/_2$ cup of cooked rice, cooked pasta, or cooked cereal.
Vegetables	1 cup In general, 1 cup of raw or cooked vegetables or vegetable juice, or 2 cups of raw leafy greens can be considered as 1 cup from the vegetable group.	Vary your toddler's veggies. Rather than serving the same types of vegetables week in and week out, vary your vegetable choices. Aim for these amounts of the various types each week: • Dark green veggies: 1 cup • Orange veggie: $^1/_2$ cup • Dry beans and peas: $^1/_2$ cup • Starchy veggies: $1^1/_2$ cups • Other veggies: 4 cups Add puréed vegetables to spaghetti sauce or soups; serve vegetables raw or lightly cooked because overcooking can make vegetables taste bitter (but make sure that the vegetable is soft enough to eliminate any choking risk).

Fruit	1 cup	When choosing canned fruits, choose fruits canned in 100 percent fruit juice or water rather than syrup; and when you're shopping for fruit juice, look for unsweetened, 100 percent juice. Look for the following words on the package: unsweetened, pure fruit juice from concentrate, no artificial flavors or colors added, 100 percent fruit juice. Real juice contains more than 20 vitamins and minerals: it's the closest thing to a real piece of fruit you can put in a glass.
	In general, 1 cup of fruit or 100 percent fruit juice can be considered as 1 cup from the fruit group.	You're probably getting a fruit drink product (which is different from fruit juice) if you see the following words: drink, punch, -ade, beverage, cocktail. These products typically contain little or no fruit juice. They are basically sugar-flavored water. Nectar, on the other hand, is all-natural 100 percent juice.
		Vary your fruit choices. Fruits differ in nutrient content.
		Don't overdo it with the fruit juice. Not only will your child miss out on the fiber that comes from eating whole fruits, children who drink a lot of juice tend to eat less of other foods. (See the section later in this chapter on other effects of fruit juices.)
Milk products	2 cups	Don't serve toddlers under the age of two low-fat milk. They still need the higher fat content of whole (homogenized) milk.
	In general, 1 cup of milk or yogurt, 1^1/$_2$ ounces of natural cheese, or 2 ounces of processed cheese can be considered as 1 cup from the milk group. A ^{1}/$_4$ cup of cottage cheese is considered ^{1}/$_2$ cup of milk.	If your toddler is lactose intolerant, serve her lactose-free milk. If your toddler is allergic to cow's milk (different from being lactose intolerant), talk to your child's health care provider or a pediatric dietitian about the best alternatives. Some alternatives may include fortified whole goat's milk, calcium-enriched soy or rice milk (for drinking); vegan cheese (for sandwiches and snacks); dairy-free margarine, vegetable shortening, or fruit juice soy butter for baking. (Use soy products as substitutions only if your child is able to tolerate soy.)
		Breast milk also falls into this category.
		Tip: 1^1/$_2$ ounces of natural cheese (hard cheese) is a piece of cheese the size of six stacked dice.

continued on p. 112

Table: 4.2 (Continued)

Food Group	Total Daily Amount from This Food Group	Important Notes: $^1/_4$ cup is roughly an egg-sized portion of food, $^1/_2$ cup is roughly an ice cream scoop portion of food, 1 cup is roughly a baseball-sized portion of food
Meat and beans	2 ounces In general, 1 ounce of meat, poultry, or fish, $^1/_4$ cup cooked dry beans, 1 egg, 1 tablespoon of peanut butter, or $^1/_2$ ounce of nuts or seeds are equivalent to 1 ounce from the meat and beans group.	All foods made from meat, poultry, fish, dry beans or peas, eggs, nuts, and seeds are considered part of this group. Certain types of fish (mainly the larger predatory fish that survive in the water the longest) are not safe for young children because they contain large quantities of environmental toxins. See www.cfsan.fda.gov/~dms/admehg3.html for more on this issue. Some toddlers reject meat initially because they don't like the taste and the texture. You can make meat more palatable by cutting it into small pieces and serving it in soups, stews, and pasta dishes. Meatloaf is also a popular meat dish for toddlers. Because it is both an excellent source of iron and it features the smoother texture that toddlers enjoy, chopped liver or liver pate may be another meat option to offer occasionally.
Discretionary calories	165 calories per day 3 teaspoons per day of healthy fats and oils	You won't have to make a conscious effort to spend your toddler's discretionary calories. Consuming higher fat milk products will take care of 130 of these calories alone each day. That leaves you with a few calories for fats and oils (see column to the left). Continue to limit your toddler's consumption of salt and sugar by not using salt and sugar to season her foods and by choosing commercially manufactured products wisely. (Look for low-sodium and sugar-free versions of products wherever possible.)

Physical fitness	60 minutes per day	Don't forget the physical fitness part of the Food Pyramid. For optimum health, toddlers should be physically active 60 minutes every day or most days. Since running, walking briskly, and dancing all count as physical activity, you can encourage your toddler to make playtime physical activity time. *Note:* Health Canada recommends that toddlers receive 30 minutes of structured physical activity (games and activities when you help your toddler learn how to move her body) and 60 minutes to several hours of unstructured physical activity (supervised time when your child plays independently or with other children).

Servings and serving sizes were calculated based on the USDA MyPyramid.gov guidelines for a two-year-old moderately active child (30–60 minutes of physical activity per day): 1,000 calories per day. *Canada's Food Guide to Healthy Eating* was being revised at the time this book went to press, but the number and types of servings and the portion sizes for toddlers this age are comparable. See *Canada's Food Guide to Healthy Eating* on the Health Canada website for details. (See Appendix B.) To modify these portions for a one-year-old, start out by offering your child less food (half the portion sizes indicated) and offer your child more food if he is still hungry. Or offer your child the same amount of food and realize that there may be food left on his plate when he's finished eating.

Every child's dietary needs are slightly different. The American Academy of Pediatrics recommends that children ages one through three consume approximately 40 calories daily for each inch of height. Even this "rule" isn't hard and fast. A more active toddler, or a toddler with a higher metabolism and a larger build, will need more food than the mythological "average" toddler.

Your child's appetite and food preferences will vary from day to day, and growth spurts will make her eating habits even less predictable, so your best bet is to expect your toddler to deviate from this chart, and then you won't be worried and stressed.

When your toddler is thirsty between meals and snacks, offer water. Get your child used to drinking water on a regular basis. Drinking water keeps your child hydrated, helps to prevent constipation, and regulates your child's energy level (stamina).

For lists of snack and meal ideas for toddlers, see Food Tools 4 and 5 at the back of the book. See Appendices A, B, and C for information on allergies, diabetes, and other important health issues.

Table 4.3

Menu Snapshot: A Typical Toddler Menu Plan

	Serving Sizes	Food Pyramid Equivalents
Breakfast	1/2 cup of cereal (either hot cereal or infant cereal or unsweetened ready-to-eat cereal)	1 serving of grains
	1/2 cup of homogenized milk (some in cereal, some in cup)	1/2 serving of milk
	4 ounces of unsweetened fruit juice	1/2 serving of fruit
Snack	1/2 slice of whole-grain toast	1/2 serving of grains
	1/2 snack-size container of yogurt	1/2 serving of milk
Lunch	1/4 cup of cooked pasta or rice	1/2 serving of grains
	1 ounce of dried beans or peas	1 serving of meat and beans
	1/4 cup of mashed or finely chopped vegetables	1/4 serving of vegetables
	1/2 medium pear (very ripe, peeled, and diced into small pieces)	1/2 serving of fruit
	1/2 cup of homogenized milk from a cup	1/2 serving of milk
Snack	2 whole-grain soda crackers	1/2 serving of bread
	6 baby carrots, cooked	1/2 serving of vegetables

Dinner	1 ounce of finely chopped meat, poultry, or fish	1 serving of meat and beans
	1/4 cup of mashed or finely chopped cooked vegetables	1/4 serving of vegetables
	1/2 cup of rice or 1/2 slice of bread	1/2 serving of grains
	1/4 cup of applesauce (unsweetened)	1/4 serving of fruit
	1/2 cup of homogenized milk from a cup	1/2 serving of milk
Bedtime Snack (optional)	Breast milk or a milk serving saved from earlier in the day	You can include servings from other groups by reworking the menu slightly.

Total food group servings for the day

Grains: 3 ounces

Vegetables: 1 cup

Fruits: 1 cup

Milk: 2 cups

Meat and beans: 2 ounces

The food pyramid officially starts at age two, but you can still use this same menu when feeding a one-year-old. Simply offer your one-year-old smaller portion sizes (start with half the portion sizes indicated above and work your way up), or offer him the same portion sizes and accept that there may be some food left at the end of the meal.

Remember that this is just a guideline. You don't have to follow it obsessively, nor do you need to weigh and measure your toddler's meals. Just eyeball the quantities to ensure that they're toddler-sized servings as opposed to grownup-sized servings. That way, you'll save yourself unnecessary worry if he eats only a portion of his meal.

If you're nursing, you may be breast-feeding at times other than bedtime. Your toddler will adjust her overall caloric consumption to account for the breast milk in her diet if you offer a variety of healthy food choices at regularly scheduled meal and snack times.

Table 4.4

What's *Not* on the Menu: Foods That *Aren't* Recommended for Toddlers

	Foods That Should Be Avoided for Food Allergy Reasons
Shellfish	Avoid until age 18 months.
	Foods That Pose a Choking Risk for Toddlers
Large chunks of table foods (e.g., meat, fish, poultry, fruits, vegetables)	Cut your toddler's food into tiny pieces to minimize the risk of choking.
String cheese	Cut string cheese into tiny pieces.
Grapes	Cut into tiny strips or wedges. You don't want any pieces that are penny- or marble-shaped.
Carrots, raw	Serve your toddler carrots that have been shredded or cooked and chopped into tiny pieces. Wait until late in the toddler years before introducing very finely cut carrot sticks and even then, don't give your toddler any carrot pieces that are thicker than her baby finger.
Gum	Choking hazard can't be eliminated. Avoid.
Hard candy, hard-to-chew candy	Avoid hard candies as well as lollipops. (The candy at the end of the stick can easily come off.) Both pose a choking risk to toddlers. Also watch out for ultra-chewy candy that your toddler may have trouble chewing and swallowing.
Nuts	Choking hazard can't be eliminated. Avoid.
Peanut butter, chunky style	Avoid. You can serve your toddler smooth peanut butter on a cracker, provided that the peanut butter is spread very thinly. Never serve a toddler or other young child peanut butter on a spoon. Observe your child carefully to make sure that she's able to chew and swallow the food without choking.

Olives	Remove pit and slice into tiny pieces.
Popcorn	Choking hazard can't be eliminated. Avoid.
Raisins	Choking hazard can't be eliminated. Avoid.
Tomatoes, cherry	Cut into tiny strips or wedges. You don't want any pieces that are penny- or marble-shaped.

Foods That Pose a Choking Risk for Toddlers

Sausages	Slice into thin strips lengthwise and then chop into bite-sized pieces crosswise. Do not cut into penny-shaped pieces. Serve only in limited amounts due to high salt content.
Weiners	Slice into thin strips lengthwise and then chop into bite-sized pieces crosswise. Do not cut into penny-shaped pieces. Serve only in limited amounts due to high salt content.

Foods That Should Be Avoided for Other Reasons

Rare ground beef, uncooked hot dogs, and luncheon meat; lox (cold-smoked fish); raw milk and raw milk cheese (such as queso fresco); soft cheeses (such as feta, Brie, Camembert, roquefort); unpasteurized apple juice; bean sprouts; alfalfa sprouts; raw eggs; uncooked dough or batter that contains raw eggs (e.g., Tiramisu)	These foods are at risk of being contaminated with harmful bacteria and should be avoided by babies, toddlers, and preschoolers as well as pregnant and breast-feeding women.

FOOD FOR THOUGHT

Toddlers don't need as much food as adults. A quarter or half a piece of toast might be enough for your toddler. Some nutrition experts suggest using serving sizes equal to 1 tablespoon per year of age or a quarter of an adult serving per year of age for toddlers and preschoolers. A serving of toast for a one-year-old would be a quarter of a piece and a serving of toast for a two-year-old would be half a piece if you use this rule. Don't assume that every serving you'll be offering your toddler will be an adult-sized serving or you'll be offering her too much food.

If your toddler is at high risk of developing food allergies, your health care practitioner may recommend a more conservative approach in introducing the foods that are responsible for most food allergies in young children. See Chapters 2 and 3 and Appendices A, B, and C for more on this issue and consult with your child's health care practitioner for advice on your child's particular risk factors.

If your child is involved in group activities like day care or play groups, it may not be safe for her to eat peanut butter at home if she'll come into contact with other children with severe peanut allergies due to the risk of cross contamination. Even trace amounts of peanuts spread via your child's clothing or skin could be enough to cause a severe allergic reaction in someone else's child. Get in touch with one of the allergy associations listed in Appendix A for guidance on this issue.

MOM'S THE WORD

"The best advice/reminder I ever received was that kids aren't what they eat at any particular time. If they refuse to eat anything other than a couple of crackers one day, they won't fall down from malnutrition. The human body is very adaptable and adept at getting fuel when it needs it. It can be really hard to keep perspective when your child hasn't had a vegetable in five days, but I try to remind myself of this all the time before freaking out. And instead of freaking out, I try to come up with ways that I can work in the nutrients she refuses to eat in soups, sauces, etc."

—*Heather, 30, currently expecting her second child*

FOOD FOR THOUGHT

Be careful how much juice you give your toddler. Too much juice can decrease your toddler's appetite for healthier foods and deprive her of necessary dietary fiber.

Excessive juice can also cause diarrhea because juice is high in sorbitol, a non-digestible type of sugar. (Check the label for sorbitol or other "sugar alcohols.") Prune, apple, pear, peach, and cherry juice tend to be particularly high in sorbitol, which is why they tend to have a particularly powerful laxative effect.

Dietitians recommend limiting toddlers to no more than 4–6 ounces per day. (You can stretch your toddler's "juice budget" a little further by diluting her juice with water.) Diluting it 50/50 will also help to minimize the risk of excess sugar that can trigger diarrhea.

Finally, do not use a bottle or a sippy cup of juice as a pacifier for your toddler during the day or at night. It's an unhealthy habit for dietary and dental reasons. You don't want her to turn to food to soothe herself every time she's feeling stressed or bored. And having her teeth constantly bathed in juice (or any beverage other than plain water) can cause tooth decay. (Offer your toddler the type of sippy cup with a built-in straw. Juice and milk is sipped past the teeth rather than pooling around the teeth.) You can side-step this problem by making juice a breakfast drink. Your toddler will learn to ask for other types of drinks at other times of day.

To minimize the risk of choking:

- Avoid serving your toddler any of the foods that pose a high risk of choking to young children, and make sure that the other key adults in your toddler's life are also aware that these foods are off limits to him for now.

- Have a rule that your toddler can eat only at the table. You'll find it easier to supervise him and he won't be able to run around while he's eating, which increases the risk of choking in young children.

Raising a Snack-Savvy Toddler

SNACKS TEND TO get a rather bad rap these days, mainly because we've lost sight of what they were designed to accomplish in the first place. We view them as something we shouldn't be offering to our kids when, in fact, they have an essential role to play in the diets of young children—helping to bridge the gap between one meal and the next.

Here are some important points to keep in mind when planning snacks for your toddler.

Treat snacks as planned mini-meals. You don't want your toddler to graze continually: you want him to learn that we eat and then we move on and do something else. He'll find it easier to make this association if you serve him his snacks in his high chair or booster seat and if you resist the temptation to give him a snack every time he's bored, unhappy, or restless. Those sorts of food associations can be hard to unlearn, particularly when they're acquired at such an early age. Give your child the gift of healthy eating by teaching him how to be a savvy snacker starting right now.

Think about the types of snacks you're serving your toddler. Rather than giving foods that are high in sugar, salt, artificial flavors, preservatives, and other ingredients like caffeine that really don't have a place in the diet of a toddler, serve healthy foods such as vegetables and fruits.

Forget that old "no snacks before meals" rule. There's nothing wrong with giving your toddler a snack right before a meal provided that snack is actually part of her meal. If she's getting totally antsy while you're trying to make dinner, sit her in her high chair and let her get a head start on the cooked carrots she'd otherwise be enjoying as part of her meal. Turn her high chair toward you so that you can supervise her while she's eating. Then you can finish up the dinner preparations while she noshes away on the veggie

---

MOTHER WISDOM

Be alert to the risk of choking while you're grocery shopping with your child. If your grocery cart contains high-risk foods like whole grapes or your cart is positioned close to the grapes in the produce aisle, your child could reach over and pop a grape into his mouth and start choking before you even realized that there was a problem. The results could be tragic for your family.

MOTHER WISDOM

Try to serve your child freshly prepared foods so that she'll acquire a taste for foods in their purest, most natural form. You're helping to establish food tastes and eating patterns that will be with her for a lifetime. It's an awesome responsibility and an exciting opportunity—your chance to give your toddler a lifelong nutritional advantage.

---

appetizer. You may want to give her a break from the high chair before dinner officially begins. Otherwise she may run out of patience long before you sit down to eat your dinner.

Toddler Feeding FAQ

"My toddler eats really quickly so that I sometimes worry that she'll choke. How can I encourage her to slow down?" Create a relaxed atmosphere at the dinner table. Talk to your toddler in a slow, calm voice and gently remind her to take time to chew her food. Limit the amount of food that you put in front of her at any given time in case she's shoving a lot of food in her mouth at once. That can increase a child's risk of choking.

"My toddler has the opposite problem. He can make a meal last forever." Some toddlers are dawdlers. The best way to handle this situation is to factor in a little extra time for mealtimes. This is particularly important if your toddler enjoys a leisurely breakfast, but you need to be somewhere bright and early. Rather than rushing her and stressing yourself—a not-so-great-way to start the day—allow yourself an extra 15 minutes or so, even if that means crawling out of bed 15 minutes earlier.

"My toddler won't eat anything but bananas these days. What can I do to encourage him to eat other foods?" It's not unusual for toddlers to develop a strong preference—some would call it a fixation—with one particular food. It might be cereal, bananas, macaroni and cheese, or the ubiquitous peanut butter-and-jelly sandwich.

The best way to deal with the situation is to continue to offer your child a variety of foods. It's fine to offer him a small serving

FOOD FOR THOUGHT

Sometimes toddlers experience food jags when their bodies are in a resting phase of the growth cycle. Because they aren't quite as hungry as they were before, they can afford to be a little extra discriminating in their dining choices. Once their growth rate picks up again and their appetite increases, they tend to eat a wider variety of foods.

---

of some of his favorite foods, but that shouldn't be the only thing on the menu. If your child is hungry and you don't get too upset about what he is or isn't eating (which may show him how much power he can wield over others by having a hissy fit over food), he'll eat the other foods that you're offering him.

"My toddler doesn't like eating solid foods. He just likes liquids, like milk and juice, and some really soft, liquidy foods." It could be that your toddler is filling up on milk, which tends to be quite filling, or that juice is dulling her appetite for other foods.

Other things to consider:

- Is your child drinking from a bottle? If he is, his tendency to overdo it with the liquid lunch (and breakfast and dinner) may be less of a problem if he has to drink from a sippy cup.

- Is your child allowed to drink from a bottle or a sippy cup all day long? This is a bad eating habit and can cause possible dental problems. It can also reduce your toddler's appetite.

"I have 18-month old twin daughters. One isn't big on veggies and the other isn't big on meat. Are they each missing out on different types of important nutrients?" Meat has traditionally played such an important role in North American society that we sometimes overestimate its importance in our diets and our children's diets, too. Many children thrive on meat-free diets. (See the appendices for some excellent resources for vegetarian and vegan parents and kids.) As long as your toddler is eating other iron-rich foods (fortified cereals and breads, spinach, beans, lentils, eggs, and certain types of fish and the dark meat in poultry, too), she should be getting enough iron from her diet. Once your toddler is a little older, you can also add iron-rich dried fruits like raisins to her diet.

FOOD FOR THOUGHT

According to Gerber's Feeding Infants and Toddlers (FITS) study, nearly one-third of infants and toddlers don't consume any vegetables at all. And the most frequently eaten "vegetable" by toddlers age 15–18 months is French fries. (Yes, fries count as a vegetable, but they certainly aren't nutritional all-stars, so offer them only occasionally if at all.)

And as for your veggie-hating twin, there's good news on that front as well. Offer sweeter-tasting veggies like sweet potatoes and carrots in the hope that she'll become more receptive to greens like broccoli and spinach over time. If she's eating a wide variety of fruit, she's getting a lot of the vitamins and fiber that she would otherwise be getting from her veggies.

"My toddler doesn't drink nearly enough milk. I know calcium is important for building strong bones. What are some other toddler-friendly sources of calcium?" Think milk products for starters unless, of course, your toddler has a milk allergy or intolerance, in which case you should talk with a pediatric dietitian about some acceptable alternatives such as yogurt, cheese, cottage cheese, and so on. Other sources of calcium include calcium-fortified soy milk, calcium-fortified 100 percent juice, broccoli, bok choy, almonds, almond butter, ice cream, frozen yogurt, tofu, and dark, leafy greens.

"How strict do we have to be with our toddler when it come to policing junk food?" Parents have different ideas about toddlers and junk food. Some prefer to keep junk food out of their homes and away from their toddlers for as long as possible so that their toddlers will hopefully develop a taste and preference for less processed foods.

"Babies/toddlers who are fed quality, fresh, organic, whole, unprocessed foods from day one do not ever know what junk food is, so they never demand it or even crave it," notes Erin, 30, mother of 15-month-old Fiona. "I have done some reading that suggests kids who are kept away from sugar, processed foods, white foods, artificial colors and flavors, etc., until they are about five years old will not really like these foods. If they do consume junk, they eat it

GROWING A HEALTHY TODDLER

While you don't want to obsess about what your child is or isn't eating, it is important to take him for regular checkups so your health care provider can monitor his rate of growth and overall development.

Research conducted at the Oregon Health and Science University and the University of Southampton, UK, has found a child's weight gain between the ages of two and eleven relates most strongly to the risk of heart disease in adulthood, not that child's actual body weight at a later age. Rapid weight gain during toddlerhood may cause a toddler to gain weight as fat rather than muscle, which could ultimately lead to an elevated risk of heart disease.

Ask your child's health care provider what she thinks about vitamin and mineral supplements for toddlers. Some pediatric health specialists and dietitians are strongly in favor of them, arguing that they provide a nutritional safety net when toddlers' eating habits get unpredictable. Others argue that these supplements are unnecessary for toddlers who are generally eating well. Some toddlers are generally considered good candidates for supplements, whether or not their health care providers have an across-the-board vitamin and mineral supplement policy or not.

In general, supplements are recommended in situations when a toddler:

- rarely eats foods that contain iron (meat, iron-fortified breads and cereals, eggs, dried fruits, cooked dried beans or lentils, and dark, leafy vegetables)

- follows a very strict vegetarian diet that does not allow for the consumption of any meat or milk products or rarely consumes meat or milk products for other reasons

- generally drinks less than 2 cups of milk each day

- consistently boycotts foods from an entire food group (e.g., no grains, no milk products, no fruits, no veggies, no meats or beans) very sparingly because it makes them feel yucky right away and they are used to feeling good after eating."

Other parents subscribe to "forbidden fruit" theory: that if you treat junk food like you would any other food and serve it occasionally, it loses some of the mystique of being a "bad" food. (By the way, that "good" food, "bad" food thinking is kind of passé. Dietitians prefer to encourage their clients to think of foods as "everyday," "sometimes," and "occasional.") If your child has a sweet tooth, you may want to limit sweet treats to twice a week. Not only will your child learn to differentiate between treats and everyday foods, but treats will retain their element of fun. (Of course, you don't want to put ice cream on a pedestal. It's all about passing along healthy attitudes about food.)

Pamela, a 33-year-old mother of two, has found a middle-of-the-road approach that works for her and her family: "I am lenient on the junk foods at other people's houses, since junk food is not a problem at home. If at a visitor's house the only thing my toddler ends up eating properly is dessert, then so be it. It is about balance and the big picture."

Solutions Central—The Last Word

While you'll want to take a "one day at a time" approach in getting through the challenges of planning meals and snacks for a toddler who may give a major thumbs-down to anything and everything you put down in front of her, you don't want to rely on a one-day snapshot of her eating patterns to decide whether or not she's well nourished. It's also important to keep an overall view of her progress in learning to accept a wider variety of foods, which is easy to lose sight of if she's currently refusing anything that shows up on the dinner table, sight unseen!

Don't forget to check out the toddler-related food tools at the back of the book and the many toddler-related food resources in the appendices.

CHAPTER 5

The Discriminating Diner: Feeding Your Preschooler

What I've noticed is "uber-advising" with occasional horrified glances at fruit snacks, and snide comments like, "Oh, I would never feed my child that."
—JESSICA, 36, MOTHER OF ONE

Some parents really brag about how adventurous an eater their child is or how much food they can pack away at a sitting.
—KIRA, 35, MOTHER OF ONE

WHEN YOU FIRST started your baby on solids, you probably assumed that you and your child would be dining on Easy Street by the time she was a preschooler. But now that time has come and you're probably discovering that your three- or four-year-old still has a few eating-related idiosyncrasies left over from her toddler days, and that she's developing some distinctly preschooler-like behaviors to boot.

And then there's you: One minute you're sane and rational about what is or isn't going into your child's mouth (it all balances out at the end of the week) and the next minute you're questioning your fitness for motherhood because one of the items in your grocery cart clearly didn't pass muster with a member of the local *momfia* (a hard-core group of moms who dropped out of play group after the organic cracker snafu, and who seem to take perverse delight in catching some other mom with a box of Twinkies perched on top of her broccoli).

This chapter is about the nutritional joys and challenges of the preschool stage. You'll find tips on dealing with some of the specific mealtime challenges you're likely to encounter during the preschool years. Then, in the next chapter, we'll take this one step further by looking at some mom-proven strategies for making meal planning, grocery shopping, and cooking as stress-free as possible.

Kitchen Confidential

THERE'S BEEN A lot of talk lately about "parenting perfectionism"— how parents (and moms in particular) feel tremendous pressure to get parenting right. And now that childhood obesity rates are skyrocketing, the issue of what types and quantities of foods to serve our kids has become ever more high stakes than ever. Sometimes parents are so concerned about preventing their kids from becoming overweight that they exercise too much control over their kids' food choices, which can backfire by causing kids to develop an unhealthy preoccupation with food.

Feeding is one of the very first things a mother does to nurture her baby, which helps to explain why such powerful emotions are triggered when a toddler or preschooler refuses to eat vegetables or starts gaining weight much more rapidly than the growth charts indicate she should. It can be difficult to separate your value as a mother from the act of feeding or the effects of your efforts to feed your child on your child's overall growth and development. So many of us have images that celebrate the golden era of "motherhood and apple pie": a 1950s mom standing in the kitchen wearing an apron, proudly showing off an apple pie or a plate of chocolate chip cookies for her kids; or a 1970s mom making yogurt from scratch so that her kids could have a healthy alternative to the sugary varieties in the grocery-store refrigerator case.

 **MOM'S THE WORD**

"I don't see much competition on the good eater vs. picky eater front. But there is some pride or bragging in terms of 'My child has never eaten X.' (X can equal sugar, refined sugar, processed meat/cheese, whatever.) There's more control over what you offer a child than there is over how much they sleep or eat, so it seems like something parents can take more credit for, and so they do."

—*Lisa, 34, mother of two*

The pendulum swings back and forth, but there are always "food rules" for mothers to follow. The pressure to do right by your kids is always there. "There's a big push to feed babies only organic foods," notes Jen, a 26-year-old first-time mother. "I even have a few cookbooks that suggest this is the *only* way to go."

While Jen embraces a lot of natural cooking methods herself, she doesn't like the pressure or the guilt to follow other people's "food rules." She feels that mothers have to be informed and confident enough to know which rules make sense for their families and which ones don't. "It's easy to feel like someone doesn't think you're a good mother if you give your child cow's milk a week before their first birthday, for instance. It's like there are these rules that exist (i.e., feed baby rice cereal first) and if you don't follow them you're a wing nut. Or if you make all your own baby food, you're some sort of hippy. You have to shrug it off and realize that all kids and parents are different."

Preschooler Brain Cam

PRESCHOOLERS TEND TO have a flair for the dramatic, an ability to telegraph their feelings about your culinary effort *du jour* in 1,001 different ways. That's what makes dining with a three- or four-year-old so entertaining and infuriating at the same time.

"My four-year-old has become more selective in the foods she eats," says Carolyn, 34, mother of two. "As a toddler, she would try anything and decide after whether or not she liked it. Now, she is more prone to judging her foods based on color, texture, or aroma before she'll even go near it. I can honestly say that she is more difficult to feed now than as a toddler."

"Emma is very stubborn and if she doesn't like the look of something, she won't try it," says Clare, a 31-year-old mother of three. "She'll convince herself that she doesn't and won't like it, and therefore won't be willing to try it. In trying to deal with it, I have to keep reminding her 'How did you know that you liked ice cream? How did you know that you liked chocolate? How did you know that you liked cantaloupe? You tried it and you liked it. You won't know if you don't like this food if you don't try it.'"

If you've ever been stuck in one of those infamous pre-schooler-parent standoffs over food, you know it's a place you don't ever want to go again. Fortunately, it is possible to sidestep many of those crazy-making power struggles over food. Here are some of the key strategies that have worked for other parents. You'll find other tips and ideas in Table 5.1 and Chapter 7.

Plan your mood as well as your food. I picked up this tip from a decidedly family-friendly nutrition book called *Food to Grow On* by Susan Mendelson and Rena Mendelson, MS, DSc, RD. The authors offer this sensible advice to parents who are tired of watching every family dinner hour devolve into a family feud. They suggest that you arrive at the dinner table determined to create a fun and upbeat atmosphere (as opposed to having a tense discussion with your partner about the last credit card bill, or with your school-aged child about the chores that didn't get done on the weekend, and/or watching your preschooler like a hawk because you just know she's going to feed her broccoli to the dog the moment you break eye contact). After all, how can anyone expect to enjoy their dinner if mom's on the rampage? And if mom's in that kind of mood, your preschooler might decide to one-up you in the battle for dinnertime domination. Yep. Things could get ugly.

Don't get locked into a battle of wills with your child over what's on her dinner plate. The more you pressure your pre-schooler to eat her dinner, the more likely she'll refuse. (It doesn't matter if she's starving because she didn't like what you served at dinner or if this is her very favorite dinner.) Preschoolers are notorious for being stubborn. And if it means she has to deal with tummy grumbles until it's time for her bedtime snack—she may decide that that's what she has to put up with in order to win this round with you.

Resist the temptation to draw comparisons between siblings. Siblings are every bit as individual when it comes to eating habits as they are when it comes to temperaments. Besides, who really cares if your preschooler's baby brother is blowing him away in the veggie department? Not your preschooler. In fact, by making his little brother out to be the Patron Saint of Sweet Potatoes, you're simply providing him with further evidence to substantiate his working hypothesis that babies aren't nearly as smart as everyone thinks. So much for sibling harmony at your dinner table.

Don't use food as a reward or a punishment. If you're looking for a healthy, kid-friendly reward, choose an activity reward instead. Tell your preschooler that you'll take her for a bike ride around the block because she did such a great job of helping you pick up all the toys in the backyard.

Encourage your kids to see food for what it is—body fuel. That doesn't mean that they shouldn't enjoy the taste of good food or the process of eating, but what you're trying to do is to make food nice and simple for your kids. If you can keep food nice and simple, they'll have an easier time developing a matter-of-fact relationship with food, as opposed to the on-again, off-again love affair that so many North Americans have with their refrigerators and their bathroom scales.

Understand that "forbidden" can be a euphemism for "fabulous" when you're a preschooler. Researchers at Pennsylvania State University founds that kids whose parents had the strictest rules about foods were the ones who tended to exercise the least control when such foods were made available to them in other situations. If you treat junk food as a forbidden food, you might be setting your child up for a binge when such foods are available. That finding makes a lot of sense to Melanie, a 29-year-old mother of one. "I get gently teased for trying to avoid giving my son junk food. But I don't mind because I am making the decisions that are best for me and my son. And in my own defense, I do allow my son to try some treat foods on special occasions so that these foods will not become coveted forbidden foods." Dietitians think it makes the most sense to put foods into three categories: (1) Everyday foods that are healthy enough to eat every day; (2) sometimes foods that are okay to have a couple of times a week; and (3) occasional foods that should be enjoyed every once in a while. You would place foods in a "never" category only if your child was allergic to them; if your family chose to avoid them for dietary reasons (e.g., your family is vegetarian); or if your family chose not to eat them for religious or cultural reasons.

Finally, don't let your preschooler's dinner diatribe lead to mealtime malaise for you. It's all too easy to allow your enjoyment of your own meal to be affected by what your preschooler has to say about her plate full of food. Who wants to listen to a non-stop monologue about how yucky dinner tastes, looks, and smells? But try not to take her food critique to heart. Remember, she's not a restaurant critic. She's a little kid. Still it doesn't hurt to try to put your mom detective skills to good use. Find out if she's objecting to the meal because it's too sour, too spicy, or too chewy and you can use that knowledge to your advantage in planning future menus.

MOM'S THE WORD

"Red grapes are fine Monday, but only green will do on Tuesday. And suddenly a crust on a sandwich will be the cause of a meltdown. So do I concede and cut the silly things off, or do I just smile and say, 'Just leave it on the side of your plate, honey' through gritted teeth?"

—*Carolyn, 34, mother of two*

Table 5.1

Typical Food and Eating Milestones and Behaviors for Preschoolers

Your Preschooler will ...	What You Can Do
... master even more eating and drinking skills, learning how to drink from a cup without a lid and how to serve himself from serving dishes on the dinner table.	Continue to provide him with opportunities to practise his skills. Preschoolers learn by doing. And remember that there's an added benefit to allowing preschoolers to serve themselves: doing so allows them to become more tuned into their signals of hunger and fullness and to learn to serve themselves accordingly.
... begin to learn some simple table manners like saying "please" and "thank you" when he asks for foods. On the other hand, your preschooler won't hesitate to be rude if he wants to get your attention in a hurry.	Encourage table manners, but keep your expectations realistic. Your child won't be dining in any five-star restaurants for a while. Besides, being respectful of other peoples' feelings is more important than knowing which fork is your salad fork. That's what you want to focus on teaching your preschooler right now.
... want to make his own food choices, including what he does with his food after it arrives on the dinner table (e.g., dousing everything with ketchup).	Build some choices into the dinner menu so that your preschooler won't feel like you're trying to be the boss of him 24/7. It can be as simple as putting out a fresh vegetable platter and inviting your preschooler to help himself or preparing two cooked veggies and giving your preschooler a choice of carrots or peas. And as for the ketchup conundrum, allow him to exercise some freedom of expression with the ketchup (or mustard or salad dressing) as long as he doesn't go totally condiment crazy.

... have a clear idea of what foods are supposed to look like and how they are supposed to be served, and will protest vigorously if you attempt to break any of his "food rules."	Strike a balance. When it's not inconvenient to serve him green peppers the way he thinks they should be served (raw and sliced in narrow strips), go for it. But if your family is dining out in a restaurant and the salad bar features them raw and finely chopped, encourage him to expand his food universe by trying something different just this once. You may not always succeed, but it's part of your job description as a parent to try.
... prefer simple foods that he can recognize.	Realize that mystery casserole isn't likely to be a hit with your preschooler. You may luck out and end up with a child who is willing to try anything and everything, but that tends to be the exception rather than the rule. Most three- and four-year-olds prefer their chicken, veggies, and noodles to be clearly identifiable and ideally on their own clearly defined place on the dinner plate.
... want a say in determining which types of foods get served for meals and snacks.	Give him a say, but not the ability to dictate the family's menus for the week. Balance his food likes and dislikes against the food likes and dislikes of other family members and your knowledge of meal planning and nutrition and then come up with a week's worth of meal and snack ideas accordingly.
... want a say in how his favorite foods are served.	Let your preschooler decide whether he wants his toast cut in quarters or halves, triangles or squares. Don't simply make that decision for him. By giving him the ability to make choices in this area of his food life, you may divert struggles in other areas where it's a bit more difficult to be democratic (like delegating decision-making authority about tonight's dinner menu!). And check with your preschooler about those toast shape preferences on a regular basis. They can and will change. You can also coach him in social skills, including manners and the art of asking nicely for what we would like and treating other people with respect. These are important skills for everyone to learn, young children included.

continued on p. 134

Table 5.1 (Continued)

Your Preschooler will ...	What You Can Do
... be eager to imitate what you're doing at the dinner table.	If you're using a regular glass, your preschooler may want to swap his sippy cup for a regular glass or maybe even your favorite coffee mug. Sometimes this can lead to frustration—if your preschooler isn't quite as adept at cutting his meat himself as you are, or if he sloshes some soup on himself while trying to feed himself soup from a soup bowl "just like dad." But it's only through experiencing some of this frustration that he has the opportunity to learn. (Your parental intuition will help you to figure out how much frustration is healthy and how much is not.)
... become increasingly aware that other families eat different types of foods and often have totally different family rules when it comes to meals and snacks.	Help him make sense of what he's observing. He may want to know why some kids are allowed to dine daily on foods that your family eats only occasionally or that your family never eats at all. Just be careful how you phrase your answers because it's quite likely that your preschooler may parrot those answers back to one of those other families at some point.

Feeding Your Preschooler: Moms' Top Worries and Concerns

You'd think after three or four years in the worry trenches, you would have run through all the food-related worries by now. Well, there are still quite a few to get through yet, at least according to the moms I know. Here's the low-down on some of the top food-related worries and concerns for the preschool stage.

"Everyone in my extended family is convinced that there's something wrong with my preschooler because there are days when he doesn't want to eat anything for dinner. Aren't appetite fluctuations fairly normal for a preschooler?"

Absolutely. In fact, if you want to get technical, those appetite fluctuations are proof positive that your preschooler is getting the amount of food that's just right for his body. He is averaging out his food intake over a period of days by paying attention to those appetite cues. If your preschooler was exceptionally hungry at lunch and ate lots of meatballs, his body knows that he doesn't need a lot of food come dinnertime. That explains why can he turn his nose up at a meal he usually loves, leaving his grandparents or other well-meaning family members worried or concerned. Your preschooler's appetite can also be affected by his mood and energy level: if he's overly excited or overly tired, he won't feel much like eating.

Here are some other points to consider when your preschooler's appetite seems to be off at a particular meal:

- **Could something be distracting him?** Is the TV blaring in the next room? Are his siblings providing so much dinnertime entertainment that he keeps forgetting to eat? Don't overlook distractions related to eating, by the way. Example: Maybe he's more fascinated by the fun of twirling the spaghetti on the fork than actually getting it into his mouth. (Solution: See if he'll let you show him how to cut the spaghetti into bite-sized pieces after he's had a chance to twirl it around for a while.)

- **Is your preschooler filling up on drinks?** Sometimes something as simple as serving your preschooler his milk after rather than during the meal can make a huge difference in terms of his appetite. Children who drink a lot of liquids (either milk or juice) are at increased risk of both failure to thrive (FTT) and obesity. (Some children who "drink" their fruit servings in the form of fruit juice don't feel as satisfied as they would if they had eaten a piece of fruit. They may therefore tend to fill up on other foods—something that can lead to a weight problem over time.)

- **Could the portion size be off?** It's generally best to start with a small portion and offer seconds—or allow your preschooler to help himself to seconds—if he still wants more to eat. This is particularly important when you're dealing with a child whose appetite is so-so at the best of times. Serve a child like this a plate that's overflowing with adult-sized portions of food and he will likely take one look and say, "Thanks, but no thanks." (An older child, on the other hand, is more likely to respond to these external food cues and may be encouraged to overeat, which is why kids should always be encouraged to serve themselves at the family dinner table.) A preschooler-sized portion can range from half the size to the full size of an adult portion. The portion size typically increases with the age of the preschooler. See Appendix B for links to some on-line tools that may be helpful in gauging portion size for a preschooler.

- **Did your preschooler drink a lot of juice during the day? Did he have a late-afternoon snack?** It's best to go easy with the juice and to avoid giving children snacks within one to two hours of dinnertime unless the snack is an appetizer (a light snack that's actually part of the meal—perhaps a small plate of raw veggies).

- **Does your preschooler tend to eat his biggest meals at breakfast and lunch?** In that case, he may require only a snack-sized dinner most evenings (and on some nights, he may not be very hungry at all). This is actually a pattern that we should all be following—eating most of our calories earlier in the day—but we gradually train ourselves to adapt to a much less body-friendly pattern of eating. So kudos to your preschooler for still being tuned into his body's natural rhythms!

- **Is your preschooler too tired to eat?** Being overly tired can cause young children to lose their appetites. Make sure your child is getting the rest he needs. If your child has a hard time settling down at bedtime, gets up too early in the morning, or is up in the night, see my book *Sleep Solutions for Your Baby, Toddler and Preschooler: The Ultimate No-Worry Approach for Each Age and Stage* for some sensible advice on sleep.

Here are a couple of other important points:

Some children have smaller-than-average appetites. If your preschooler falls into this category, offer her nutritious, high-energy snacks between meals such as cheese, higher-fat yogurt, whole milk, muffins, and peanut butter (unless, of course, nut allergies are a problem for your preschooler, other family members, or any of the other children she is in regular contact with) as well as nutrient-rich foods such as meat, beans and lentils, peas, and whole-grain and enriched cereals.

Make sure you feed your preschooler when he's hungry, not when you're hungry or when you think he should be hungry. If he asks for a snack an hour before mealtime because he's hungry, let him get a head start on dinner by eating some veggies or a bowl of soup. If you disregard his hunger cues, you'll be teaching him that it's more important to pay attention to the time on the clock than his body's signals of hunger or fullness, which is not exactly the message you want to convey.

FOOD FOR THOUGHT

Don't try to talk your preschooler into eating if he's not hungry. One of your most important jobs as a parent is to help your preschooler to tune into his internal signs of hunger and fullness, which enable him to determine how much food his body actually needs. You want him to remain tuned into those signals for a lifetime, and for his body to continue to send him reliable hunger and fullness cues.

Table: 5.2
What's on the Menu?: The Preschooler Food Pyramid

Food Group	Total Daily Amount from This Food Group	Important Notes: *1/4 cup is roughly an egg-sized portion of food, 1/2 cup is roughly an ice cream scoop portion of food, 1 cup is roughly a baseball-sized portion of food*
Grains	5 ounces	Make half of your preschooler's servings from this group whole grains. You can increase your toddler's intake of whole grains by choosing foods with one of the following ingredients first on the label's ingredient list: brown rice, bulgur, graham flour, oatmeal, whole-grain corn, whole oats, whole rye, whole wheat, wild rice. Foods that are labeled with the words "multi-grain," "stone-ground," "100 percent wheat," "cracked wheat," "seven-grain," or "bran" are usually not whole-grain products. (These are still healthy foods, of course.) One ounce of grains equals one slice of bread, 1 cup of ready-to-eat cereal or 1/2 cup of cooked rice, cooked pasta, or cooked cereal.
Vegetables	1½ cup In general, 1 cup of raw or cooked vegetables or vegetable juice, or 2 cups of raw leafy greens can be considered as 1 cup from the vegetable group.	Vary your preschooler's veggies. Rather than serve the same types of vegetables week in and week out, make a conscious effort to serve your preschooler a variety of vegetables. Aim for these amounts of the various types each week: • Dark green veggies: 1½ cups • Orange veggies: 1 cup • Dry beans and peas: 1 cup • Starchy veggies: 2½ cups • Other veggies: 4½ cups

Fruit	1¹/₂ cups	When choosing canned fruits, choose fruits canned in 100 percent fruit juice or water rather than syrup; and when you're shopping for fruit juice, look for unsweetened, 100 percent juice.

Fruit

1¹/₂ cups

In general, 1 cup of fruit or 100 percent fruit juice can be considered as 1 cup from the fruit group.

When choosing canned fruits, choose fruits canned in 100 percent fruit juice or water rather than syrup; and when you're shopping for fruit juice, look for unsweetened, 100 percent juice. Look for the following words on the package: "unsweetened," "pure fruit juice from concentrate," "no artificial flavors or colors added," "100 percent juice," or "nectar." Real juice contains more than 20 vitamins and minerals: it's the closest thing to a real piece of fruit you can put in a glass.

You're probably getting a fruit drink product (which is different from fruit juice) if you see the following words: "drink," "punch," "-ade," "beverage," "cocktail." These products typically contain little or no fruit juice. What you're purchasing is basically sugar-flavored water.

Vary your preschooler's fruit choices. Fruits differ in nutrient content.

Don't overdo it with the fruit juice. Not only will your child miss out on the fiber that comes from eating actual fruit: children who drink a lot of juice tend to eat less of other foods.

Milk

2 cups

In general, 1 cup of milk or yogurt, 1¹/₂ ounces of natural cheese or 2 ounces of processed cheese can be considered as 1 cup from the milk group; ¹/₄ cup of cottage cheese is considered ¹/₂ cup of milk.

Preschoolers can start to drink low-fat or fat-free milk, yogurt, and cheese.

If your child is lactose intolerant, serve her lactose-free milk. If your child has an allergy to cow's milk (different from being lactose intolerant), talk to your child's health care provider or a pediatric dietitian about the best alternatives. Some alternatives may include calcium-enriched soy or rice milk (for drinking); vegan cheese (for sandwiches and snacks); dairy-free margarine, vegetable shortening, or fruit juice soy butter for baking. (Use soy products as substitutions only if your child is able to tolerate soy.)

If your preschooler does not drink milk, talk to a dietitian or your child's health care provider about alternative ways of providing calcium and vitamin D to your child. Milk is the main dietary source of vitamin D.

continued on p. 140

Your preschooler's food consumption at any one meal is far less important than his total food consumption over the course of the day or a couple of days. If you're worried about what your child is or isn't eating, keep track of his food intake over a couple of days and compare his food consumption to the food guidelines in Table 5.2.

"Do Preschoolers Need Vitamins?"

It depends on who you ask. Some dietitians and pediatricians routinely recommend vitamins for all preschoolers. They think of vitamins as a form of dietary insurance—a way to provide a nutritional safety net on those days when your preschooler's appetite has gone AWOL or she's having a "nothing but bananas" kind of day. Others argue that vitamins are generally unnecessary, even for the pickiest of eaters, and that healthy nutrition should come from foods, not a pill.

If you decide to purchase a vitamin supplement for your child, it's important to purchase the right one. Vitamins are typically meant for children in a particular age range and the particular composition of vitamins and minerals varies from brand to brand. Look for one that includes iron and calcium: many preschoolers don't receive enough of these nutrients from dietary sources alone. (See also the section of this chapter that talks about milk.)

One final, all-important note: Store vitamins safely out of your child's reach. Because vitamins are designed to taste like candy in order to make them more appealing to children, children have been known to eat them like candy, and eating too many vitamins can be dangerous. And, of course, it goes without saying that you should never refer to a vitamin as candy. That could lead to a vitamin overdose.

"Will My Preschooler Ever Try New Foods?"

Ever? That's a pretty open-ended time frame. So I'm going to take my chances and say yes!

Some kids are adventurous eaters right from their baby days. (These are the ones who cry between spoonfuls of rice cereal if mom or dad misses a beat in the spoon-feeding momentum.) And then there are others who are just as skeptical about the whole process as those other babies are enthusiastic. They'd rather just stick with the breast or bottle. And while some of those culinary skeptics do get with the solid foods program quite quickly, others carry that food critic-like attitude well into the toddler and preschool years, treating all but a few carefully chosen foods as the enemy. (I'm assuming your three- or four-year-old is a member of this camp.)

So what do you do if your preschooler doesn't want to try new foods? Should you let her stay within her food comfort zone indefinitely or should you gently encourage her to expand her food repertoire, adding new foods, experimenting with new ways of preparing her old favorites, and sampling the cuisine of other ethnic groups and cultures?

Even though allowing your preschooler to dine indefinitely on familiar favorites is definitely the path of least resistance, you've got an important role to play in encouraging her to try new foods.

And, believe it or not, the situation may not be as hopeless as you might think. There's plenty you can do to encourage your child to accept new foods. Here are a few ideas. (You'll find more tips in Chapter 7.)

- Let her see you trying a variety of new foods on a regular basis, including whatever foods you're serving to her.

- Introduce new foods when she's with other kids (siblings, cousins, friends from play group) in the hope that some of them will start eating that food with great gusto. Kids who may be reluctant to try any new foods on their own are often surprisingly willing to experiment if a trusted peer is munching on that particular food.

- Try to serve foods that measure up to your preschooler's criteria for yumminess—the food is attractive (e.g., it features different colors, shapes, and textures of food) and it doesn't violate any of

"My Four-Year-Old Used to Eat All Kinds of Vegetables When He Was a Baby. Now He'll Eat Only a Couple Types of Vegetables and Only If They're Raw. Help!"

Many preschoolers are also big fans of raw cauliflower and broccoli, so you may want to serve those to your preschooler, too, assuming she hasn't already vetoed them.

Other tips:

- Try puréeing small quantities of other nutrient-rich veggies that your preschooler isn't so keen on (e.g., spinach) and add them to soups, pasta sauces, and stews. (Keep the veggie ratio low so that the flavor of the veggies doesn't overpower the other food or your preschooler is likely to refuse the entire entrée.)

- Some preschoolers who hate veggies served any other way love them when they're grilled on the barbecue. Of course, if your preschooler goes ballistic if her toast is the least bit golden brown, you may want to pass on this idea. Grill marks are unlikely to be her thing. And go light with the seasonings in the marinade. Your preschooler's taste buds are much more sensitive than yours, so that pepper medley spice blend may be unbearably hot to her.

- Don't give up on cooked veggies for good. Try serving them to her again, but cook them lightly, so that the vegetables are crisp and flavorful. Overcooking can make vegetables taste bitter. Just make sure that the vegetable is soft enough to eliminate any risk of choking. And if your preschooler prefers raw veggies, serve her those instead. In many cases, raw vegetables provide more nutrients than their cooked counterparts.

See Chapter 6 and Food Tools 4, 5, and 6 for more tips on encouraging your preschooler to try a greater variety of vegetables.

"My Three-Year-Old Hates Milk. Any Ideas on How I Can Make Milk More Appealing and Encourage Her to Drink More of It?"

Milk has an important role to play in the diets of young children (as opposed to dairy products in general). While other milk products (such as cheese and yogurt) are rich in calcium, they don't contain vitamin D, which kids need to develop strong bones and healthy teeth.

Sometimes a two-tiered strategy works best in dealing with this particular nutritional challenge: making milk a more appealing beverage and finding other ways of working milk into your preschooler's diet.

Make milk more appealing:

- **Consider how much juice your preschooler is drinking.** If your preschooler is drinking a lot of juice, that could be one of the reasons he's decided to give milk a major thumbs-down. Limit juice to 4–8 ounces maximum and continue to dilute that juice with water. If your preschooler has been drinking juice out of commercially manufactured juice boxes, you may have to gradually wean him off the full-strength stuff by switching to reusable plastic juice box containers and adding your own water.

- **When in Rome ...** If your preschooler loves juice this much, use that fact to your advantage. Serve her a fruity cow—milk with some concentrated fruit juice mixed in. (Make sure the fruit juice is 100 percent unsweetened.)

- **Whip up a smoothie.** Add fruit, yogurt, milk, and ice and you've got a beverage that even a hard-core milk-hater will have a hard time resisting. You can add more than one type of fruit (bananas and berries make a particularly delicious combo) and you can vary the thickness by simply adjusting the ratio of ingredients.

"Are Snacks Still Important for Preschoolers?"

Absolutely! It's difficult for preschoolers to squeeze all the nutrients their growing bodies need into just three meals a day because their stomachs are still relatively small. That's why snacks continue to play an important role in the diet of a three- or four-year-old, functioning as a nutritional bridge from one meal to the next.

If you think of snacks in those terms—as nutritional bridges rather than fillers—you'll see why most dietitians recommend offering preschoolers mini-meals rather than nutritionally empty snack foods when snack times roll around.

Here are some other important points to remember when planning snacks for your preschooler. (You'll find a list of snack ideas for preschoolers in Food Tools 4 and 5.)

- **Beat the clock.** Pay attention to the timing of your child's snacks. Ideally, don't offer a snack within two hours of a meal or you'll take the edge off your child's appetite.

- **Think of snack time as an opportunity for taste testing.** Because snack-sized servings are much smaller and hence less intimidating than meal-sized servings, snack time is the ideal time to introduce your toddler to new foods.

- **See double.** To make snacks nutritious as well as filling, try to include at least two food groups in a snack. For example, serve your preschooler a glass of chocolate milk and an apple at snacktime.

- **Consider giving your child choices at snack time.** That way, he can practise making healthy food choices, which isn't always possible to quite the same degree at mealtime. Present your child with a couple of healthy snack options and let her decide which she'd like, but let her know that once she makes her choice, she needs to stick with that choice for that snack time. Otherwise, you might end up making both snacks and throwing one away—and your preschooler wouldn't learn anything about making food choices.

- **Serve snacks that go the distance.** Every time you combine protein with carbohydrates, you increase a snack's staying power. Sliced turkey (protein) and cheese (protein) on a whole-grain cracker (complex carbohydrate) would be an example of a snack that would provide your preschooler with long-lasting energy.
- **Make it water or milk.** Think of juice as a breakfast drink and limit the juice to 4–8 ounces maximum per day. Research has shown that kids who drink more than $1^{1}/_{2}$ cups of juice each day are three times more likely to be overweight than children who drink less juice.

"Should I Let My Preschooler Help Herself to Snacks Whenever She's Hungry? Is It Okay If Those Are Healthy Snacks?"

Nutritionists have carefully balanced the pros and cons of this particular question. It sounds like such a great idea in principle (allowing your child to have total control over when she eats and what she eats, provided that those snacks are healthy), but the problem is that allowing preschoolers unlimited access to the snack cupboard or the refrigerator encourages some children to look for food whenever they feel bored or restless. Don't give your preschoolers free rein in the kitchen. If your child is hungry, she can, of course, let you know that she'd like something to eat. If it's not quite time for a snack, you might offer a glass of water and some veggies to see if she's *really* hungry. (In most cases, a preschooler who is simply bored will decide to hold out for something else unless, of course, the preschooler totally loves vegetables.) Then when her actual snack time rolls around, you can offer her something more substantial. Encourage her to respond to her natural hunger cues by eating when she's hungry and encourage her to train her body to feel hungry at certain predictable times of day (as opposed to engaging in an all-day grazefest!).

MOTHER WISDOM

If you allow your preschooler to spend time on the computer, that computer time should be counted toward your child's total screen time budget. It doesn't matter if your child is parked in front of the most educational, genius-making software package ever invented: he still needs time for active play.

- Look at your daily schedule and see if you can find blocks of time in your day that get gobbled up by chores that could be post-poned until later or shared with other family members. Do you have to clean the kitchen right after dinner, or could you use those 30 minutes to do something active with your preschooler?

- If your schedule is overloaded, hire a teenager to help with chores for an hour after dinner and use that time to go for a walk or a bike ride with your preschooler. Think of it this way: you wouldn't have a problem paying the teenager to babysit your child. You're paying her to clean up your kitchen instead.

- Make it a multi-family or multi-generational effort. Involve other people you know so that you'll be more likely to stick with your family fitness commitment. Start your own after-dinner walking club. Go to the park every evening as a group. Do whatever it takes to get and stay motivated.

- Plan for the off-season. The warm weather doesn't last forever, at least in some parts of North America. Go to ParentingLibrary.com and download the tip sheet on "Winter Family Fitness" so that you can keep your family in motion all year round: www.parentinglibrary.com/tipsheets.html.

Don't overdo it with the ultra-organized extracurriculars. Helping a young child to be physically active doesn't have to mean hours of shuttling kids to extracurricular programs. (If you need a PalmPilot to keep track of your preschooler's schedule, it's time to ease up a little!) Fun, spur-of-the-moment activities in which parents can be involved tend to have greater appeal for preschoolers. There will be plenty of time to sign up your child for organized sports when she's a little older. For now, let her have fun rolling down hills, kicking around a ball in the backyard, and working on her

FRIDGE NOTE

Looking for ways to increase your own opportunities for physical activity while you're motivating your kids to be active? Visit the "We Can! Ways to Enhance Children's Activity and Nutrition" website: www.nhlbi.nih.gov/health/public/heart/obesity/wecan.

---

swimming or skating skills during the family swim time at the community center.

Move outside your own comfort zone. Encourage your child to try new things by trying new things yourself, too. That way, she can see that it's okay to be a beginner at something—that it's all part of the fun.

Look for ways to become more active as a family. This means working more formal and informal physical activity into your regular routine (see Table 5.3) and also looking for ways to work some extra activity into special times like birthday parties, get-togethers with the neighbors, camping trips, and family vacations (see Table 5.4). To keep your family fitness program fun, stick with a core group of activities that you love, but always look for ways to try something new and different. That's what will keep your family fitness program fun and fresh, and increase the odds that you'll stick with it over the long run. And, by the way, not being active with your kids isn't an option these days—not with childhood obesity rates skyrocketing and kids being less fit than any generation before. Consider motivating your kids to be active to be part of the parenting job description—a task that is far too important to let slide.

Continue to work toward your family's healthy eating goals at the same time. See Chapter 6 for helpful tips on planning and preparing healthy family meals with minimum time, stress, and hassle.

Don't make too many changes all at once, and don't expect perfection of yourself or your kids. That kind of thinking tends to lead most adults and kids to head for the couch and/or the refrigerator. If you feel yourself losing your motivation, remind yourself of all the great benefits your kids are reaping because you are encouraging them to make physical fitness part of their lives.

Table 5.3
The Family Fitness Buffet: Activities That Are Fun for Preschoolers and Their Parents, Too

	Lower Intensity Fitness Activities	Higher Intensity Fitness Activities
Free or almost free	• Play outside • Play Frisbee • Swing on a swing • Go down a slide • Show your preschooler how to fly a kite • Take an after-dinner walk • Play follow-the-leader • Go for a bike ride	• Dance in your living room • Encourage your preschooler to jump up and pop the bubbles you are blowing with bubble solution • Run around your backyard • Make a backyard obstacle course using items you already own • Kick a ball around the backyard
Low to moderate cost	• Go bowling • Make a skating rink in your backyard (or make one as a neighborhood project) • Go for a walk at the zoo or take an indoor walk at a children's art gallery or museum • Purchase a family membership at a community center, health club, or the YMCA. (Make sure the facility welcomes kids!)	• Sign your family up for a fundraising walk for charity • Go on a family hike or nature walk • Go sledding • Take the kids swimming

Table 5.4

Pump Up the Fun Factor: More Fun Ways to Be More Active as a Family

	Everyday Fun	Special Occasions
Your house	*Home gym*: Create the world's least expensive indoor gym. Use canned goods for weights, a full or partial set of stairs as a stair machine, and a skipping rope for the aerobic workout.	*Party perfect*: Plan your child's next birthday party around an activity theme, like "the Backyard Games." The party guests can have fun playing wacky games like pool noodle hockey (hit a beach ball with a pool noodle) and get some exercise at the same time. As your child gets older, you can stick with the physical activity theme, but switch to different activities, e.g., bowling, skating, rollerblading, etc.
Your street	*Weekend warriors*: Challenge the neighbors to a friendly game of Frisbee every night after dinner. The winning family gets to keep the Frisbee at their place overnight.	*Bicycle rodeo*: Get together with the other parents on your street to organize a bike and trike rodeo. It will give your kids a chance to work on their bike skills and get plenty of exercise at the same time.

continued on p. 158

Table 5.4 (*Continued*)

	Everyday Fun	Special Occasions
Your neighborhood	*I spy:* Try a more active variation of that old game "I spy." With this version of the game, your family goes for an after-dinner walk around the block. You say, for example, "I spy with my little eye something that is red" and the other members of your family have to guess what it is. The person who guesses correctly gets to go next. Before you know it, your walk will be finished and you will have seen your block through different eyes—"I spy" eyes.	*Mom power:* Get together with a group of moms in your neighborhood who are looking for fun ways to be more active with their kids. Commit to getting together once a week to do something active. Here are a couple of ideas to get you started: *Sock walk.* Slip a pair of woolly socks over a pair of sneakers and go for a walk through a meadow. In a matter of minutes, you'll have enough seeds to start your own wildflower garden. *Motherhood zoo.* Pack a healthy lunch and take the kids for a walk and picnic lunch at the zoo.
Your community	*You've got mail!* Get on the e-mail list for community calendars and bulletins for local associations that organize fun runs, nature walks, games days, and other outdoor activities where families are welcome. Use interactive tools like group calendars and shared to-do lists to keep everyone organized. (See Appendix B and Motherofallsolutions.com for some mom essentials.)	*It's where you live:* Find out if anyone has published a guide or on-line directory listing all the fabulous activities for families to do in your community. Once you've tracked down this information, send me an e-mail and I'll post what you've found on the blog for this book so that other parents will have access to the information. (Go to Motherofallsolutions.com for the link.)

Being physically active helps kids to build strong bones, strengthen their muscles, help their bodies stay flexible, reach and maintain a healthy weight, get their hearts pumping, acquire good posture and balance, achieve healthy fitness levels, relax and eliminate stress, feel good about themselves, and grow and develop in healthy ways. It's also a fun social activity that can be enjoyed with friends and family and that leaves kids feeling better about their bodies and themselves. It's the ultimate investment in your kid's future.

Limit the amount of screen time. When we were kids, TV was the enemy. Now that we're parents, we're trying to drag our kids away from anything with a screen: TVs, video game consoles, computers, and any hand-held entertainment device that can captivate a child and keep him on the couch. Sometimes it feels like a hopeless battle.

The good news is that we parents aren't fighting this battle alone. All the leading pediatric health authorities are on our side. Both the American Academy of Pediatrics and the Canadian Paediatric Society recommend that parents limit TV viewing time to a maximum of one to two hours per day. (Babies and toddlers shouldn't be watching television at all.) The time that your child spends parked in front of the tube or the computer is time that might otherwise be spent swinging on a swing or riding up and down the sidewalk on his tricycle.

And here's another good reason to limit your child's access to the tube. A Tufts University School of Nutrition study of TV viewing habits found that children from families who watched a lot of TV made less healthy food choices than those who watched less TV. The kids from families who watched a lot of TV derived 5 percent more of their calories from pizza, salty snacks, and soda and 5 percent less of their calories from fruits, vegetables, and juices. It's hardly surprising that kids' eating habits are affected by what they see on TV. According to the National Academy of Sciences' report on *Food Marketing to Children and Youth* (www.nap.edu), the food and beverage industry spends approximately $10 billion each year marketing its products to children; most of these products are high in calories, sugars, salt, and fat and low in nutrients; and food marketing influences the food preferences and food requests of children as young as two years of age. It's up to us moms, as the family's key nutritional gatekeepers, to refuse to heed our kids' requests for the latest (but by no means greatest) fast food and convenience foods. Our kids can whine and ask for those products, but those products won't find their way into our homes and into our kids' bellies unless we agree to bring these products home.

Note: Chapter 6 offers you all kinds of practical solutions for navigating the mealtime maze, whether you're dining in or dining out, so if you're looking for ideas and inspiration, there's good stuff coming your way.

Solutions Central—The Last Word

THIS CHAPTER TALKED about the joys and challenges of feeding preschoolers and dealing with the sometimes frustrating situations that arise if your preschooler is less than impressed by what's on the menu. We also talked about moms' important role as fitness role models for their kids. Now we'll talk about planning and preparing meals for your family. Fortunately, the next chapter is full of helpful shortcuts, tips, and solutions, whether you're a culinary queen or a kitchen conscript. We'll even ensure you get time off for good behavior, or at least time away from the kitchen. (The chapter includes a section on dining out with young children.)

CHAPTER 6:

Dining in and Dining out

*We eat way too much takeout. When Tristan was about
22 months old, a canvasser came to the door collecting for some
charity or another. I hunted for my wallet, found five dollars,
and made a donation. I closed the door to see Tristan standing
on the step watching me expectantly. He looked at me with
his big blue eyes and asked, "No pizza?"*
—DANI, 36, MOTHER OF TWO

SOME OF US were born to cook, and some of us find our way
to the kitchen more out of necessity or a sense of maternal
obligation: we realize that we have to get meals on the table
or our kids will starve. And for those of us who weren't exactly born
with a soup ladle in one hand, the thrill of cooking homemade
everything for our little ones can start to wear off around the same
time that they lose their fondness for puréed everything.

Fortunately, doing battle with the mealtime monster doesn't
have to be nearly as exhausting, overwhelming, or time-consuming
as it seems at first. Just as you quickly get into "the motherhood
groove" as you move from stage to stage, you'll quickly master
aspects of planning and making healthy, kid-friendly meals once
you get some practice.

You'll probably spend less time worrying about making dinner,
dashing out to get missing ingredients, or ordering takeout if you

take the approach to meal planning and preparation mapped out in this chapter. And you might start eating better and have the chance to reconnect with some of your long-lost girlfriends.

You'll also get the low-down on how eating dinner together is an important part of your family's life (even if you can't do it every single night) and how to make dining out a fun (rather than totally crazy-making) experience for yourself and your little ones.

What's on the Menu?

HERE'S A QUICK crash course on mapping out your family's menus.

- Figure out how many dinners you'll make and serve during the upcoming week and how many meals you'll make ahead of time. Consider what's on sale and what's in season so that you can stretch your grocery budget further and enjoy fresher-tasting foods.

- Decide what to make for dinner. Strike a balance between the need to get dinner on the table in a reasonable amount of time and the need to make healthy meals for your kids.

- Remember the types of foods that you want to work into your child's meal at dinnertime such as age-appropriate-sized servings of milk (to work in a calcium serving), vegetables, meat and beans (to ensure your child is getting enough iron), a serving of grains, and possibly a serving of fruit. Your child may not eat all this food. Your job is to make it available to her.

- Sign up for on-line recipe clubs and e-mail lists that will send you recipe ideas each week. Have them sent to a free e-mail account so that you can delete the messages you don't want and keep your meal-planning mail all in one spot.

- Take advantage of recipe websites that allow you to search for recipes by the type of ingredient. This can be a huge timesaver if your child has food allergies or is a choosy eater and you have to eliminate 95 percent of the recipes you come across by the time you reach the third or fourth ingredient.

- Choose recipes that can be prepared and served in under 30 minutes for those nights when you'll be preparing dinner at dinnertime (as opposed to cooking ahead).

- Look for ways to "cook once, eat twice." Barbecue extra chicken breasts one night and serve the extra chicken as part of a chicken vegetable salad two days later. Make multiple batches of anything that involves making a mess. That way, you get multiple meals, but you'll clean up the mess only once.

- Have breakfast or lunch-style meals for dinner: a vegetable omelette or scrambled eggs with some raw veggies on the side, soup and sandwiches, etc. You might even consider serving something as simple (and healthy) as a peanut butter and banana sandwich and a glass of milk, especially since peanut butter is off limits at most daycares these days, because of concerns about nut allergies. (Of course, if someone in your family is allergic to nuts, you'll need to come up with an alternative sandwich spread.)

- Save the more involved recipes for those times when you can do some batch cooking (perhaps on the weekend or one night during the week). Then mark that block of time off on your calendar since your family's meals for the week depend on you keeping this culinary commitment to yourself.

- Always have a few ultra-speedy backup menus in mind for those evenings when you discover at the last minute that a family member has noshed through the cheese that you needed for the menu *du jour* without telling you. You can either dig into your stash of frozen entrées or reach for one of the following winning combos: soup and salad (top it with some sort of protein); soup and sandwiches (with whole-grain bread and a broth-based soup unless you're trying to boost your child's milk consumption, in which case you might go with a cream-based soup); or a pasta and bean salad served with fresh veggies and yogurt dip. (See Food Tool 5 and Appendix B for links to different recipes and recipe sites.)

MOM'S THE WORD

"My favorite recipe book is Google.com! I type in what I'm looking for and survey all the results for the one that looks closest to what my taste buds want."

—*Karen, 41, mother of one*

MOTHER WISDOM

Taking care of yourself will make it easier for you to make healthier meals for your family. Healthy meals are one of the first things to go when parents are overloaded. It's easier to pop a frozen pizza in the oven or to call for takeout than to come up for an idea for dinner or to ensure that you have the necessary ingredients on hand. If you don't have the time or the energy to get healthy meals on the table right now, call for backup. Ask friends and family members to come over one weekend to help you to juggle kids and casserole dishes while you prepare a half-dozen different entrées for the freezer. Or, better yet, ask if they can do some cooking for you while you catch up on some badly needed rest.

- To make it easy to come up with dinner ideas for future weeks, save your weekly meal plans. You can reuse certain meal ideas or mix and match menu ideas, perhaps replacing that new recipe that was too much work with a tried-and-true favorite. Note any modifications you made to your menus and recipes so that you won't forget what you did three months from now.

- If you constantly resurrect the same, predictable dozen mealtime menus over and over again, try the following suggestions from other moms for achieving a little mealtime moxie:

  o Keep track of your family's favorite recipes. Chances are you use only a small fraction of the recipes in each cookbook you've accumulated over the years (except for those few favorite cookbooks that you cook from again and again). Note the page number of the best recipes in that book in one central location, perhaps a card file in a recipe box or in an electronic database. Either photocopy the recipe page, slip it into a plastic sheet protector and place it in a binder or a photo album (plastic pages can be easily sponged off), or key the recipe into your computer using cookbook software, recipe database software, electronic scrapbooking software, graphic design software—*whatever!*

- Swap recipe suggestions with other moms. Ask friends, relatives, coworkers, and other moms if they can recommend useful cookbooks and recipe sites. (And don't forget to check out some of the recommendations in Appendices B and C.)

Secrets of (Grocery) Shopping-Savvy Moms

SHOPPING WITH LITTLE ones can be a welcome break in the middle of your day—or an experience to be endured rather than savored, depending on the age and stage of your kids, their temperaments, and all kinds of other fascinating (and often unpredictable) variables.

"I actually love grocery shopping with Noah," says Leslie, 27, mother of one. "He's always very cooperative, and I think that's because (a) he's used to it, and (b) he's very involved."

"Once when the girls were about one year old and I was staying at home with them full time, I had to tell my partner not to 'do me a favor' by picking up groceries on his way home from work," adds Lesley, the 32-year-old mother of two-and-a-half-year-old twins. "We lived just around the corner from the grocery store, which is quite a neighborhood hub, and it was the highlight of some days for me to trundle over to the grocery story with the girls, soaking up all the attention we would get and connecting with my neighbors. Some weeks would see me go the grocery store every day for one thing or another!"

That's not how things have played out for Clare. "When it comes time to go food shopping, if it's feasible it's definitely easier not to take any children with me," the 31-year-old mother of three explains. "It's faster and I don't have to listen to the complaints of their hunger, tiredness, or need to use the facilities or desire to look at the toys. Whoever designed the shopping trolleys where I shop certainly cannot have children! The carts have two levels, which is great if you don't have children because you can put the delicate stuff up top. However, if you've got your child in the children's seat, your child can turn around and start picking at everything or throwing it out of the trolley!"

MOM'S THE WORD

"Treat grocery shopping as a team sport if you've got a lot to buy. If I need a lot of things, I generally make sure I have my husband with me. Also, make sure the kids aren't hungry and aren't tired (and you're not either) and things will go much better!"

—*Jennifer, 25, mother of two*

Dollars and Cents

Here's how to save time at the supermarket and get the most nutritional bang for your grocery buck.

- Don't shop when you're tired or hungry, or you'll crave the energy burst that comes from high-fat, high-sugar, high-carb foods—poorer nutritional choices than the foods your family actually needs.

- Always shop from a list that has been structured around your meal plan for the upcoming week. That will reduce the number of impulse purchases, which is a good move nutrition- and budget-wise.

- Make your grocery list after you've planned your meals for the week. If you're using cookbook or recipe software, your software package may generate a preliminary grocery list for you. Of course, you'll need to check this list against the contents of your kitchen cupboard to see what you already have on hand, but it's a quick and easy way to let your computer do some of the thinking for you. If you'd rather create your own grocery list from scratch, you can start with one of the numerous templates available for download on-line (see Motherofallsolutions.com for links) or you can make your own based on the breakdown of aisles in your grocery store. (This is one of the advantages of shopping at the same grocery store on a regular basis.)

- Hang your grocery list on your refrigerator. You can check off the items that you need this week, or use a highlighter to mark off the items you need. (You'll probably find it easier to shop

FOOD FOR THOUGHT

Grocery shopping with your preschooler? Set some ground rules about the types of foods you are and aren't willing to purchase before you hit the grocery store. A study reported in the March 2003 issue of the *International Journal of Pediatric Dentistry* found that children can exert a significant amount of pressure on their parents to purchase sugary snacks. The researchers, who studied a group of seven- and eight-year-olds in the U.K., found that parents' efforts to limit children's intake of sweet snacks and beverages are being undermined by earlier and earlier outside influences in children's lives (think TV marketing messages!) and children's access to money from outside sources, most notably grandparents.

---

from a highlighted grocery list.) You can manually add on any additional items. (Be sure to add them to the computer master list so that your working copy will always be updated.)

- To ensure that any perishable items stay as fresh as possible, try to time your grocery-shopping day as close as possible to the batch-cooking day. If you hit the grocery store right after dinner, you might avoid the crowds. (It's always a good idea to shop during off-peak hours if you can.)

- Plan to purchase fresh produce twice a week if you can swing it. If you can't manage two trips to the store, you may want to purchase fruits and vegetables that have a slightly longer shelf life for the second half of the week (apples, carrots, parsnips, beets, and broccoli), or to purchase frozen fruit, canned fruit, or unsweetened applesauce, frozen vegetables, or fruit and vegetable juices.

- Consider shopping on-line, by fax, or by phone for groceries if this is an option in your community. Even if you don't want to do this all the time, it's handy to find out if you can have your groceries brought to your door when it's more difficult to get out and get them yourself (e.g., when your child has the stomach flu). Compare prices and balance off the convenience factor against the added expense. You may decide that it's worth it sometimes.

PLAY IT SAFE

Kitchen sanitation may not be the sexiest of topics, but once you or a family member has had a bout of poisoning, you'll never want to go there again. *Ever.* Here's how to prevent this kind of misery from hitting your household.

- Stop kitchen bacteria before it has a chance to make your family sick. Clean and sanitize cutting boards, countertops, kitchen sink drains, and other kitchen surfaces on a regular basis with soap and hot water and then sanitize with either a store-bought kitchen cleaner or a mild bleach-water solution (1 teaspoon of bleach to 3 cups of water). Cleaning with baking soda and vinegar may be an environmentally friendly cleaning solution, but it doesn't kill kitchen bacteria. You need a product like Clorox Anywhere Hard Surface daily sanitizing spray or Benefect Botanical Disinfectant. Allow surfaces to air dry, if possible, or dry all surfaces with clean kitchen towels.

- Clean and sanitize food processors, meat grinders, and blenders immediately after use.

- Plastic cutting boards are best for raw meat, poultry, and seafood because they can be cleaned in the dishwasher. Clean and sanitize all cutting boards after each use.

- Think about purchasing a second cutting board for your kitchen. That way, you can designate one for raw meat, poultry, and seafood and one for ready-to-eat or cooked foods.

- Defrost meat and poultry in the refrigerator rather than on the counter. This means you have to think about tomorrow night's dinner the night before—a small price to pay for preventing a nasty case of food poisoning.

- Don't allow plates and food containers that have been used for raw food to come into contact with cooked food.

- Wash your hands thoroughly with soap and water (scrub your hands for at least 20 seconds) after you have handled raw food, particularly meat, poultry, or seafood.

- If you have an infection or open cut on your hands, wear gloves or a bandage when you are cooking. Wash your gloves as often as you would wash your bare hands while you are cooking because your gloves can pick up bacteria while you are cooking, too.

- Replace kitchen sponges often. They can quickly become a breeding ground for bacteria.

- Air dry dishes as much as possible because kitchen towels can pick up bacteria.

- Store food in sealed containers to minimize food spoilage and contamination, and to avoid attracting insects and small animals.

- Foods that should be refrigerated to minimize food spoilage should be put away first when you arrive home from grocery shopping. They shouldn't be left unrefrigerated for more than two hours.

- Store raw meat, poultry, and seafood that you will be using during the next two days on the bottom shelf of the refrigerator in containers that are large enough to prevent any juices from dripping on to other foods. If you will not be using meat within the next two days, freeze it instead.

- Don't overload your refrigerator. An overstuffed refrigerator won't function properly. Cool air must circulate around the foods in your fridge to keep these foods cool.

- Make sure that your refrigerator is functioning properly. (Use a refrigerator thermometer to ensure that your fridge is operating at or below 40°F.)

- Keep frozen foods at or below −40°F.

- Clean out your refrigerator and freezer regularly to get rid of spoiled foods.

- Scrub all fresh fruits and vegetables before serving.

- Be aware of any government food safety alerts. These are widely publicized in the news, but you can also stay in the loop by visiting the U.S. Food and Drug Administration and Health Canada websites.

- If you buy a large quantity of canned or packaged goods in bulk, date these items before storing them in your pantry. (You can make a bunch of dated stickers using the printer on your computer. Or stamp a bunch of stickers using a date stamp from a stationery store.)

FRIDGE NOTE

Consumers aren't being deterred by the fact that organic foods cost 50–100 percent more than their non-organic counterparts. According to ConsumersReports.org, nearly two-thirds of U.S. consumers purchased organic foods and beverages in 2005, a sizeable leap from the approximately one-half who purchased such products in 2004.

One of the most budget-friendly ways to purchase organic foods is by frequenting farmers' markets. (For links to farmers' markets in your community, visit LocalHarvest.org or marketplace.chef2chef.net/farmer-markets/canada.htm.)

Another option is to buy a share in an organic farm, which may cost $300 to $500 for a season's worth of fresh produce. You may be expected to do some of the work in growing or distributing that produce, and you often don't get to pick and choose which types of produce your family receives. This can be a plus because your family will be encouraged to try veggies that you might not otherwise give a second look at in the grocery store. Once they're sitting on your kitchen counter, you'll have an incentive to flip open your favorite vegetarian cookbook or to hit the web for a recipe that will show you how to use that unusual variety of squash or greens.

- If you shop on-line, archive your list so that you can reuse it in future. You won't have to re-key it the next time around.

- Go big and then go home. Plan to do a big grocery shop whenever you experience grocery store karma (you're by yourself in a grocery superstore or warehouse store, and you've actually got a few spare dollars stashed away in your checking account). Load up on mealtime staples (e.g., rice, chickpeas, black beans, and other non-perishables with a long shelf life) so that you don't have to lug this stuff home week after week when you're doing your regular grocery shopping (possibly with an unhappy tot or two in tow).

MOTHER WISDOM

Is your kitchen organized in a way that works for you? Your kitchen is efficient, time-saving, and family-friendly if:

- you can prepare a meal with minimal fuss and confusion (e.g., your refrigerator door opens in a direction that makes sense, your pots are within easy reaching distance of the stove, you can reach the dish soap while your hands are in the sink, you have a safe and clean workspace, etc.)

- you can easily access the tools, materials, and ingredients needed for meal preparation (For tools and time-saving appliances that other moms find particularly useful, see Appendix B)

- you are using your cupboard space as efficiently as possible

- your kitchen has been thoroughly childproofed, but is still a warm and welcoming environment for your kids

- your kitchen allows you to make meals and supervise your baby, toddler, or preschooler at the same time

---

How to Make Dinner with a Baby in Your Arms (and Other Secrets of Kitchen-Savvy Moms)

HERE'S AN AGES-and-stages guide to surviving the suppertime insanity.

- Ask yourself what your child needs from you before you start making dinner. Consider both her physical needs (Does she need to be nursed? Does she need her diaper changed? Does she need a quick snack or a glass of water?) and her emotional needs at this time of day:

  ○ If you've been away all day, spend some time reconnecting with your child before you start making dinner. That way, she may not feel quite the same need to cling to your leg as you make dinner.

- o   If you've been together all day, maybe she would benefit from a change of scene (and maybe you would, too). What about taking a walk around the block or spending a few minutes playing catch in the backyard? Then, when you get back from the park, encourage your child to settle into a quieter activity so that she won't be too revved up by the time dinner is served.

- If your baby wants to be held when you're chopping veggies or heating something in the microwave or on the stove, consider:

   - o   sitting her in the high chair, a baby seat, or the baby swing, safely out of reach of anything dangerous or sharp.

   - o   singing to her while she plays on a mat on the other side of the kitchen.

   - o   carrying her in a baby carrier, baby sling, or baby backpack, but only if you can keep her safely away from anything hot, sharp, or dangerous; safety must come first.

- If your toddler or preschooler wants your time or attention:

   - o   set him up with a project or activity at the kitchen table so that he can do something and be close to you at the same time.

   - o   involve him in meal preparation (helping you to wash and dry vegetables in the sink or in a basin of water on the counter or at the kitchen table, or helping to place the cutlery on the kitchen table).

   - o   create a toy cupboard in the kitchen that your child can access when you're busy making meals, or give him free rein of your plastic container cupboard. (Just be sure to wash any containers before you put food in them or your leftovers may end up being tucked away with a bonus serving of toddler drool.)

MOTHER WISDOM

If your preschooler is starving while you're trying to make dinner, offer her a healthy snack such as a fruit or veggie platter, which encourages preschoolers to fit in servings that they may have missed earlier in the day.

- Consider hiring a neighborhood teenager to pitch in once or twice a week while you make dinner. The teenager could either help entertain your toddler while you focus on food preparation or assist with some of the food preparation tasks that require two hands if your baby is having a "Mommy, hold me" moment—or maybe do a little of both. A little bit of hands-on help a couple of times per week can relieve the stress of getting dinner ready, particularly if you're a single parent or your partner works long hours or is out of town a lot on business trips.

- Think about doing some of the mealtime preparation earlier in the day, if you have that option. Some moms who are at home during the day find it works best to hit the kitchen during naptime: "I try to prepare as much of dinner as I can while my son naps to minimize the time I have to spend preparing it when he wakes up and is hungry," says Melanie, 29, who is currently expecting her second child. "Making meals when my son is hungry is awful because he tends to hang around the kitchen, whining and hanging off my legs."

Save Time in the Kitchen

WHETHER YOU LOVE to cook or you consider it a necessary evil, these time-saving kitchen shortcuts and cook-smart tips will put valuable minutes back in your day.

- Empty the dishwasher and the sink before you start making dinner so that cleanup will be that much quicker, and try to stay on top of the cooking mess as you go. (Put ingredients away as you finish using them and pop pots and utensils into a sink of hot soapy water to soak while you finish cooking. Use cold water if the stuck-on food is carb-based.)

- Keep a large bowl or an empty pail on the counter (out of reach of your baby, toddler, or preschooler, of course) so that you can toss in any items for the compost while you're cooking. This will help to keep your work area clear while you chop and prepare foods.

MOTHER WISDOM

Understand the difference between multitasking and flirting with disaster. Rather than trying to tackle five different recipes at once, see one recipe through to its logical conclusion before diving into the next. (Theresa Albert-Ratchford, author of *Cook Once a Week: Eat Well Every Day,* suggests that you wait until you've at least got recipe number one to the simmer stage before you move on to recipe number two.) Otherwise, you're likely to get the wrong ingredients in the wrong recipe or leave out some ingredients entirely, which can be a huge waste of time and money.

- If you're planning to do some heavy-duty batch cooking later in the week, do some of the preparation work ahead of time. For example, pre-chop the onions or pre-brown the ground beef for that double- or triple-batch of lasagna you're planning to make this weekend.

- Cut green onions and sun-dried tomatoes with a clean pair of kitchen scissors rather than chopping them on a cutting board. It's quicker and easier.

- Spray mixing spoons and blender and food processor blades with non-stick cooking spray before you mix or blend ultra-sticky foods. It will minimize the sticking and the cleanup. If you'd prefer not to use commercial non-stick sprays, try making your own by adding olive oil to a kitchen pump or spray bottle (available for purchase in kitchen supply stores).

- Spray plastic storage containers with non-stick cooking spray to prevent them from staining.

- Purchase a wide-mouthed funnel. It will eliminate a lot of the splatters and spills that occur when you're pouring soups and other messy foods into storage containers and freezer bags.

(You Can Never Have) Too Many Cooks in the Kitchen

WHO KNEW THAT connecting with other moms could make cooking easier and more fun? Well, previous generations of women certainly knew this, but our generation has only recently rediscovered

MOTHER WISDOM

Keep a pencil handy so that you can jot notes in your cookbook as you go. Make margin notes of any batch calculations (if you doubled or tripled the recipe), substitutions, and cooking time or temperature adjustments. And, if the recipe was a complete flop or a huge hit, you'll probably want to note that on the page, too.

You may also want to think about starting a recipe journal, either on paper or in electronic form. If you keep a recipe journal or blog on the web, you can share your cooking triumphs and culinary disasters with friends, relatives, and anyone else who drops by your blog. It can be a lot of fun. You can get a free blog by signing up with Blogger.com.

There are also a growing number of cooking sites with active cooking communities where you can swap cooking ideas with other cooks—everyone from culinary novices to experienced chefs. (Check out ReluctantGourmet.com if you're a less-than-inspired cook.)

---

this long-lost secret, which explains why any group cooking experience is suddenly catching on like wildfire. Here are some fun ways to get more cooks in your kitchen, and to reap some major culinary rewards as a result.

Double up with another mom. She can bring over her own groceries and the two of you can cook up a storm while chatting, sipping coffee (or other beverages), and listening to some Mom Music (see Motherofallsolutions.com). (You can't stray far from the kitchen when you're waiting for the timer to ding, so you've got the perfect excuse to relax and enjoy your friend's company.) And if you both have babes in arms, you might even turn it into an old-fashioned girlfriend sleepover party (or a try-to-get-some-sleep sleepover party).

Do a straight dinner swap. Here's a variation on the same theme. Your friend brings you dinner on Tuesdays and you bring her dinner on Thursday. Or you send your hubby to pick up dinner and she sends her partner. Or whatever. The idea is that you each get a night off from cooking one night a week because you've each cooked a double batch of the same entrée on a different night.

Brainstorm menu ideas with a whole group of moms. (The more the merrier, right?) Ask each mom to bring a list of her family's top seven recipe ideas, along with information on the source of each recipe (e.g., the web link, if the recipe is available on-line; the page reference and the name of the cookbook if the recipe comes from a cookbook; or a copy of the recipe if she doesn't mind sharing).

Break the rule that says cooking has to feel like work. Take the "friend in the kitchen" idea and add a whole bunch more mom friends. Organize a cooking club or a dinner swap—two ways of working cooperatively to make cooking more fun and less of a chore.

- **Cooking club:** A cooking club can either mean cooking together and taking home your meals to enjoy with your families later on (imagine a cooking spree with some wine and snacks on the side), or cooking some dinners to take home and then enjoying a yummy meal that has been prepared by the mom who is playing host that month—one part cooking spree and one part dinner party. Here are some tips on getting a cooking club up and running.

  ○ Think about who to invite. Obviously, dietary compatibility matters. However, don't be afraid to stretch your culinary horizons a little. Your friend with the slightly exotic eating habits might expose you and your kids to recipes you might not otherwise even think about trying.

  ○ Establish some recipe ground rules. Are you aiming for healthy, low-fat menus? Do you want a certain percentage of the meals to be vegetarian? Are there any foods that everyone in the group absolutely loathes? There are the types of issues that need to be hammered out up front.

  ○ Look for recipes that can be tailored to the taste preferences of each individual family after the fact: e.g., the garlic lovers can pump up their favorite spice when they reheat their share of the vegetable soup; the cheese junkies in the group can add a layer of their can't-live-without-it condiment when they cook up their serving of the chicken casserole at home; the olive lovers can go olive-crazy with the pasta salad and the olive haters won't get stuck playing olive roulette.

MOTHER WISDOM

If you've got more moms than your kitchen can possibly accommodate, maybe it's time to take your idea on the road. See if there's a community center, church, synagogue, or other faith group that might be willing to rent its kitchen facilities to your group once or twice a month so that you can do some batch cooking. Because these facilities have mile-long countertops and more than one stove, you and your friends should be able to whip up an extraordinary number of lasagnas, casseroles, or other entrées in record time.

Or see if there's a dinner-preparation store (a.k.a. a once-a-month cooking store) where you can go to cook your meals. These facilities will even do the shopping for you: you just show up ready to cook and enjoy some bonding time with your girlfriends. (Some encourage you to bring wine so you can turn the cooking time into fun time.) You can either tackle a single entrée at each get-together or have one group of moms prepare one dish and another group tackle another so that each mom will leave with one of each (either fully cooked, if you have time for that, or ready to cook in her own oven). The Easy Meal Preparation Association (www.easymealprep.com) maintains an online directory of members. There were 252 companies and 652 outlets represented as of early March 2006, including SuperSuppers, DreamDinners, SupperWorks, and Dinner Revolution.

---

o   Look for ways to give everyone's favorite family recipes a healthier twist. (See Food Tool 7.) You don't have to sacrifice flavor to make healthy eating a habit for your family.

o   Decide whether you'll each bring your own groceries (not terribly efficient) or whether you'll take turns shopping (if everyone brings her checkbook, you can settle up for each mom's share of the groceries while you're cooking up all those delicious dishes).

o   Decide ahead of time what kinds of pots, pans, and cooking utensils each person needs to bring to that particular cooking club get-together. You may want to take advantage of electronic party-planning tools like Evite.com or electronic to-do list systems like Rememberthemilk.com to help everyone stay organized.

"Kaylei, my two-year-old, and I eat at friends' houses almost weekly. My fellow mommy friend and I have husbands who travel frequently, so to keep our sanity, we formed the Deserted Housewives Club. When we learn our husbands' travel schedule, we send out an SOS e-mail and, if the trips coincide, we get together for takeout and wine. I find I always pick up new ideas when we eat with other people and their kids, whether it's a meal idea or a tip of some sort. So far, no disasters!"

—*Michelle, 37, mother of one*

- ○ Treat the cooking club as a night out for you. If that doesn't work and it ends up being a Saturday morning with the kids, you'll need to assign one mom to "kid patrol" so that you don't end up playing "dodge the toddler" while you're carrying hot pots and sharp knives. (Obviously, if you're breast-feeding and your baby is still quite young, it may be just as convenient to have baby in the sling when you're at the cooking club, rather than worrying about rushing home for a feeding. Figure out what works best for you in terms of logistics.)

- • **Dinner swap:** Cook up a triple or quadruple batch of dinner and then swap dinners with other moms. Most of the tips that apply to organizing a cooking club also apply to a dinner swap. Make sure you choose your dinner swap partners with care (compatibility counts in cooking as in love) and be as organized as possible. See Appendix B for links on co-operative and batch cooking if you're interested in going this route.

The Big Chill

DON'T FEEL THE burn (the freezer burn, that is). Make sure the fruits of your cooking labors are packaged appropriately for the freezer—either in freezer bags, plastic containers with well-fitting lids, or serving dishes that are designed to go from freezer to microwave/oven to table. (Never heat or store food in containers that were not designed for this purpose. Single-use containers like margarine containers can warp or melt in the microwave, causing some of the container's materials to seep into the food.)

Before you pop those goodies in the freezer, label the package with the date and type of entrée. Finally, keep track of what's inside your freezer as your stock of ready-made meals builds up. Keep a freezer inventory in a binder in your kitchen or right beside your freezer—wherever you think you'll be most likely to update your records.

Make Family Mealtimes Matter

EATING MEALS TOGETHER as a family is important, but, for most families, getting everyone home for dinner each night seven nights a week can be a bit of a scramble if mom or dad is a shift worker or self-employed or has to spend a couple of nights a week taking care of a sick or aging relative, for example.

So does that mean that you should give up on the idea of family dinners? Not at all! Instead, you could have other family mealtime rituals—perhaps a fun and leisurely Saturday breakfast or a Sunday afternoon brunch. It doesn't matter what meal it is or when it happens. What matters is that it happens and that you have a chance to connect with your kids around the table. Here is the "recipe" for a successful family meal:

- **To reduce conflicts about what's for dinner, serve a few variations on the same basic dinnertime theme.** That way, everyone can have a dinner they enjoy. The more adventurous eaters can have all the ingredients in a chicken or vegetarian stir-fry sautéed together so that maximum flavor transfer can occur. The less adventurous eaters can have the same ingredients sautéed separately, so that the chicken tastes like chicken, the veggies taste like veggies, and none of the ingredients are touching one another. It may mean a few extra pots to wash, but it's a lot easier than making multiple dinners. You can apply the same divide-and-conquer cooking strategy to pasta dishes (serve meat, pasta sauce, veggies, and noodles separately to those who like it that way and as a combined dinner to those who don't mind if their various foods are on slightly friendlier terms) and many of your other favorite recipes. Of course, you'll want to strike that balance between making reasonable concessions and challenging your toddler or preschooler to stray outside his culinary comfort zone from time to time. Let your knowledge of your child and what you know about the importance of helping him to develop healthy eating habits help you to find the sensible middle ground.

- **Minimize interruptions.** That means turning off the TV (a 2004 survey by *Parenting* magazine found that 77 percent of families have the TV on during dinner), unplugging the phone, turning off cell phones and other electronic gadgets (unless they are absolutely necessary), and letting other people know when you have dinner so that they're less likely to ring the doorbell during that time (something that results in an instant dinner table mutiny when you've got toddlers and preschoolers).

- **Check your worries at the kitchen door.** That means focusing on the conversation with your three-year-old—or the Herculean efforts that your baby is making to chase that piece of cereal across the tray of her high chair—as opposed to letting your mind drift away to the worries of the day.

FOOD FOR THOUGHT

Having your preschooler give your cooking a thumbs-down night after night can certainly put a damper on dinner. But while you might be tempted to hand him a cheese sandwich, plop him in front of the television set, and declare an end to family dinners forevermore, it's definitely worth persevering. Studies have shown that when families eat meals together on a regular basis, children benefit in all kinds of powerful and unexpected ways:

- nutritionally (they're twice as likely to get their recommended five servings of fruit and vegetables per day; they are more likely to consume higher levels of fiber, calcium, iron, and essential vitamins; and they are less likely to drink soft drinks and eat fried foods).

- socially and academically (thanks to all that dinnertime conversation with their parents, they have more advanced vocabulary skills than their peers and they tend to do better in school).

- psychologically (they tend to feel better about themselves, which provides a buffer against illicit drug use and depression as they head into the teen years).

FOOD FOR THOUGHT

You are what you eat—and what you watch, too. A study reported in the January 2001 issue of the medical journal *Pediatrics* found that children whose families watched a lot of TV consumed 5 percent more of their daily calories from pizza, salty snacks, and soda and 5 percent less of their energy from fruits, vegetables, and juices than children whose families didn't watch a lot of television.

- **Do what you can to minimize the stress of family mealtimes.** Keep the mood light and fun, and make sure your expectations of your child are age-appropriate and realistic. (It's not fair to expect a two-year-old to have the food-handling skills and social graces of a five-year-old.)

- **Offer age-appropriate portions to your child rather than grown-up-sized portions.** Children tend to eat more when larger quantities of food are presented to them.

- **Enjoy the pleasure of your child's company rather than obsessing about what she is or is not eating.** Trying to control your child's eating behavior isn't healthy for her or for you. Besides, it's a strategy that tends to backfire and make a bad situation worse. (For more on this topic, see Chapter 7.)

- **Look for ways to make mealtimes fun.** Make one of your menus for the week a special picnic dinner that can be enjoyed in the picnic area at a local park, or in your living room if the weather is bad.

- **Look for the humor in the most crazy-making situation.** If you've temporarily misplaced your sense of humor, find it again—and fast. It's a parenting essential.

The Savvy Parent's Guide to Dining out

HERE'S AN INSIDER'S guide to handling the two biggest challenges parents with young children face when dining out in restaurants: dealing with "whining and dining" and finding reasonably healthy menu options for their little ones.

More Dining, Less Whining

If you can keep the whining-to-dining ratio tolerable, you'll reduce the number of glares, smirks, and tsk-tsks from your fellow diners and you'll enjoy your dinner more.

Remember that your child's age can have an important impact on how well the meal goes. "Dining out was 'easy' (it's all relative) when my daughter was a newborn," recalls Cathleen, 33. "We'd just tote her in, car seat and all, and she'd sleep through most of the meal. And then when she was old enough to sit in a high chair and eat solid food while we ate our food, it was also 'easy.' The hardest part was the in-between period when she was old enough to want to be involved, but not old enough to sit and eat independently. With only two of us at dinner, we'd take shifts: I would hold her on my lap and wrestle with her as she tried to grab everything in sight, while my partner shoveled food into his mouth as fast as possible before his turn was over!"

Consider feeding your child before you get to the restaurant. "I feed Cooper before we go out if dinner is scheduled late or the food is notoriously slow," says Ali, 32, mother of 19-month-old Cooper. "Then he can snack on bread, etc., to feel a part of the group. If I'm unsure about the menu, I might even bring some sandwiches or a jar of baby food just in case."

Have a seating plan. "The best thing we did was to have our child sit in a high chair while at the restaurant," says Josée, 35. "This is what we did with our son until he was almost two and a half. This way he couldn't get out of his seat. He never complained about it either. Now that he just uses a regular chair, we have him sit where it's not so easy for him to get out (e.g., the back of a booth) so the temptation for him to get up and walk around is lessened." "We choose a booth table so he can stand up at the table without tipping a chair over, he feels like a big boy, and it keeps him entertained," adds Ali, 32, mother of one.

BYOS: Bring your own seat. Don't count on the restaurant to have a safe, clean, suitable, or available high chair or booster seat. "The First Years makes an amazing fold-up booster seat that we keep in the trunk of our car. It folds down to the size of a chair cushion and has saved us from many a miserable dining experience," says Dani, 36, mother of two.

Bring lots of other stuff, too. "I nearly always bring along a small container of dry cereal and a small thermos of milk to stave off emergency hunger, thirst, or boredom. A small toy, a pencil and paper, and/or a book also help pass the time waiting for a table or food, or if Isaac finishes eating before the rest of us. We leave a change of clothes in the car as a matter of habit. You only have to drive your naked-except-for-his-diaper child home once to learn that lesson. Thank goodness it was July, not the middle of an Edmonton winter." And if you forget your restaurant survival kit at home? "You can play 'I–Spy' or other games to occupy young ones until the food comes," says Elizabeth, 36, mother of two.

Have reasonable expectations of your junior dining companions. "We're pretty rigid about some rules (screeching during a meal is never acceptable, nor is standing on your chair or running around during a meal), but more relaxed about others when we're out (a longer meal in a restaurant may be more tolerable for all concerned with a few breaks to read a story or go for a walk with daddy to see the fish tank)," says Jennifer, 30, mother of two.

 MOM'S THE WORD

Restaurant survival kit (a.k.a. Dora the Explorer backpack):

- One coloring book
- Crayons/markers
- Dora the Explorer velcro Xs and Os
- Snack (e.g., crackers, granola bar, plus a unique, special treat in case of emergency, i.e., total meltdown brewing)
- Water in a sippy cup
- Extra diaper/wipes
- Other small toys or books that are easily transportable.

—Heather, 30, currently pregnant with second child

MOM'S THE WORD

"When you get to the restaurant, ask for your food to come to your table with the bill and in takeout containers. That way, if all is well, you can sit and eat there, but if not, it's ready to go and your bill is ready to be paid. Ever notice that when your children are fussy, the servers are nowhere to be found with your bill?"

—*Bonnie, 31, mother of two*

Be prepared to switch from dining in to take-out if eating out is not working out. "If a child continues to act up, is overtired, is not feeling well, or is having a bad day, be prepared to just pay the bill, have your food wrapped up, and leave," says Bonnie, 36, mother of four-year-old Lauren. "This accomplishes three things: your child learns that certain behaviors aren't tolerated in a restaurant (and likewise their feelings, if they are sick, are being recognized and respected); you aren't stressed out over their behavior; and other patrons aren't subjected to unruly behavior."

Don't expect a post-kid dining-out experience to be what a pre-kid dining-out experience used to be. "With two under two, I got the bright idea of taking my husband to our favorite restaurant for his birthday because we hadn't been out in so long," recalls Lisa, 34, mother of two. "Then we remembered why. I had built up our night out to something like the fun, romantic evenings we had pre-kids ... and it didn't happen, *of course*. Eating out with kids can be fun, but it is not relaxing and it is not couple time!"

Finding the Carrot Stick in a Haystack of French Fries

Restaurants have come a long way in terms of adding healthier fare to the grown-up portion of the menu, but the "kiddie menu" still has a long way to go. Here are some tips on finding healthy meal options for your kids when you're dining out as a family.

- **Say "nay" to the buffet.** Restaurant buffets are rarely budget friendly or belly friendly when you're dining as a family. You often have to pay for your child's portion, even if she eats only a single dinner roll or one bite of fruit from the entire buffet. And if the restaurant allows kids to eat for free, it's generally because parents pay a premium. (Remember, there's no free lunch.)

- **Don't just stick to the children's options on the menu.** See if there are some healthy side dishes or small adult portions that could be combined to make a healthy, kid-friendly meal. Many restaurants offer kids only high-calorie, high-fat options. And if you do end up ordering off the adult menu because there's nothing suitably healthy for your child, take a moment to explain why. You might help to convince the restaurant to add some healthy kid-sized entrées to its menu.

- **Don't be afraid to request substitutions that aren't on the menu.** For example, you could ask if it would be possible to substitute fruit or vegetables, for all or a portion of your child's order of fries. You may have to pay a few extra dollars for the menu substitution, but at least you'll boost the nutritional value of your child's dinner.

- **If the meal that your child has ordered is too large, split it between two siblings or take half of it home.** Your child can enjoy a bonus meal for lunch or dinner the next day. (Ask for the takeout container before your child starts eating his dinner. This will help with portion control and keep the other half of his dinner from coming in contact with saliva from his fork or spoon, which causes food to spoil more quickly.)

- **Consider the food-preparation method.** Order meals that are prepared in the healthiest manner possible (baked, grilled, or barbecued as opposed to fried, sautéed, battered, or breaded). And if a menu item sounds reasonably healthy, but comes drenched in high-fat gravies or sauces, ask the chef to hold the sauce.

- **Consider taking fast food home rather than eating it in the restaurant.** That way, you're not forced to mix and match menu options to make an entire meal. You can introduce some healthier side dishes by supplementing the fast-food takeout item with a healthier item from the grocery store, e.g., a bag of salad or some fresh fruit.

Table 6.1

What's on the Restaurant Menu? Making Healthier Choices

Less Healthy Options	Better Bets
Breakfast Foods	
Croissant, biscuit, muffin	English muffin, toast, bagel
Full breakfast (eggs, bacon, sausages, home fries, toast)	Vegetarian omelette and whole-grain toast
Sausages, bacon, ham	Have a small serving on occasion (order low-salt, extra lean versions, if available) or order low-fat yogurt instead
Pancakes with butter and syrup	Pancakes with fresh fruit
Waffles topped with butter, syrup, and whipped cream—and maybe even chocolate sauce	Waffles topped with fresh berries
Breakfast cereals, sugary ready-to-eat varieties	Oatmeal, unflavored or ready-to-eat breakfast cereals that are low in sugar (sugar isn't one of the first three ingredients)
Lunch and Dinner	
Soft drinks, milkshakes, other sugary beverages, fruit juice	Milk or water (if they serve the beverage in a fancy glass with a straw, it will still have plenty of kid appeal)
Deep-fried breaded chicken and fish sandwiches, chicken nuggets, and chicken fingers	Broiled chicken breast or fish fillet, grilled hamburger
Jumbo-sized hamburgers with all the fixings	The smallest hamburger or cheeseburger without any fixings or with small amounts of ketchup, mustard, or barbecue sauce
Fried chicken	Chicken without the skin
Thick-crust pizza with all the fixings	Thin-crust pizza with vegetarian toppings: ask for more sauce and less cheese and blot the pizza with a napkin to absorb extra grease

Less Healthy Options	Better Bets
Lunch and Dinner	
Potato salad, macaroni salad, creamy coleslaw, and other high-fat salad bar fixings	Greens (ideally dark greens) with lots of vegetables, fruit, and beans; skip the salad dressing (or have a small serving), and pass on the bacon bits and the croutons
French fries	Baked potato, raw vegetables, salad, corn on the cob, baked beans, or broth-based soups
Smart Substitutions	
Mayonnaise, tartar sauce, salad dressing	Lose the sauce
Fried versions of food (especially foods that have been breaded or coated in batter and fried)	Broiled, grilled, or barbecued versions of these foods

Solutions Central—The Last Word

COOKING MEALS DOESN'T have to be a tortuous chore if we reduce the total amount of time we spend preparing meals. By joining forces with other time-pressed moms and swapping mealtime solutions, we will have more time for ourselves, our families, and our friends; improve the quality of the meals our families are eating; and have a lot of fun at the same time. Likewise, dining out with young children doesn't have to be the stuff of which late night comedy routines are made. You can eat out with kids and enjoy it, provided everyone (including you) is well rested and in the right frame of mind.

CHAPTER 7

No More Food Fights

*If I gave my daughter full control over her food choices,
she'd eat macaroni and cheese 24/7. I do give her choices,
though: "Would you like carrots or broccoli?" The more
involved she is in the decision, the less she feels controlled.*
—BONNIE, 36, MOTHER OF ONE

AVING A TODDLER or preschooler who hates everything on the menu can make family mealtimes something to be survived rather than savored.

If it's any consolation, you're certainly in good company. A study conducted by the University of Tennessee Nutrition Department found that 50 percent of moms described their 24-month-olds as picky eaters. And a recent article in *Parenting* magazine reported that as many as 40 percent of children under the age of five are anything but easy to please at dinnertime.

So how do things get so difficult on the feeding front? One minute your child is breast-feeding enthusiastically and before you know it, your child hates everything. A dislike of new foods typically sets in at around age two, peaks around age three, and gradually tapers off, generally disappearing entirely by the time kids reach high-school age. (Of course, some people continue to be suspicious of new foods for their entire lives.)

If your child is a less-than-adventurous diner by nature, you'll want to learn some strategies for encouraging him to expand his food repertoire while managing (or at least coping with) his mealtime behaviors. That's what you'll find in this chapter. (You can also find additional age-specific information on coping with challenging eating behaviors in Chapters 2 through 5.)

No More Whining and Dining: Strategies for Parenting a Picky Eater

LOOKING FOR WAYS to minimize the stress of family dinners that are peppered with constant outbursts of "Yuck"? Here are some tips from other parents in the know.

- **Talk to other parents who are facing similar dinnertime challenges and find out what is and isn't working for them.** There's no point comparing notes with parents whose kids have always been enthusiastic eaters. They'll either have no clue what you're dealing with (so any advice that they offer will be null and void) or—*worse*—they'll offer patronizing advice that implies that you need to do less of what *you're* doing with your kids and more of what *they're* doing with theirs.

- **If you swear you're raising the poster child for picky eaters, make sure she's not learning any of those behaviors from her parents!** You want to be sure that you're modeling a willingness to try new foods. "My husband and I desperately want our children to eat a variety of things as my husband is extremely picky and even he doesn't want the kids to turn out that way!" says Jennifer, 25, mother of two.

- **Use your knowledge of your child to pinpoint some of the possible causes for her lack of interest in eating certain foods—or her lack of interest in eating at all.** See Table 7.1 for a list of some of the most common causes of picky eating behaviors in young children.

- **Find low-key ways to involve your child in dinner preparations and to promote your child's interest in food.** Read books and sing songs about food, nutrition, and eating. Take your child grocery shopping and encourage her to pick out new foods to try.

Table 7.1
Why Is My Child a Picky Eater?

What You've Noticed	What May Be Happening	What to Do about the Problem
Your child doesn't have much of an appetite.	She may be filling up on juice or milk/formula, which can reduce her appetite for solid food.	Note how much juice and milk/formula she is consuming and adjust her fluid intake if necessary. (See Chapters 2 through 5 for guidelines on the amount of liquid babies, toddlers, and preschoolers of various ages should be consuming.)
	Her snacks may be too large (meal-sized), too frequent (she may be grazing all day long as opposed to having pre-planned meals and snacks), or too close to mealtime.	It's fine to offer your child "bonus" snacks on days when she's extra hungry (that's teaching her to respond to her own internal hunger cues—a healthy thing to do), but you also want to encourage healthy eating patterns (a regular routine of pre-planned meals and snacks) rather than a refrigerator and snack cupboard free-for-all. If you want your child to eat well at mealtime, pay attention to the timing and size of her snacks.
	She may not be getting enough iron in her diet. Being iron deficient can lead to a decrease in appetite.	Your health care provider can screen your child for anemia (iron deficiency) by doing either a finger-prick blood test or by taking a sample of blood from her arm.
Your child is distracted.	TV sets, boisterous conversations, emotional stress, and other distractions can turn a child off eating.	Try to minimize mealtime distractions, particularly if your child isn't an overly enthusiastic eater.

Your child is uncomfortable.	Look at the way your child is sitting during mealtime. Does she start to slouch and wiggle? Does she seem comfortable or uncomfortable?	Make sure your child's feet are supported (as opposed to dangling). Think how uncomfortable it is for you to sit at a stool without any foot support. It's uncomfortable for your child, too.
Your child has a hard time handling foods of certain textures or sizes (e.g., they cause her to gag or choke).	The foods that you are serving your child may seem perfectly edible to you, but obviously your child is having difficulty with them.	Cut your child's food into smaller pieces or, if she's still a baby, mash or purée it to a smoother consistency. This will make it easier for the digestive enzymes in your child's mouth to break down food. Over time, gradually adjust the consistency so that your child can practise chewing and swallowing foods with a more challenging consistency.
Your child is extra sensitive to texture and finds anything other than smooth, highly processed foods difficult to eat.	Does your child react strongly to other types of textures? Does he protest if fabric is itchy or a tag on his sweater is rubbing his neck? He may be extra sensitive to textures. (Of course, it's also possible he has a canker, sore gums, or a sore throat. Never overlook the obvious, particularly if the problem has just cropped up out of the blue.)	Consider the textures of the foods you are serving your child. Is your child accustomed to them and are the textures of the food consistent? Gradually encourage your child to accept a wider variety of textures, but don't make these changes too rapidly or you may experience a total backlash: back to liquid purées.
Your child doesn't like the smell of the food.	Your child starts complaining about dinner the moment she can smell it cooking from the other room.	Don't tolerate rude comments, but do realize that her extra-sensitive sense of smell is for real. She's highly tuned into scents—even scents of foods she dislikes.

continued on p. 192

Table 7.1 (Continued)

What You've Noticed	What May Be Happening	What to Do about the Problem
Your child doesn't like the taste of the food.	Your child hates anything other than very bland foods, or has other narrowly defined food tastes. Babies are born with a preference for certain types of foods—sweet, fatty, creamy foods (like breast milk or ice cream) as opposed to sour, stronger, more complex-tasting foods (like sour pickled cabbage). When children are young, their taste buds are highly sensitive, which can make spicy, bitter, and acidic foods so overwhelming that strong-tasting foods taste awful. This heightened sensitivity to certain tastes becomes less pronounced as they grow older.	Scientists have discovered that some people are "super-tasters." They are born with extra-acute taste buds, so the Brussels sprouts that you find mildly bitter may taste horrendous to your child. Serve her vegetables that aren't quite as bitter.
Your child doesn't like the appearance of the food—most likely its color!	Your child has developed a strong dislike of anything green, which is unfortunate because green is very good in the world of veggies.	Read some books and sing some songs about vegetables (but in a fun, low-key way) so that she'll understand that certain types of vegetables are supposed to be green. Continue to offer green vegetables on a regular basis, perhaps accompanied by some orange and yellow sidekicks to make them a little less scary. Your child may be more inclined to try them that way.
Your child doesn't like the temperature of the food.	Your child complains that the food is too hot or too cold.	Try to accommodate your child's temperature preferences within reason. Obviously, there are food safety considerations and other practicalities that you have to factor in.

Your child doesn't like the way she feels after she eats certain foods.	She may not have the words to tell you about the yucky feeling she gets after drinking milk or eating eggs, but this could be what's going on.	Look for consistent patterns and talk to your child's health care provider about what you've noticed. He may want to have your child assessed by a pediatric dietitian or allergist to confirm your suspicions, particularly if a potentially severe allergy (e.g., an allergy to peanuts or shellfish) is suspected.
Your child has learned that kicking up a fuss about food is a good way to get more attention or she's decided to play the role of the picky eater at the dinner table (perhaps in a co-starring role with an equally picky older brother or baby sister).	Consider how you react to your child's food-related behaviors. Do you act unduly concerned if he's not eating? Do you show signs of anger or frustration? Do you go overboard with rewards and attention when your child eats well? Or do you manage to play it cool?	Try to take a relatively low-key approach to your child's eating habits. Try not to show worry or concern in front of your child. Getting upset gives your child the power to control you by eating or not eating—and most kids will exercise that power. And if there are siblings involved, you don't want the mealtime pickiness to escalate as the siblings play off on one another's extreme mealtime behavior.
Your child has developmental delays, a medical condition, a physical impairment, or a history of feeding problems that are interfering with or affecting his enthusiasm for eating.	If your child's feeding difficulties are persistent or extreme, it could be that an underlying problem is making it difficult for your child to eat or swallow food.	Consult with your child's health care provider. A team of professionals, including a speech-language pathologist, a dietitian, and pediatricians, may be able to devise a treatment plan for your child that can improve the situation.

- **Limit the liquids. Too much juice can lead to a poor appetite, poor weight gain, and diarrhea.** Even drinking too much milk can fill up a young child. (See Chapters 4 and 5 for age-specific dietary recommendations.) Watch your child's overall juice consumption and pay attention to the times of day when your child is drinking juice. (Juice should ideally be a breakfast drink only.)

- **Serve your child age-appropriate-sized portions.** A child with a so-so appetite can be put off dinner entirely by a huge serving of food.

- **Look for quick and easy ways to make food look fun and appealing.** (See the list of ideas in the box that follows.)

- **Consider instituting the "one-bite" rule: an expectation that your child will try one bite of new foods.** In her book, *How to Get Your Child to Eat ... But Not Too Much,* Ellyn Satter explains the rationale behind the one-bite rule: "All you are trying to accomplish with the 'one bite' rule is to get her to taste [the new food] so she can decide if she wants to eat it. You are not trying to get her to *eat* it. That is crossing the line into forcing, and the net result will be to decrease the likelihood that she will learn to like it. You'll be doing even better with this rule if you allow her the option of taking the bite back out again if she doesn't like it." And if her verdict after trying the new food is a definite nay? Accept her decision and move on. Don't pressure your child into trying another bite or try to sell her on how great those parsnips will really taste if she'll just keep eating them. If you keep pushing, your child won't try a single bite the next time around.

MOM'S THE WORD

"Madison has always hated fruit. I don't think she's ever going to be one of those kids who prefers fruit over vegetables. And while I'm on the fruit subject, why do they only make medicine in fruit flavors? Madison would prefer pea-flavored Tylenol any day."

—*Shaila, 21, mother of one*

CREATIVITY COUNTS!

Try a few fun food things every now and again that will make meals palate-pleasing and eye-catching to your extra-choosy baby, toddler, or preschooler. (Not all of these foods are suitable for babies and younger toddlers. See Chapters 2, 3, and 4 for advice on what foods are definitely off-limits for younger children.)

- Use cookie cutters to give a sandwich a whole new personality. Maybe the "gingerbread man" grilled-cheese sandwich will be greeted with a bit more enthusiasm than his square-shaped counterpart.

- Use small, child-safe pieces of grated or chopped fruit, vegetables, cheese, meat, or bread to dress up other foods or to make pictures on your child's plate. It can be fun to do this every once in a while. And don't forget to give your toddler or preschooler the chance to try making "food art," too.

- Place an ice cream scoop of egg salad, tuna salad, or salmon salad on a colorful plastic plate. Treat this "blob" as the body of an animal, a face, or whatever else your imagination envisions. Decorate accordingly.

- Use fun "dishes." Serve yogurt in a miniature plastic pail (a brand new one, of course) or oatmeal in a colorful plastic bowl from your picnic set. (Don't microwave anything that's not designed for use in the microwave. Make the oatmeal in a microwave-safe dish and then place it in the plastic dish.)

- Make "toast art." Anything you put between two slices of toasted whole-grain bread will be more fun if the toast has fun and funky pictures on it. Check out Poparttoaster.com and you'll see that toaster art has come a long way.

- Cut food into "fingers." Finger-shaped sandwiches, fruit slices (just be conscious of the choking hazard), and other foods are always big hits with the preschool set.

- Take advantage of the many shapes and colors of pasta to come up with truly edible art. And while you're at it, think of cheese as another edible art supply. It comes in all kinds of lovely colors and textures. It can be chopped, carved, grated, sliced, and diced. And it melts, too. Too cool!

continued on p. 196

CREATIVITY COUNTS! *(Continued)*

- Serve whole-grain pancakes in different shapes. (Purchase a squeeze bottle to draw a heart or to write your preschooler's initial in pancake batter.)

- Dress up the dinner table. Make homemade placemats with your child. Place a giant sheet of brown craft paper on the dinner table so that restless toddlers and preschoolers can doodle while they dine or have fun sticking stickers on the "table." (Just make sure that this won't become too much of a distraction. You'll have to use your discretion here.)

- Come up with creative names for your culinary creations. Give your dinners a theme and choose some appropriate music to go along with the theme or make "food" the theme. (You can find all kinds of children's songs about food.)

See the Food Tools and Appendix B for additional sources of culinary inspiration.

- **Don't reward your child for trying a new food.** It puts too much pressure on your child and gives him the sense that he's being conned. After all, if you have to give him a treat or a reward for trying that piece of cauliflower, there must be something wrong with it (or so your child may assume).

- **If at first you don't succeed, try offering that food again.** It may be welcomed with greater enthusiasm at another time, date, or place—or in a different form. ("You may find out that they love asparagus raw—just not cooked or in a soup, says Kimberly, 40, mother of one.) Never say never—or at least don't say never until you've reintroduced that food 10 to 20 times—the number of times it may take your child to decide for sure whether or not she actually likes it. And don't forget that offering it again may mean taking a break before re-introducing the veggie non-grata, offering it in a slightly different form, or teaming it up with a more popular sidekick.

- **Don't let what your child is or isn't eating become the focus of family mealtime.** "Look at the *child,* not the plate," says Leslie, 27, mother of one. Enjoy the dinnertime conversation and your own meal. Think of anything but the fate of the piece of broccoli that may or may not be making its way to your child's mouth.

- **Accept that there will be some foods that your child doesn't like—just as there are some foods that you don't like.** "My daughter doesn't like peas," says Mary Lynn, 35, mother of one. "She eats plenty of other veggies, so I just accept that I shouldn't feed her peas. I may try every few months to get her to try them again, but if she doesn't want to, that's okay."

- **Don't make your child special meals or offer your child junk food to get him to eat something.** If everything on the dinner table is healthy, her choices are healthy, healthy, and healthy. If she chooses not to eat any of those foods, she'll be presented with more choices at the next scheduled snack, and then at the next planned meal, and then at the next planned snack, and so on. Obviously, you're not going to offer her a smorgasbord of horrible foods (or foods she considers horrible!). If you include at least one food she likes at each meal or snack, she can nibble on that while deciding whether to try the other foods. Maybe she'll try them; maybe she won't. Ultimately, that's her decision to make.

- **Steer clear of the "good food, bad food" trap.** If your family eats dessert, consider serving dessert at the same time as the rest of dinner. Serve a healthier choice like fruit (as opposed to ice cream) for dessert or stick to small servings of "the goodies," but by having fruit salad along with your main meal, you'll be treating dessert in a matter-of-fact way, which may encourage your child to eat other parts of his dinner once he's had his dessert. (You'll have to experiment to see if this strategy works with your child or not.)

MOTHER WISDOM

Is breakfast almost as much of an ordeal as dinner? Sometimes toddlers and preschoolers don't feel like eating when they first wake up. Try working more time into your morning routine so that your child can work up an appetite for breakfast. You may find it also works well to serve a light breakfast (perhaps a fruit and yogurt breakfast smoothie) followed by a decent-sized mid-morning snack.

MOTHER WISDOM

Concerned that your child's overall rate of growth may be lagging behind? Set up an appointment with your child's health care provider. She can check your child's overall growth and development over time to see if your child is gaining weight at the expected rate, or if your child's weight gain is lagging a little; check your child for signs of iron-deficiency anemia (a common cause for low appetite in young children), infection (particularly infections of the urinary tract, ears, sinuses, tonsils, adenoids, and/or lungs), gastrointestinal problems, allergies and asthma, and more serious medical conditions (heart disease, cystic fibrosis, diabetes, thyroid disorders, and neurological disorders).

- **Don't tolerate rude comments from your toddler or pre-schooler about what you've prepared for dinner.** Ditto for whining and screaming at the dinner table and other obnoxious mealtime behavior. It's important to teach your child how to behave at the dinner table so that everyone looks forward to dinner rather than dreading it.

- **Remember that your child is not rejecting you when he rejects the dinner.** Don't invest too much of your self-esteem in the meals that you prepare for your child or you could end up feeling great when your child eats well and lousy when everything you prepare is greeted with protests and tears.

- **If you can't stand the heat, get out of the kitchen.** Well, at least for a while. Dealing with a child who is extra-challenging at mealtime requires exceptional patience, so take planned and impromptu breaks every once in a while. Hire a child care provider and escape for dinner without kids, or leave someone else in charge of the dinnertime fracas and take a momentary timeout to regain your cool. Then, when you're feeling like you can listen to another passionate monologue on the evils of eggplant or the perils of parsnips, you can head back into the culinary front lines.

- **Present a united front.** Make sure that you, your partner, and all of the key adults in your child's life (grandparents, day care providers, and anyone else responsible for feeding your child) are playing by the same "food rules." The reason is obvious. If you're trying to establish one set of mealtime rules and behaviors and everyone else in your child's life is headed off in an entirely different direction, it will be difficult to make any progress on the mealtime front. Don't be surprised if you get into some heated discussions with your partner about how lenient or lax you should be about what your child is eating, whether alternate meals should be prepared, and what role, if any, parents should play in encouraging the child to eat. It's okay for parents to disagree, but have these discussions out of earshot of your child and away from the dinner table. By the time you start dishing out your child's meal, both parents should be clear on the mealtime strategy and rules and should be prepared to present a united front.

- **Consider the big mealtime picture.** If you're freaking out about what your child is or isn't eating, look at your child's food consumption over a period of days rather than during a single meal. If you're concerned, keep a food diary for a week and then share it with your child's health care provider or a pediatric dietitian. You'll be able to get some objective feedback on whether, in fact, there is cause for concern right now. If you find it difficult to estimate your child's portion sizes or keeping track of everything he's eaten, consider taking snapshots of his meals and snacks using a digital camera or the photo feature that can be found on many cellphones. Then you can spend a little time after he's in bed at night making more accurate notes to share with the health care provider or dietitian.

🔊 **MOM'S THE WORD**

"From a young age, Emma always loved Kraft Dinner, but she would never eat the broken ones (the noodles that were flat rather than round because they'd split for whatever reason). Even if she hadn't seen it, she could taste it and knew it was there and next thing you know, she'd throw up. She can't even look at the broken ones. For a time I would try and get them all out, but I always seemed to miss one or two and there would then be trouble. Now that she's five, she won't even go near Kraft Dinner for fear of the broken ones, I guess."

—*Clare, 31, Mom of three*

When Picky Becomes a Problem

WE'VE ALL KNOWN at least one picky eater who drove his parents around the bend with his food preferences. But raising a garden-variety picky eater is an absolute cakewalk as compared to raising a child with a full-blown feeding disorder—a child who has difficulty chewing or swallowing; who chokes, coughs, gags, or vomits at every meal; and whose food repertoire is limited to as few as three foods. Your child may also be flagged as having some sort of growth-related concern if his rate of growth is consistently poor (e.g., his height and weight keep falling off the pediatric growth charts curve). The medical term applied in such cases is "failure to thrive."

So what's behind these pediatric feeding disorders? Sometimes these children have medical issues, physical impairments, developmental delays, or sensory integration problems (a disorder in which the brain has difficulty making sense of sensory input from the body) that make eating by mouth extremely difficult. In other cases, a medical problem may have resulted in a delay in the introduction of solid foods or any type of food by mouth (the child may have been fed intravenously or through a feeding tube) for a period of time and now that the child has been given the green light to start taking some or all of his food by mouth, the child is finding it difficult to make this transition.

If you suspect that your baby, toddler, or preschooler has a feeding problem, have your child assessed and treated. A treatment plan will focus on improving your child's eating skills and chewing patterns, increasing your child's tolerance for different food tastes and textures, and helping your child to be more receptive to eating. Generally, children with severe feeding problems require treatment from a team of specialists. Sometimes treatment is administered on an out-patient basis. At other times, such treatment is provided in a hospital. To learn more about pediatric feeding disorders, see Lori Ernspenrger, PhD, and Tania Stegen-Hanson's book, *Just Take a Bite: Easy Effective Answers to Food Aversions and Eating Challenges* (Arlington, Texas, Future Horizons, 2004).

Solutions Central—The Last Word

Coping with a child who is a picky eater can be a major source of worry and frustration. Compare notes with other parents and have a game plan for dealing with your child's food issues so that you're not flip-flopping your strategy from moment to moment or from meal to meal.

Whether your child's food issues are minor or major, it's important that you and your partner function as a team. Otherwise what started out as an eating and/or behavior problem can quickly escalate into a major source of conflict between you and your partner. If you can keep your focus on making mealtimes fun and relaxing (as opposed to allowing them to devolve into parent-child power struggles over food), you'll likely find your child's eating habits much easier to cope with over the long run.

CHAPTER 8

When Your Child Is Sick

*Try to stay calm. It is so hard not to freak out and
get upset when your kid is so sick.*
—KIRA, 35, MOTHER OF ONE

"AN APPLE A day keeps the doctor away." If it were that
simple, you would have been giving your child the apple
advantage from the moment she started solids, offering
your baby puréed apples, your toddler unsweetened applesauce,
and your preschooler apple slices three times a day, just to hedge
your bets, but it's impossible to ward off every cold and flu bug
that's making the rounds of play groups, day care, or toddler
gym-and-swim, especially not when little ones are so apt to share
the germy love!

And when kids get sick, their appetites often go AWOL. Like
the rest of us, they don't feel much like eating when they've got a
sore throat or an aching belly. That can send our worry-o-meters
kicking into overdrive. Hey, we're moms. We worry. It's natural.
And, of course, sometimes the health-related issues are much more
complicated.

I don't have the space in this very tiny final chapter to get into
all the possible pediatric health issues that can affect feeding and

nutrition. Encyclopedia-length books are written on this subject, after all. But, in addition to the garden-variety illnesses such as colds and flus (which may include ear infections), nausea and vomiting, and diarrhea, I also wanted to talk about some common issues that may arise in young children, and that may necessitate significant changes on the feeding front: gastrointestinal reflux disease, food allergies, and diabetes. While I have the space to mention these conditions only briefly, I include them for two reasons: firstly, so that you would be aware of them in case your child is having health problems that warrant further investigation, and you're looking for clues; and secondly, in case your child has just been diagnosed with one of these problems, so that you won't feel quite so alone.

I've also included a brief discussion on childhood obesity because I want to stress the importance of taking a three-pronged approach to dealing with this issue: emphasizing healthy nutrition, active living, and positive body image.

Feed a Fever ...

FORGET THAT OLD adage about feeding a fever and starving a cold. Well, at least forget the "starving a cold" bit. Children still need to be fed, even when they're not feeling well (see Table 8.1).

When your child is sick, he may not be as hungry as usual and the foods he's usually crazy about may not appeal to him at all.

"When Katie is sick, I focus on getting lots of liquid into her and I don't worry about the food. As long as she is drinking lots, I am happy," says Shana, 32, mother of 19-month-old Katie.

Table 8.1

Feeding Your Sick Child

Type of Illness	Tips on Feeding and Caring for Your Sick Child
Cold and cough	Encourage your child to drink extra fluids. Runny noses, sneezing, and coughing causes your child to lose more fluids than usual.
	Your toddler or preschooler may be more willing to consume liquids and soft foods than solids because his throat may be sore.
	• Add honey to warm water. Honey can really help to soothe a sore throat. *Note:* Remember that honey is not recommended for children under one, due to the risk of botulism.
	• Apple juice, flat ginger ale, popsicles, gelatin, pudding, yogurt, and ice cream may be soothing to your child's throat.
	• Broth, soup, and warm cereal may also be welcome choices.
	• If your child is willing to consume slightly more solid foods, try offering lightly buttered toast, mashed potatoes, rice, and canned fruits.
	Continue offering the breast to your breast-fed baby.
	• It may be difficult for your baby to nurse when her nose is stuffed up. To make nursing easier for her, try to keep her as upright as possible while you're feeding her.
	• Use saline drops, a squirt of breast milk, or a suction bulb to clear out your baby's nose before you sit down to feed her.
	• To suction your child's nose, lay her across your lap with her head resting on your upper arm. Tuck your baby's inside arm behind your back, use the arm that is supporting her head to hold her other arm. Tip her towards you so her head can't bob around and use your free hand to operate the suction bulb. Quick motions are most effective.

continued on p. 206

| Nausea and vomiting | Seek medical attention immediately if your child seems extremely ill, is lethargic, or is showing signs of dehydration (sunken eyes, no tears, dry mouth, or decreased urination, which, in babies and young toddlers, means fewer wet diapers). |

Feeding tips:

- Don't offer your child anything to eat when she is vomiting. Give her stomach a chance to settle down. After an hour, offer a few sips of liquid. If she can keep that liquid down, offer more fluids over the next few hours. If she can tolerate that liquid, slowly offer her other stomach-friendly foods that are part of her usual repertoire of foods. Feedings should be small and frequent.

- Your child may be scared to eat because she's afraid of throwing up again. Soothe and comfort your child before, during, and after the feeding.

- Try not to convey your worry about how much your child is or isn't eating.

- Don't become frustrated with your child if she can't keep the liquid down.

- Give your child opportunities to rinse her mouth and help her to brush her teeth, both to protect her tooth enamel and to get rid of the yucky taste in her mouth.

Pediatric hydration formulas:

- Your doctor may recommend a pediatric hydration formula that contains electrolytes. If you're breast-feeding and your baby is nursing well, your health care provider may simply suggest that you continue breast-feeding.

- If your doctor recommends that your child start on a hydration formula, start out by offering your child a small amount (1–2 ounces) to see if your child can keep the liquid down. Once your child is tolerating larger servings well, your health care provider will likely suggest that you reintroduce easy-to-tolerate solids such as dry toast and crackers (provided your baby is already eating these foods).

- Pediatric hydration formulas are intended to be used only for two to three days. If your child is not able to keep the formula down or isn't able to get back on solid foods within a couple of days, contact your child's health care provider.

Table 8.1 (*Continued*)

Type of Illness	Tips on Feeding and Caring for Your Sick Child
Diarrhea	Diarrhea occurs most often in children between the ages of one and three. It can lead to dehydration quite rapidly, particularly if the toddler or preschooler is also vomiting. Seek medical attention immediately if your child seems extremely ill, is lethargic, or is showing signs of dehydration (sunken eyes, no tears, dry mouth, or decreased urination, which, in babies and young toddlers, means fewer wet diapers).
	• To prevent dehydration, make sure that your baby is consuming plenty of liquids. Offer the breast to your breast-fed baby often. If your baby is drinking formula, ask your health care provider if he recommends diluting the formula to provide extra fluid or temporarily switching your baby to a lactose-free formula (if your child usually drinks a formula that contains lactose). When a child has diarrhea, the intestinal enzyme that is responsible for digesting and absorbing lactose can be temporarily damaged, triggering additional diarrhea when products containing lactose are eaten.
	• Offer your child smaller feedings more often. If your child still has difficulty tolerating these feedings, your health care provider may suggest a pediatric hydration formula (sometimes called "pediatric rehydration formulas").
	• Well-meaning friends and family members may suggest that you offer your child apple juice and ginger ale to keep your child well hydrated, but the high sugar content in these products can lead to further diarrhea and diaper rashes.
	• Others may suggest that you put your child on the BRAT diet (bananas, rice, applesauce, and toast). While this is a diet that has yet to be scientifically proven to prevent diarrhea, many dietitians, pediatricians, and moms swear by this diet.

Fever

If your baby is still quite young and has developed a fever, it's important to have your baby seen by a doctor so that the root cause of the fever can be identified (e.g., an ear infection). Your doctor will likely suggest that you feed your baby at least every two hours—more often if your baby wants to nurse more often—in order to meet your baby's increased need for fluid and calories while she is fighting off a fever.

Older children should also be offered plenty of cool liquids such as water, fruit juice, and ginger ale. Start adding puréed fruit, fruit juice slush drinks, yogurt, and pudding as your child's temperature starts to return to normal. (Your child's health care provider can provide you with specific guidance, given the severity of your child's illness and your child's age and dietary needs.)

Note: Don't push solids if your child's appetite is off. She'll regain that appetite as soon as her body is ready for solid food. Focus on offering liquids instead.

Don't push food before your child is ready, stresses Jennifer, 30, the mother of two-and-a-half-year-old Isaac and nine-month-old Alex. "Be gentle and slow, and heed your child's cues. Kids seem to have trigger-tummies, and putting too much in is more than likely just going to result in it coming out—everywhere! When they're feeling better, you can catch up on the veggies."

Of course, it's important to ensure that your child receives enough fluid to avoid becoming dehydrated. A child under 22 pounds needs 1.5 ounces for each pound of body weight. A child between 23 and 45 pounds needs 33 ounces of liquid plus 0.67 ounces of liquid for each pound of body weight. To make it easier to keep track when you're missing out on sleep (as is often the case when your child is ill) use a sippy cup with measurements on the side so you can keep track of the volume of liquids going in. That should provide you with some estimate of liquids in.

Gastroesophageal Reflux Disease (GERD)

GASTROESOPHAGEAL REFLUX DISEASE (GERD) occurs when the contents of a baby's stomach flow backwards up into the esophagus, reaching as high as the mouth or nose, contributing to extreme fussiness, sleeping and feeding problems, and other health-related problems in some cases, including insufficient weight gain and pneumonia. Certain feeding strategies have been proven to minimize the symptoms of GERD in young babies:

- Offer smaller, more frequent feedings.
- Keep your baby's head elevated (at a 45° angle) during feedings as well as for 20 to 30 minutes after the meal to prevent regurgitation.
- Burp your baby frequently.
- Keep records of your baby's feeding schedule so that you can identify what patterns seem to work best for your baby. Many

parents find that gaps of two to two-and-a-half hours between feedings work well with babies with GERD, as opposed to constant grazing. However, every baby is unique, so it's important to remember that, too.

You can obtain helpful information on coping with GERD by visiting the following websites:

- Children's Digestive Health and Nutrition Foundation (www.CDHNF.org)
- North American Society for Pediatric Gastroenterology, Hepatology, and Nutrition (www.NASPGHAN.org)

For sleep advice, see *Sleep Solutions for Your Baby, Toddler and Preschooler: The Ultimate No-worry Approach for Each Age and Stage*.

Food Allergies

A FOOD ALLERGY is an adverse reaction to food that triggers a reaction from the body's immune system. (Other types of adverse reactions to foods that do not trigger a reaction from the immune system include food intolerances like lactose intolerance, which are caused by enzyme deficiencies; food poisoning; and a pharmacological reaction like what you experience when you drink too much coffee.) A young child with food allergies may experience such symptoms as abdominal cramps; vomiting; diarrhea; hives; swelling of the face, lips, throat, eyes, and extremities; eczema; asthma; runny nose; difficulty breathing; low blood pressure; shock. Most reactions are immediate.

It's important to have food allergies diagnosed accurately so that an appropriate nutrition plan can be created for the child, particularly if a child has multiple allergies. Children with severe allergies should carry an epinephrine kit so that they can receive injections immediately, in the event of a reaction, which should be treated as a life-threatening emergency.

See Appendices A and B for some helpful resources related to food allergies.

MOM'S THE WORD

"There should be a support group for mothers who have to give up peanut butter and all things nutty because their baby is allergic. Seriously. I find this harder (and I'm not joking) than giving up alcohol when I was pregnant. Peanut butter is such a staple to me ... doing without over the past year has been difficult. And nuts are in a lot of things. The fact that Alec isn't allowed to have them has forced us as a family to give up nuts entirely. This is the way to go for me because if I had temptation in the house, I'm sure I'd crack...."

—*Jen, 26, mother of one*

Diabetes in Young Children

DIABETES IS A disease in which the body is not able to produce or make proper use of insulin, the hormone that converts sugar, starches, and other food products into body fuel. Approximately 5–10 percent of diabetics have Type 1 diabetes, which occurs when the body fails to produce insulin. The remaining 90–95 percent of diabetics have Type 2 diabetes, which results from insulin resistance (a condition when the body fails to make proper use of insulin) combined with insulin deficiency. When diabetes occurs in babies, toddlers, and preschoolers, it is most often Type 1 diabetes, but both types of diabetes can occur in people of all ages.

The warning signs of diabetes include extreme thirst; frequent urination; drowsiness/lethargy; sugar in urine; sudden vision changes; increased appetite; sudden weight loss; fruity, sweet, or wine-smelling breath; heavy, labored breathing; being dazed or "out of it"; and passing out. If you notice some of these signs in your child, talk to your health care provider.

If your baby, toddler, or preschooler has been diagnosed with diabetes, you will need to learn how to check your child's blood sugar levels and to administer insulin shots to keep your child's blood sugar levels as stable as possible, which is necessary to ensure healthy brain development and to protect her other body systems. (Untreated diabetes can result in damage to the cardiovascular system, kidneys, eyes, nerves, blood vessels, gums, and teeth.)

FRIDGE NOTE

No one enjoys having a finger pricked or getting or giving a needle. You can make the process easier on your child by:

- letting your child know that the pinprick needle is coming so that she doesn't start to associate being picked up with "a sneak attack"

- offering lots of cuddles before, during, and after the blood sugar check or insulin shot

- giving your toddler or preschooler some choices (e.g., "Which finger do you want the pinprick in?")

- having your child help you keep track of injection sites by sticking stickers on a life-sized cut-out of herself. (She can stick stars or other stickers on after each needle.)

For other tips on making injections as child-friendly as possible, download a copy of www.diabetes.org/uedocuments/DiabetesInfantsToddlers.pdf from the American Diabetes Association website.

One of the best ways to keep your child's blood sugar levels as stable as possible is to serve meals and snacks at predictable times. Ideally, your child would consume roughly the same amount of food at the same time of day, from one day to the next, but as you already know from reading this book, that's a Utopian food fantasy when you're talking about babies, toddlers, and preschoolers. What you, as the parent, can control is the timing of the meal or snack and the size of the corresponding insulin dose. You can't control the amount of food that goes into your child's mouth. You'll also want to pay attention to the types of foods that your child eats. Believe it or not, fruit juice can cause blood sugar levels to rise more rapidly than most solid sources of carbohydrates. Therefore, children with diabetes should consume only small quantities of juice.

It's also important to be aware of the signs that your child may be becoming hypoglycemic (experiencing low blood sugar): a distinctive cry, sweating or trembling, becoming pale, crankiness, clumsiness, developing a bluish tinge on the fingers or the lips. If you detect these signs, do a blood check right away. If you can't do a blood check, assume that your child is experiencing hypoglycemia and give your child $^1/_4$ cup to $^1/_2$ cup of apple juice or orange juice, 4 to 5 ounces of milk, or a source of emergency glucose (see childrenwithdiabetes.com).

For additional information about diabetes in young children, see Appendices A and B for some recommended resources.

Weighty Matters

THE LATEST STATISTICS about weight problems among very young children are alarming, to say the least. Ten percent of two- to five-year-olds are overweight. Children who are overweight are at increased risk of physical health problems, including Type 2 diabetes, and of experiencing social and psychological problems such as teasing and poor self-esteem. They are more likely to become overweight teenagers and adults, and therefore face an increased risk of the serious—even deadly—health problems associated with being overweight or becoming obese.

Sometimes we get so panicked by bad news that we forget that we parents have a powerful opportunity to help our kids to beat those odds as a result of the actions we take in our own families. In addition to promoting healthy nutrition (see Chapter 6 and the appendices for tips and resources) and giving your child plenty of opportunities to be physically active (see Chapter 5 for some practical suggestions on becoming more active as a family and the appendices for more resources that can support and inspire you in your efforts), you want her to develop a positive attitude toward her body. You can do that by:

- giving her opportunities to move her body and to experience the joy of being physically active

- encouraging her to focus on all the amazing things her body can do (as opposed to the shape or size of her belly or how her body compares to that of other children she knows)

- accepting that children come in all shapes and sizes (the pressure to have "the perfect body" is starting to hit kids at a younger and younger age, so it's important that we arm our kids with body positive messages from early childhood onward)

FRIDGE NOTE

Kids need to be weighed and measured regularly to ensure that their rate of growth is on track. You can download growth charts for children from birth to age 36 months and BMI-for-age (body mass index for age) charts for children and adolescents, ages two through 20, from www.cdc.gov/growthcharts/. In general, you can expect your baby to double his birth weight by age four to six months and triple it by age one year. He'll then gain about 4–6 pounds during each of the toddler and preschool years. This growth doesn't happen at a steady rate. In fact, you may notice that your child goes through periods when he's a little leaner and times when he's a little chubbier. This is perfectly normal.

- not allowing your child's body size or eating habits to dominate your relationship with or feelings about your child
- striving to be a healthy role model yourself when it comes to fitness, nutrition, and body confidence

Solutions Central—The Last Word

IT DIDN'T TAKE your newborn baby long to start thinking of "mom" as a synonym for "food." Forget the scent of freshly cooked anything from the oven. When you're a new baby, nothing beats the scent of your own mom!

But our role in feeding and nurturing our families doesn't end when we wean our little ones—or they wean us—whatever the case may be. Whether we work outside the home or in the home, most of us play a major role in planning meals, cooking for our families, and deciding what ends up in the cupboards and the refrigerator.

I hope you'll use the resources in the back of this book as a launching pad for coming up with your own unique smorgasbord of solutions for nourishing yourself and your family during the crazy-busy but wonderful years when you're raising a family. Not only are you a nutritional role model for your child (you are the secret ingredient in the recipe for a healthy kid!), you want to be in the best possible health so that you can enjoy motherhood as your child moves from stage to stage.

So here's one final bit of advice: Get together with a group of mom friends and share ideas at "the motherhood buffet"—a place where moms "dish" with other moms by swapping strategies for eating well, finding time for fitness, and nurturing themselves mind, body, and soul. Bon appetit!

Food Tools

Food Tool 1: Basic Baby Food Purées

To MAKE EACH of the following baby food purées, wash, peel, core, and remove any seeds from the produce and cut into small cubes or slices to reduce cooking time. Check food while it is cooking to see if food has reached the desired texture (see Food Tool 2). To purée, run the food through a blender, food mill, ricer, or food processor until it is smooth or force the food through a sieve. Then refrigerate or freeze your baby food. (See Chapter 2 for food storage tips.)

	Ingredients	Preparation Instructions
Fruit		
Apples	4 cups apples, peeled and sliced ¹/₂ cup water	Cover and cook over medium heat until fruit is tender: 15–20 minutes. Purée.
Apricots, fresh	4 cups apricots, peeled, pitted, and chopped ¹/₂ cup water	Cover and cook in a steamer basket until fruit is tender: 7–9 minutes. Purée.
Bananas	4 very ripe bananas, broken into small chunks	No cooking necessary. Purée.
Blackberries	1 pint or 2 cups blackberries (fresh or frozen)	No cooking necessary. Purée and then force mixture through a mesh sieve using a plastic spatula.

continued on p. 216

	Ingredients	Preparation Instructions
Fruit		
Blueberries	1 pint or 2 cups blueberries (fresh or frozen)	No cooking necessary. Purée and then force mixture through a mesh sieve using a plastic spatula.
Cantaloupe	4 cups cantaloupe, peeled and chopped into little pieces	No cooking necessary. Purée.
Honeydew	4 cups honeydew melon, peeled and chopped into little pieces	No cooking necessary. Purée.
Kiwi fruit	4 cups kiwi fruit, peeled and sliced	No cooking necessary. Purée.
Mangoes	4 cups mangoes, peeled and sliced $1/3$ cup water	No cooking necessary. Purée.
Nectarines	4 medium-sized nectarines	Cover and cook in a steamer basket in a pot over low heat until fruit is tender: 2–4 minutes. Purée.
Papaya	4 cups papaya, peeled and sliced $1/3$ cup water	No cooking necessary. Purée.
Peaches	4 cups fresh peaches, peeled $1/2$ cup water *Note:* If you can't find fresh, ripe peaches (or if they are out of season), use frozen or canned unsweetened peaches instead.	Cover and cook in a steamer basket in a pot over low heat until fruit is tender: 2–4 minutes. Purée.

	Ingredients	Preparation Instructions
Fruit		
Pears	4 cups pears, chopped and peeled $^1/_2$ cup water *Note:* Unsweetened canned pears can substitute for fresh fruit. Simply purée the canned fruit with a proportionate quantity of liquid.	Cover and cook in a steamer basket in a pot over low heat until fruit is tender: 8–12 minutes. Purée.
Pineapple	1 pineapple, peeled and chopped (or unsweetened canned pineapple)	No cooking necessary. Purée and then force mixture through a mesh sieve using a plastic spatula.
Plums	4 cups plums, peeled and chopped	Cover and cook in a steamer basket in a pot over low heat until fruit is tender: 2–4 minutes. Purée.
Prunes	2 cups prunes $^2/_3$ cup water	Cover and cook over low heat or steam until fruit is tender: 15–20 minutes. Purée.
Raspberries	1 pint or 2 cups raspberries (fresh or frozen)	No cooking necessary. Purée and then force mixture through a mesh sieve using a plastic spatula.
Strawberries	1 pint or 2 cups strawberries (fresh or frozen)	No cooking necessary. Purée and then force mixture through a mesh sieve using a plastic spatula.
Watermelon	4 cups watermelon, chopped and seeded	No cooking necessary. Purée.
Vegetables		
Asparagus	1 bunch asparagus $^1/_2$ cup water	Cook over medium-low heat until water comes to a boil. Then simmer for 15–20 minutes or until tender. Purée.

continued on p. 218

	Ingredients	Preparation Instructions
Vegetables		
Avocado	1 avocado, chopped and peeled	No cooking necessary. Purée.
Beans, green or yellow	4 cups green beans $1/2$ cup water	Cook over medium-low heat until beans come to a boil. Then simmer for 15 minutes or until tender. Purée and then run through a sieve to achieve a smoother texture.
Beets	2 cups beets $1/2$ cup water	Cook in a steamer basket over a pot of boiling water for 45–60 minutes or until tender. Purée.
Broccoli	4 cups broccoli $1/2$ cup water	Steam for 10 minutes or until tender. Purée.
Carrots	4 cups carrots, peeled and sliced $1/2$ cup water	Cook over medium-low heat until carrots come to a boil. Then simmer for 20 minutes or until tender. Purée.
Cauliflower	4 cups cauliflower $1/2$ cup water	Steam for 10–20 minutes or until tender. Purée.
Lima beans	2 cups lima beans $1/4$ cup water	Cook over medium-low heat until lima beans come to a boil. Then simmer for 20 minutes or until tender. Purée.
Peas	3 cups peas 2 cups water	Cook over medium-low heat until peas come to a boil. Then simmer for 5 minutes or until tender. Purée.
Potatoes	1 cup potatoes $1/4$ cup water	Cook over medium-low heat until potatoes come to a boil. Then simmer for 15–20 minutes or until tender. For best results, use a food mill or sieve rather than a blender or food processor when you're puréeing sweet potatoes. Purée. *Note:* Potatoes don't freeze well.

	Ingredients	Preparation Instructions
	Vegetables	
Pumpkin	8 cups pumpkin, peeled and cooked	Cut a small pumpkin into large chunks and cook in a large pot with approximately 1 cup of water. (The idea is to steam the pumpkin chunks rather than to boil them.) Cook for 20–30 minutes or until tender. Drain the pumpkin, reserving the liquid as a base for other baby food purées. When the chunks are cool enough to handle, remove the peel and purée the flesh.
Spinach	1 package fresh spinach, washed and cleaned or 1 package frozen $^1/_2$ cup water	Cook over medium-low heat, until leaves start to wilt (about 3 minutes). Purée.
Squash	4 cups squash $^1/_2$ cup water	Cook over medium-low heat until squash comes to a boil. Then simmer for 20 minutes or until tender. Purée.
Sweet potatoes	4 cups sweet potatoes $^1/_2$ cup water	Microwave on high for 7–9 minutes, or until tender. (Pierce with a fork before microwaving.) For best results, use a food mill or sieve rather than a blender or food processor. Purée.
Yams	4 cups yams $^1/_2$ cup water	Microwave on high for 7–9 minutes, or until tender. (Pierce with a fork before microwaving.) For best results, use a food mill or sieve rather than a blender or food processor. Purée.

continued on p. 220

Ingredients	Preparation Instructions
Meats and Beans	
Beans, red kidney, black, or white	1 large can of beans (look for salt-free or low-salt varieties), drained and well rinsed	No cooking required. Simply purée. If consistency is too thick, add a small amount of water or vegetable stock.
Beef	1 cup cooked beef, chopped into small pieces $^1/_2$ cup water or vegetable stock	*Variation:* To achieve a less grainy texture, purée beef and liquid with cooked potatoes and cooked carrots.
Chicken	1 cup cooked chicken, chopped into small pieces $^1/_2$ cup water or vegetable stock	Purée until smooth. *Variation:* To achieve a less grainy texture, purée chicken and liquid with potatoes and carrots.
Chickpeas (also known as garbanzo beans or celi)	1 large can of chickpeas (look for salt-free or low-salt varieties), drained and well rinsed	No cooking required. Simply purée. If consistency is too thick, add a small amount of water or vegetable stock.
Lentils	7 ounces small red lentils $^1/_2$ cup water	Bring lentils and water to boil over medium-high heat. Simmer until the lentils are thoroughly cooked (about 14 minutes). If the lentils are already the desired texture, you don't have to do anything else. Otherwise, add more water and purée.
Cereals and Grains	
Barley	1 cup barley, whole 3 cups water	Bring barley to a boil over medium heat and then simmer until tender (about 90 minutes). Allow to cool slightly and then purée, adding more water, if necessary, to adjust texture.

	Ingredients	Preparation Instructions
	Cereals and Grains	
Bulgur	1 cup bulgur 2 cups water	Bring bulgur to a boil over medium heat and then simmer until tender (about 1 minute). Allow to cool slightly and then purée, adding more water, if necessary, to adjust texture.
Couscous	1 cup couscous 2 cups water	Bring couscous to a boil over medium heat and then simmer until tender (about 90 minutes). Allow to cool slightly and then purée, adding more water, if necessary, to adjust texture.
Oats	1 cup oats, rolled 2 cups water	Bring oats to a boil over medium heat and then simmer until tender (about 5 minutes). Allow to stand for 10 minutes.
Quinoa	1 cup quinoa 2 cups water	Bring quinoa to a boil over medium heat and then simmer until tender (about 20 minutes). Allow to cool slightly and then purée, adding more water, if necessary, to adjust texture.
Rice, brown	1 cup brown rice 2 cups water	Bring brown rice to a boil over medium heat and then simmer until tender (about 45 minutes). Allow to cool slightly and then purée, adding more water, if necessary, to adjust texture.

continued on p. 222

	Ingredients	Preparation Instructions
Cereals and Grains		
Spelt	1 cup spelt 3 cups water	Bring spelt to a boil over medium heat and then simmer until tender (about 90–120 minutes). Allow to cool slightly and then purée, adding more water, if necessary, to adjust texture.
Wheat, whole	1 cup wheat, whole berries 3 cups water	Bring whole wheat to a boil over medium heat and then simmer until tender (about 90–120 minutes). Allow to cool slightly and then purée, adding more water, if necessary, to adjust texture.

Notes:

To maximize nutrients, set aside some of the water that you have used to steam your fruit or vegetables so that you can use this water rather than plain water as liquid in the blender. You can also add pure, unsweetened fruit juice to fruit purées.

Some parents prefer to add breast milk to their fruit purées. You can do that if you're puréeing fruit as you serve it to your baby, but not if you're making a large batch of baby food for the freezer.

The proportion of food to liquid is just a starting guideline. To achieve a smoother texture, add more liquid. Just remember that your baby will obtain more nutrients per bite if you limit the amount of water that you add to the baby food, and you want to encourage her to move on to foods with more challenging textures in order to promote healthy eating skills.

You may still want to run your final purées through a food strainer or sieve to achieve the desired texture, depending on your baby's age and stage.

The purées in this chart have been listed in alphabetical order, not in the order in which foods should be introduced to babies. See Chapters 2 and 3 for information on which types of foods are not suitable for babies of various ages.

The cereal purées should be served only occasionally. They should not be considered a substitute for iron-fortified infant cereals, which play an important role in baby's diet into the toddler years.

Technically, avocados and pumpkins are fruits, but because most of us tend to treat them like vegetables when we're cooking, I've included them in the vegetable portion of this chart.

For other baby food purées, see the recipe links in Appendix B.

For tips on cooking with various whole grains, visit the nutrition section of Harvestcoop.ca or Wholegrainscouncil.org.

Food Tool 2: Baby Food Cuisine: Mix and Match Purées

ONCE YOUR BABY has become accustomed to a variety of different purées, you can start mixing and matching those purées to add variety to your baby's diet and maximize nutrients and taste. Here are some combinations that babies love

Base Purées	Mix with One or More of These Foods	
	Fruit	
Apples	Apricots	Raspberries
	Blueberries	Squash
	Carrots	Strawberries
	Chicken	Sweet potatoes
Bananas	Avocados	Prunes
	Blueberries	Raspberries
	Cottage cheese	Squash
	Mango	Sweet potatoes
	Nectarines	Tofu
	Papaya	Yams
	Peaches	Yogurt
	Pineapple	
Pears	Apples	Peaches
	Apricot	Peas
	Bananas	Plums
	Blueberries	Prunes
	Carrots	Squash
	Cauliflower	Sweet potatoes
	Cottage cheese	Yams
Prunes	Apples	Pears
	Bananas	Sweet potatoes
	Carrots	Yogurt
	Cottage cheese	
	Vegetables	
Avocados	Bananas	Papaya
Carrots	Pears	Squash
	Pineapple	Yogurt

continued on p. 224

Base Purées	Mix with One or More of These Foods	
Vegetables		
Potatoes	Apples	Peas
	Broccoli	Sweet Potatoes
Sweet potatoes	Cauliflower	
Squash	Apples	Peaches
	Carrots	Pears
Meats and Legumes		
Beef	Asparagus	Peas
	Beans	Pineapple
	Carrots	Potatoes
	Cauliflower	Sweet potatoes
Chicken	Apples	Peas
	Beans	Pineapple
	Broccoli	Potatoes
	Carrots	Rice
	Nectarines	
Chickpeas	Black beans	Chicken
	Carrots	
Lentils	Beans (red kidney, black, white)	
Cereals and Grains		
Infant cereals, (iron fortified, commercially manufactured) or single-grain cereal purées (homemade)	Fruit purées Vegetable purées Yogurt	Cottage cheese, puréed

Notes:

Before you start mixing and matching foods, always make sure your baby can tolerate each of the foods you intend to mix. (See Chapters 2 and 3.)

You may need to add liquid (e.g., vegetable stock, fruit juice, breast milk, infant formula) to achieve the desired texture.

This chart only hints at the exciting food combos that are possible. For more ideas and inspiration, talk to other moms, see the other food tools and appendices, and try some culinary experiments of your own, for example, combining pork purée with applesauce.

Food Tool 3: Baby Food Textures Guide

AS YOUR BABY'S chewing and swallowing skills improve, she'll be able to handle foods with increasingly sophisticated textures. Here's a quick overview of what's on the baby food texture menu.

Baby Food Texture	How to Create This Texture	What You'll Notice about Your Baby's Eating Abilities
Thin purées	Start with highly diluted infant cereals or baby foods (commercial or homemade) that have a very watery texture.	Your baby initially tries to suck the food off the spoon. (She's trying to transfer her breast- or bottle-feeding skills to solid foods.)
Thicker purées	Thicken the purées by adding less water to infant cereals or homemade baby food. If you serve your baby commercial baby foods, continue to buy pure foods (e.g., blends without any fillers). You can thicken them by adding infant cereal or other cereals and grains that your baby has proven she can tolerate.	Your baby uses a combination of sucking and chewing motions to eat the food on the spoon. Your baby can also practise her chewing skills by chewing on toast crusts and other soft foods. She's starting to figure out how to use an up-and-down chewing motion.
Ground, grated, and mashed foods	Rather than puréeing all of your baby's foods, serve some of her foods ground, grated, or mashed (e.g., mashed potatoes or other fruits and vegetables, grated cheese, small-curd cottage cheese). This is when it can be very handy to have a food mill or small food chopper. If your baby is eating most of the same foods you are, you can run small servings of some of your table foods through the food mill.	Your baby is able to move food from side to side using her tongue. Your baby will find it difficult to handle mixed textures (e.g., lumpy foods mixed with smooth foods), so keep this in mind when you're planning her menus.

continued on p. 226

Baby Food Texture	How to Create This Texture	What You'll Notice about Your Baby's Eating Abilities
Chopped foods (finger foods)	Offer your baby finger foods that are easily chewed. (Chop your baby's food into small, fine pieces.)	Your baby's chewing abilities are getting better by the day and she is becoming much more interested in feeding herself.
Table foods	Start introducing other tastes and textures, including crunchy and chewy foods. (Monitor your child closely and ensure that you offer appropriately sized morsels of these foods.)	Your baby or young toddler's chewing abilities are well developed at this point. Other than watching out for the foods that are known hazards to young children (see Chapters 2, 3, and 4), you can offer your child most of the foods that you dine on, while adjusting for the fact your baby or toddler's taste buds are much more sensitive than your own.

Notes:

Start introducing thin purées at age six months (or whenever you and your health care provider think your baby is ready) and continue to introduce increasingly complex textures on an ongoing basis as your baby proves she is capable of handling them.

Don't forget that your baby also needs an opportunity to practice her self-feeding skills from babyhood onward—skills that will become more sophisticated as her hand-eye co-ordination, grasping, and other fine motor skills continue to improve. See Chapters 3, 4, and 5.

Food Tool 4: Meal and Snack Ideas for Babies, Toddlers, and Preschoolers

HERE ARE SOME meal and snack ideas for babies who have moved beyond basic purées and who are starting to experiment with increasingly complex textures (see Food Tool 3), as well as toddlers and preschoolers, who are likely to have a fair bit of experience with foods of varying tastes and textures by now. Let your knowledge of your child's eating stage, food repertoire, and taste preferences be your guide in deciding what types of foods are appropriate for your older baby, toddler, or preschooler, and how each food should be served (e.g., grated, chopped, diced, sliced, mashed, or served whole). You want to strike a balance between offering your child textures that you know he can handle and encouraging him to experiment with slightly more challenging textures. (See Chapters 2, 3, 4, and 5 for more guidelines and tips, including reminders of which foods are not recommended for babies, toddlers, and preschoolers.)

Breakfast

- Iron-fortified infant cereal with puréed fruit
- Hot cereal with applesauce or banana tidbits
- Ready-to-eat cereal (low-sugar, whole-grain varieties)
- Whole-grain pancake with fruit
- Whole-wheat waffle with fruit purée
- Whole-grain toast with hummus
- Homemade muffins
- Scrambled eggs (yolks only for babies) and fruit salad
- French toast (egg yolks only for babies)
- Yogurt and fruit

Lunch

- Vegetable lentil soup with a toasted mini-bagel with cream cheese
- Black bean soup with whole-grain crackers
- Split pea soup with mini-bagels, toasted
- Grilled cheese and apple sandwich
- Cucumber and cream cheese sandwich
- Turkey sandwich with sweet-potato oven fries
- Peanut butter and banana sandwich (only for toddlers and preschoolers who don't have allergies and who won't be coming into contact with other children who are allergic to nuts)
- Ham and cheese melt on a pita
- Turkey, cheese, and broccoli turnovers
- Egg salad pinwheel sandwiches with fruit and vegetable wedges
- Macaroni and cheese with broccoli or other vegetables
- Pasta and bean casserole
- Broccoli, ricotta cheese, and pasta
- Broccoli, cauliflower, and rice with cheese sauce
- Pasta salad with beans and vegetables
- Vegetable frittata
- Ham and cheese quiche
- Fruit, vegetables, yogurt dip, and cheese

Dinner

- Black bean and couscous stew
- Brown rice, lentils, and vegetables
- Macaroni and cheese with vegetables (raw or cooked)

- Fish cakes with mashed potatoes and mixed vegetables
- Baked fish with sweet potato fries (oven-baked) and green beans
- Tuna, carrot, broccoli, and cauliflower casserole
- Chicken nuggets with fruit and vegetable wedges
- Chicken cubes, diced carrots, and diced potatoes
- Chicken, rice, and apple casserole
- Chicken tortellini with vegetables
- Chicken, rice, beans, and vegetables
- Pork tenderloin with apple purée, diced potatoes, and squash
- Beef or chicken mini-meatballs with rice
- Beef, potato, and vegetable meatloaf
- Spaghetti with tomato sauce and mini-meatballs (beef with grated carrots)
- Shepherd's pie (beef with grated vegetables)
- Burritos (vegetarian, chicken, or beef)
- Chili (vegetarian, chicken, or beef)
- Lasagna (vegetarian, chicken, or beef)
- Pizza (vegetarian, chicken, or any flavor combination)
- Quesadillas (vegetarian or chicken)
- Stew (vegetarian, chicken, beef, or lentil)
- Meatloaf (lean ground turkey with grated carrots and chopped spinach)

Snacks

- Ready-to-eat cereal (low-sugar, whole-grain varieties)
- Whole-grain crackers and cheese

- Muffins (low sugar, high fiber, with fruit or grated vegetables blended in)
- Fresh fruit salad (apple, banana, cantaloupe, pear, watermelon, etc.)
- Fresh veggie salad (shredded carrots, chopped lettuce, chopped cucumber)
- Vegetable plate (with yogurt dip, for toddlers and preschoolers)
- Plain yogurt flavored with fruit purée or mashed fruit
- Eggs, hard-boiled, cut into wedges (for toddlers or preschoolers only)
- Hummus or bean dip on a mini-pita
- Tortilla with bean dip and sliced or diced green peppers
- Rice cakes with melted cheese
- Fruit and yogurt smoothie
- Cottage cheese with fruit
- Chocolate fondue (75% cocoa-style chocolate) with fruit
- Tofu with peaches
- Sandwich fingers and fruit tidbits
- Oatmeal cookies and apple slices
- Granola bars (non-hydrogenated oils)
- Tiny portions of anything you might serve at mealtime, including breakfast

Looking for recipes and meal suggestions? See Food Tool 5, the cookbook suggestions in Appendix C, and the recipe links in Appendix B. Many of the links lead to searchable databases containing thousands of on-line recipes and sites that will allow you to download entire recipe books for free. For health and safety reasons, always keep your child's age and stage in mind, as well as any known or potential food allergies, when you're assessing the suitability of a possible recipe.

Food Tool 5: Moms' Favorite On-line Recipes for Babies, Toddlers, and Preschoolers (Plus a Few Mom-Invented Recipes, Too)

On-line Recipes

H ERE'S A ROUNDUP of the recipe links that arrived in my in-box when I asked the members of the parent advisory panel for this book to share some of their baby, toddler, and preschoolers' favorite on-line recipes.

(Recipe sites are notorious for moving their links around on a regular basis. That's why you'll also find an on-line version of this chart at Motherofallsolutions.com [use the on-site search tool to search for "Food Tool 5" or look for a link in the blog]. I'll keep this chart updated as links break or I'll provide links to similar recipes if some of these recipes eventually become unavailable.)

As I noted in Food Tool 4, you are the best judge of what foods are right for your child right now. What's suitable for someone else's child may not be suitable for your child at all. You may need to slice, dice, grate, chop, or purée some of these foods to make them suitable for your child. And some of these foods may not be suitable at all because of allergies. If in doubt, consult with a dietitian or your child's health care provider.

Baby Food

Baby Cereal Cookies
www.wholesomebabyfood.com/text/snackprint.htm

Chicken and Peach Delight
www.recipesource.com/special-diets/babyfood/
chicken-peach-delight1.html

Creamy Apples and Carrots Baby Food
www.vegetarianbaby.com/recipes/creamyapples.shtml

Fresh Baby: Fresh Ideas Archive Newsletter and Recipe Archive
www.freshbaby.com/healthy_eating/archive.cfm

Super Baby Food Recipes
www.superbabyfood.com/recipes.htm

Wholesome Baby Food Meat Recipes
www.wholesomebabyfood.com/MeatRecipes.htm

Breakfast

Banana French Toast
www.vegetarianbaby.com/recipes/bananafrenchtoast.shtml

Easy Cheesy Skillet Frittata
www.mealsmatter.org/RecipesAndMeals/Recipes/
recipes.aspx?RecipeId=10174

Morning Mush
vegweb.com/recipes/breakfast/8025.shtml

Pumpkin Pancakes
www.nickjr.com/food/meal_finder/breakfast/
pumpkin_pancakes.jhtml

Lunch

Chick Pea and Tomato Soup with Pasta
www.kaboose.com/food/recipe_lunch.html?recipe=4

Cream of Carrot Soup
chefmom.com/recipebox/recipes/911.htm

Cupid's Soup (Apple and Beet Spice Soup)
www.vegetarianbaby.com/recipes/cupidsoup.shtml

Vegetable Barley Soup
www.nickjr.com/food/meal_finder/lunch/
vegetable_barley_soup.jhtml

Wholesome Toddler Food Lunch Ideas
www.wholesometoddlerfood.com/lunch.htm

Dinner

Chicken Stew
www.toronto.ca/health/vf/vf_maindishes_chicken_stew.htm

Healthy Meat Loaf
www.mealmaster.com/recipes/r254.htm

Honey Dijon Chicken
www.thescramble.com/newsletter/sample/

No-Nonsense Nuggets
www.mealmakeovermoms.com/recipes/recipes.html#nuggets

Orzo, Chicken, and Sage Simmer Pot
www.chatelaine.com/applications/recipe/
article.jsp?recipeId=4166

Porcupine Meatballs
www.kraftfoods.com/recipes/PorkBeefEntrees/GroundBeefOther/
PorcupineMeatballs.html

Sweet Potato Fries
www.dietitians.ca/english/kitchen/recipes/recipe12.html

Tasty Tofu Nuggets
www.mealmakeovermoms.com/recipes/
recipes.html#tasty_tofu_nuggets

Turkey Shepherd's Pie
www.recipesource.com/main-dishes/dinner-pies/00/rec0069.html

Vegetarian Spaghetti Sauce
www.nhlbi.nih.gov/health/public/heart/other/syah/vegspasa.htm

Snacks

Baking Recipes
www.kingarthurflour.com/recipes/

Best Oat Cookies That Ever Existed
vegweb.com/recipes/sweets/6310.shtml

Good-for-You Corn Bread
www.nhlbi.nih.gov/health/public/heart/other/syah/cornbrd.htm

Incredible Edible Veggie Bowls
www.kidshealth.org/kid/recipes/recipes/veggie_bowls.html

Low-Fat Banana Bread
www.epicurious.com/recipes/recipe_views/views/4331

Pumpkin Muffins
vegweb.com/recipes/appetizers/2302.shtml

Recipes

A FEW BOOK panel members also shared some of the recipes they invented in order to find yummy ways to squeeze more nutrients into their baby's or toddler's diets. (Necessity is, after all, the mother of recipe invention.) Thanks to Jenn Goodwin and Pam Baribeault for sharing their mother recipe wisdom, and to Wendy Reingold, RD, the consulting dietitian for this book, who managed to find time to dig up a few of her family's favorite recipes in between her newborn twins' round-the-clock feedings!

Alec Eats His Vegetables

4 large carrots, peeled

2 parsnips, peeled

1 handful of broccoli

1 apple, peeled (you don't need to core it as long as you take out the seeds)

Steam vegetables and apple. Purée, adding a little of the cooking water if desired. Makes enough to freeze in an ice cube tray.

 MOM'S THE WORD

"This is a one-bowl all-food-groups lunch that I used a lot."

—*Pam, 27, mother of one*

MOM'S THE WORD

"This is a great one if you're like me and worried your baby can't possibly be getting enough vegetables, especially when he reaches the point where he likes sweet things more than vegetables!"

—*Jenn, 26, mother of one*

Carrot Cake Purée

2 tbsps wheat cereal powder

2 scoops formula powder

enough water to form a thick paste

$^1/_4$ cup puréed carrots

$^1/_4$ cup applesauce

tiny dash of cinnamon

Crush wheat cereal into powder. Then combine formula powder. Mix with water to form a thick paste. Add carrots, applesauce, and cinnamon.

Sesame-Flax and Ginger Green Bean Purée

$^1/_4$ cup sesame seeds

$^1/_4$ cup flaxseeds

$^1/_4$ tsp ginger powder

1–4 tbsps puréed green beans (or other vegetable)

Heat ingredients in a frying pan until sesame seeds darken and you hear popping sounds. Allow to cool. Then grind in a blender or food processor until very fine.

Add green beans until you achieve the desired texture for your child.

MOM'S THE WORD

"I invented this to get more protein, iron and fiber into my daughter, but it also conveniently masks the strong taste of green beans, or even spinach."

—*Pam, 27, mother of one*

Recipe Notes:

• If you have a family history of allergies, don't try this last recipe until you are positive that allergies aren't a problem for your child. Sesame seeds are one of the most common food allergens.

• It's important to grind nuts and seeds for children under age four to prevent choking.

Wendy's Easy and Delicious Bran Muffins

1 cup whole wheat flour

1 cup natural bran or oat bran

3 tbsps wheat germ (refrigerate upon opening)

$1/3$ cup packed brown sugar

1 tsp baking powder

1 egg (Omega-type)

$1/3$ cup vegetable oil

$1/2$ cup orange juice (with added calcium and lots of pulp) diluted with water

1 tsp vanilla extract

1 cup raisins or blueberries or apricots, etc.

Preheat oven to 350 degrees. Combine wet ingredients and mix thoroughly. In a separate bowl, mix dry ingredients. Add dry ingredients to wet ingredients, stirring until just mixed. Add raisins. Bake approximately 18 minutes. (Check with a toothpick to avoid overcooking.)

Makes 12 muffins.

MOM'S THE WORD

"Double these recipes and freeze the remaining muffins for delicious snacks on the go."

—*Wendy Reingold, RD, a breast-feeding mother of two-month-old twins and Mealtime Solution's consulting dietitian*

Wendy's Fantastic Banana Muffins

3–5 ripe bananas

$1/3$ cup vegetable oil

$1^1/2$ cup all purpose flour

1 tsp vanilla extract

1 tsp baking powder

1 tsp baking soda

$1/2$ cup sugar

1 omega egg or egg substitute (substitute $1/4$ cup egg substitute for each egg)

Preheat oven to 350 degrees. Whip ripe bananas. Add all other wet ingredients and mix thoroughly. In a separate bowl, dry ingredients. Add dry ingredients to wet ingredients, stirring until just mixed. Bake approximately 18 minutes. (Check with a toothpick to avoid overcooking.)

Makes 12 muffins.

Wendy's Awesome "Makes-Me-Feel-Full" Oatmeal Soup

12 cups low sodium chicken broth

4 diced parsley roots – in shape of little silver dollars! (just the root part, not the parsley part, if parsley root is unavailable, substitute with parsnips)

6 diced carrots

1 cup green peas (canned, rinsed)

1 cup diced onion

2 cups rolled oats (Quaker Quick Oats, not instant oatmeal)

2–3 mashed garlic cloves

2 tbsps soya sauce (use low sodium soya sauce)

2 tbsps canola or olive oil

FOOD FOR THOUGHT

Using egg whites in place of eggs tends to make baked goods rubbery, because egg substitute has no fat. To improve the product's texture, add one teaspoon of canola oil for each egg replaced.

Bring chicken broth to a boil. Let simmer for 30–40 minutes, stirring frequently. Then add the remaining ingredients. Season to taste. *Note:* You can also add ground flax seeds into this soup to provide additional fiber, if desired.

Wendy's Easy and Delicious Chicken Loaf

2 lbs lean ground chicken

1¹/₂ cups low sodium chicken stock

2 omega eggs

2 tbsp chopped parsley or cilantro

1 tsp curry powder (optional)

1 tsp garlic powder

1¹/₂ cups bread crumbs

Combine all ingredients in a bowl, adding the bread crumbs last. Mix well and add to a loaf pan. Bake at 350 degrees for approx. 1 hour.

MOM'S THE WORD

"This chicken loaf recipe is so easy, and yet so yummy and nutritious. Enjoy with some steamed veggies or a green salad for a balanced meal."
—Wendy Reingold, RD, a breastfeeding mother of two-month-old twins and *Mealtime Solution's* consulting dietitian

Food Tool 6: Quick Tips on Shopping Smart for Healthy Convenience Foods

Convenience Food Label Decoder

Who ever said "convenience" had to be a synonym for "unhealthy"? Here are some quick tips on decoding food labels so that you'll be able to zero in on the healthiest convenience foods in the grocery store aisles.

Find out who's starring and co-starring. Like stars on a movie bill, ingredients on packaged goods are listed in order of appearance, with the star players (in this case, the ingredients that make up most of the item by weight) listed first on the ingredient label. Also note who's co-starring on the label. The next few ingredients matter, too.

Learn to spot "the good guys" and "the bad guys" when it comes to fat. Fat aids in the absorption of vitamins A, D, E, and K, so it's important to have some fat in your diet. (It's particularly important for kids because fats assist in the development of your child's brain and other organs.) Steer clear of products that contain the following types of fats: hydrogenated vegetable oils, vegetable oil shortenings, and palm kernel oils. These are trans fats, which have been getting so much bad press lately because it's so difficult for the body to burn and break them down. Having fat stay in the body is never a good thing because it can lead to elevated cholesterol levels and obesity. Instead, look for products that include healthier fats such as canola oil, flaxseed oil, olive oil, non-hydrogenated oils, and grape seed oil.

Consider how much nutritional bang the product delivers, and consider whether your child will eat a full serving or a partial serving. If, for example, your toddler eats half of a serving of a product that delivers 2 percent of the daily requirement of vitamin A per serving, the fact that product contains vitamin A isn't worth getting too excited about. You'd be better off with some real fruits and veggies instead. (One medium raw carrot will give you 172 percent of your daily requirements!) Here's how to decide whether a particular convenience food delivers the goods nutritionally.

- **Calories:** Treat the banana as your nutritional benchmark when deciding whether or not a particular product has many or few calories. A banana has roughly 100 calories and is a powerhouse of energy, potassium, and fiber.

- **Fat:** Look at both the *type of fat* and *the total amount of fat.* Choose products with less than 2 grams of saturated and trans fats combined.

- **Sodium:** Look for products with 500 milligrams or less of sodium per serving. Remember that salt is often used as a preservative in packaged items, so read food labels carefully.

- **Fiber:** Choose products that deliver the fiber your child needs for heart health, healthy bowel functioning, and to feel full longer. To find out how many grams of fiber your child needs each day, add 5 to your child's age. Adults need 25 to 35 grams of fiber each day. A one-year-old would require 1 + 5 or 6 grams of fiber daily. (When calculating your child's fiber intake, remember that fiber can also be found in fruits, vegetables, whole-grain breads, and cereals.) Finally, remember, fiber needs water to work.

- **Sugars:** Stick to foods that deliver 5 grams or less of sugar per serving. Children do not require a lot of added sugar (or salt) to enjoy their foods because their taste buds are highly sensitive. To figure out how many teaspoons of sugar are in a single serving of a particular product, divide the number of grams of sugar on the product nutrition label by four. Some packaged foods contain as much as 40 grams of sugar (10 teaspoons of sugar) per serving. No one needs that much sugar.

(Prepared in consultation with Wendy Reingold, RD.)

Food Staples for Older Babies, Toddlers, and Preschoolers: Grocery Store Best Bets

You'll never be left wondering what to serve your child at mealtime or snack time if you keep the following types of foods in the house.

Canned and Packaged Goods

Applesauce (unsweetened)

Beans and lentils (canned and dried)
  Black beans
  Chickpeas (garbanzo beans)
  Kidney beans
  Lentils
  Navy beans
  Split peas
  White beans

Bread
  Bagels
  Pitas
  Whole-grain breads
  Whole-grain buns

Cereals
  Infant, iron-fortified, various whole-grain and mixed-grain varieties
  Hot, cooked, whole-grain varieties
  Ready-to-eat, whole-grain varieties

Condiments and spices

Crackers (whole-grain)

Fish
  Salmon (canned, water-packed)
  Tuna (canned, water-packed)

Fruit (canned, packed in juice)
  Fruit cocktail
  Peaches
  Pears, etc.

Grains (whole)
  Barley
  Cornmeal
  Flour (unbleached, whole-wheat)
  Oats, etc

Pasta (whole-grain)
  Spaghetti
  Other types of pasta

Pasta sauce (prepared or canned)

Rice (long-grain)
  Brown
  White

Rice cakes

Soups (canned, various varieties)

Tomato products
  Crushed tomatoes
  Tomato paste
  Tomato sauce

Vegetables (canned, unsalted, or low-salt)

Produce

Fresh fruit
  Apples
  Bananas
  Oranges, etc.

Fresh vegetables
    Broccoli
    Carrots
    Onions
    Potatoes
    Sweet potatoes, etc.
Pre-washed salad mix
Pre-washed spinach

Refrigerator

Cheese (including some grated cheese)

Eggs (yolks only for babies)

Hummus (pre-made, low-fat)

Juice (unsweetened; non-citrus for babies)

Margarine or butter

Milk or soy beverage (breast milk or formula only for babies)

Tofu

Turkey and other lean cold cuts (sliced)

Yogurt (plain)

Frozen Foods

Fruit

Fruit juice (unsweetened, concentrated)

Meat, poultry, and fish

Vegetables

Food Tool 7: Old Recipe, New Twist: Making Favorite Family Recipes Healthier

THE TYPES OF recipes that get passed around at family reunions may score big points on the taste front, but they don't always measure up quite so well nutritionally. Here are some strategies to give some of your favorite recipes a nutritional makeover. Just one bit of advice: If you're used to the recipe the old way, you may want to make the changes gradually rather than making a lot of dramatic ingredient swaps all at once. The cold turkey approach may be too much for your palate!

Recipe Makeover Nutrition Booster	What You Need to Know
Basic Cooking Techniques	
Cook with liquids other than water.	Cook rice, couscous, and other grains in carrot or tomato juice (or dilute your favorite vegetable juice with water); use carrot or tomato juice to steam fish; use carrot or tomato juice as a base for soup.
Bake; don't deep fry.	Instead of deep-frying potatoes, chicken, fish, and other foods, try baking these foods in the oven instead. Foods like chicken and fish can be coated in seasoned breadcrumbs (add grated parmesan cheese to the bread crumbs to boost calcium). Foods like potatoes can be spritzed with vegetable oil (use a spray bottle) and baked on high heat (475°F).
Mealtime	
Replace the high-fat, low-nutrient ingredients in your salads with healthier choices.	Replace artificial bacon bits, croutons, and cream-based salad dressings with fresh fruit, lentils, chickpeas, quinoa, and other natural flavorings. These ingredient substitutions will improve the flavor of your salads while boosting the fiber and nutrient content too. When your child gets old enough to safely chew and swallow seeds, nuts, and dried fruit, toss these in, too.

Recipe Makeover Nutrition Booster	What You Need to Know
	Mealtime
Replace some or all of the meat in casseroles and other entrées with beans.	Add beans to spaghetti sauce or stew and cut back on (or eliminate) the meat in the recipe.
Find alternatives to regular ground beef.	Replace regular ground beef with lean ground beef or combine beans, lentils, and vegetables to take the recipe in an entirely different direction. And don't forget to try using lean ground turkey and lean ground chicken in recipes like meat-balls. They are much lower in fat.
Look for opportunities to boost the nutritional content of meals like spaghetti, lasagna, and macaroni and cheese.	Choose whole-grain pastas, purée vegetables into pasta sauces, and add diced vegetables to macaroni and cheese.
Use different types of pasta rather than plain pasta.	Look for pastas made from kamut, spelt, rye, quinoa, rice, buckwheat, and vegetables such as corn and artichoke.
Give your pizza crust a makeover.	Replace half of the flour in your pizza crust recipe with whole-wheat flour.
Add more vegetables to shepherd's pie.	Use a blend of sweet potatoes and white potatoes in the potato layer of shepherd's pie, and add a layer of vegetables. (Vary the vegetables each time you make the recipe.) Or try making your shepherd's pie with a puréed cauliflower topping for maximum nutritional bang per bite.
Turn your favorite quiche recipe into a frittata.	Turn your quiche into a frittata by cooking your "quiche" in a frying pan and losing the crust. If you're used to making your quiche with cream, replace the cream with condensed milk or regular milk. (Use yolks only for babies.) You can also "up" the egg white content by using a mix of egg whites and whole eggs for toddlers and preschoolers.

continued on p. 246

Recipe Makeover Nutrition Booster	What You Need to Know
Mealtime	
Reduce the fat content of your favorite guacamole recipe.	Replace one-quarter of the avocado with puréed white beans.
Baked Goods	
Use whole-wheat flour in your baked goods.	Whole-wheat flour can be substituted for up to one-half of the all-purpose flour in most baked goods recipes.
Use vegetable oil instead of solid fats like shortening, lard, or butter in baked goods.	Corn oil, canola oil, and certain other types of liquid vegetable oils can substitute for solid fats in recipes. When you use liquid vegetable oils rather than solid fats, you can use one-quarter less than what the recipe calls for.
Reduce the amount of oil in your baked goods.	You can generally reduce the amount of oil by one-quarter to one-third without affecting the taste or the texture. You can also add a corresponding amount of puréed or grated vegetables or fruit.
Reduce the amount of sugar in your baked goods.	Reduce the amount of sugar by one-quarter to one-third and substitute flour for the missing sugar. (Don't try this with yeast-based baked goods because the sugar is needed to make the yeast work.)
Replace cream cheese in desserts with a blend of low-fat cream cheese and dry-curd cottage cheese.	Blend equal parts of low-fat cream cheese and dry-curd cottage cheese. Flavor with lemon juice. You will need 1/2 teaspoon of lemon juice for every 1/2 cup of cream cheese-cottage cheese mixture.

For more tips on remaking your recipes in healthy ways, see Appendices A, B, and C.

Directory of Organizations

Breast-feeding

AMERICAN

La Leche League
1400 N. Meacham Road
Schaumburg, IL 60173-4808
Phone: 847-519-7730
E-mail: llli@llli.org
Website: www.lalecheleague.org

CANADIAN

La Leche League
12050 Main Street W.
P.O. Box 700
Winchester, ON K0C 2K0
Phone: 613-774-1842
Breast-feeding Referral Service:
800-665-4324
Fax: 613-774-1840
E-mail: ofm@LLLC.ca
Website: www.lalecheleaguecanada.ca

INTERNATIONAL

International Lactation Consultant Association
1500 Sunday Drive, Suite 102
Raleigh, NC 27607
Phone: 919-861-5577
Fax: 919-787-4916
E-mail: info@ilca.org
Website: www.ilca.org

World Health Organization
Avenue Appia 201211
Geneva 27, Switzerland
Phone: 41-22-791-21-11
Fax: 41-22-791-3111
E-mail: info@who.int
Website: www.who.int

Child Development

AMERICAN

National Institute of Child Health and Human Development
P.O. Box 3006
Rockville, MD 20847
Phone: 800-370-2943
TTY: 888-320-6942
Fax: 301-984-1473
E-mail:
NICHDInformationResourceCenter@
mail.nih.gov
Website: www.nichd.nih.gov

Zero to Three: National Center for Infants, Toddlers and Families
2000 M Street NW, Suite 200
Washington, DC 20036
Phone: 202-638-1144
E-mail: www.zerotothree.org/
ztt_aboutus.html
Website: www.zerotothree.org

CANADIAN

Canadian Institute of Child Health
384 Bank Street, Suite 300
Ottawa, ON K2P 1Y4
Phone: 613-230-8838
Fax: 613-230-6654
E-mail: cich@cich.ca
Website: www.cich.ca

Invest in Kids
425 Adelaide Street W., 6th Floor
Toronto, ON M5V 3C1
Phone: 877-583-KIDS or 416-977-1222
Fax: 416-977-9655
E-mail: mail@investinkids.ca
Website: www.investinkids.ca

Nutrition

AMERICAN

American Dietetic Association
120 South Riverside Plaza, Suite 2000
Chicago, IL 60606-6995
Phone: 800-366-1655
E-mail: knowledge@eatright.org
Website: www.eatright.org

Nutrition.gov
National Agricultural Library
Food and Nutrition Information Center
Nutrition.gov Staff
10301 Baltimore Avenue
Beltsville, MD 20705-2351
E-mail: info@nutrition.gov
Website: www.nutrition.gov

Vegetarian Resource Group
The Vegetarian Resource Group
P.O. Box 1463
Dept. IN
Baltimore, MD 21203
Phone: 410-366-VEGE
E-mail: vrg@vrg.org
Website: www.vrg.org

CANADIAN

The Canadian Council of Food and Nutrition
3800 Steeles Avenue W., Suite 301A
Woodbridge, ON L4L 4G9
Phone: 905-265-9124
Fax: 905-265-9372
E-mail: info@ccfn.ca
Website: www.ccfn.ca

Dietitians of Canada
480 University Avenue, Suite 604
Toronto, ON
M5G 1V2
Phone: 416-596-0857
Fax: 416-596-0603
Website: www.dietitians.ca

Food Health and Safety

AMERICAN

U.S. Food and Drug Administration
5600 Fishers Lane
Rockville, MD 20857-0001
Phone: 888-INFO-FDA or 888-463-6332
E-mail list signups:
www.fda.gov/emaillist.html
Website: www.fda.gov

CANADIAN

Canadian Food Inspection Agency
59 Camelot Drive
Ottawa, ON K1A 0Y9
Phone: 613-225-2342
Fax: 613-228-4550
E-mail: cfiamaster@inspection.gc.ca
E-mail list signups:
www.inspection.gc.ca/english/tools/
listserv/listsube.shtml
Website: www.inspection.gc.ca

Health Canada
Address Locator 0900C2
Ottawa, ON K1A 0K9
Phone: 866-225-0709 or 613-957-2991
TTY: 800-267-1245
Fax: 613-941-5366
E-mail: www.hc-sc.gc.ca/
home-accueil/contact/general_e.html
Website: www.hc-sc.gc.ca/
fn-an/index_e.html

Pediatric Health

AMERICAN

**American Academy of Pediatrics
National Headquarters**
141 Northwest Point Boulevard
Elk Grove Village, IL 60007-1098
Phone: 847-834-4000
Fax: 847-434-8000
E-mail: (list of key contacts)
www.aap.org/visit/contact.htm
Website: www.aap.org

**National Association of Pediatric
Nurse Practitioners**
20 Brace Road, Suite 200
Cherry Hill, NJ 08034-2634
Phone: 856-857-9700
Fax: 856-857-1600
E-mail: info@napnap.org
Website: www.napnap.org

CANADIAN

Canadian Paediatric Society
2305 St. Laurent Boulevard
Ottawa, ON K1G 4J8
Phone: 613-526-9397
Fax: 613-526-3332
E-mail: info@cps.ca
Website: www.cps.ca

Canadian Nurses Association
50 Driveway
Ottawa, ON K2P 1E2
Phone: 800-361-8404 or 613-237-2133
Fax: 613-237-3520
E-mail: info@cna-aiic.ca
Website: www.cna-nurses.ca

Health—Other

AMERICAN

**American Academy of Asthma,
Allergy, and Immunology**
555 East Wells Street, Suite 1100
Milwaukee, WI 53202-3823
Phone: 414-272-6071
Patient Information and Physician
Referral Line: 800-822-2762
E-mail: info@aaaai.org
Website: www.aaaai.org

**American Cleft Palate-Craniofacial
Association/Cleft Palate Foundation**
1504 East Franklin Street, Suite 102
Chapel Hill, NC 27514-2820
Phone: 800-24-CLEFT or
919-933-9044
E-mail: info@cleftline.org
Website: www.cleftline.org

American Diabetes Association National Call Center
1701 North Beauregard Street
Alexandria, VA 22311
Phone: 800-DIABETES or
800-342-2383
E-mail: AskADA@diabetes.org
Website: www.diabetes.org

Food Allergy and Anaphylaxis Network
11781 Lee Jackson Highway, Suite 160
Fairfax, VA 22033-3309
Phone: 800-929-4040
Fax: 703-691-2713
E-mail: faan@foodallergy.org
Website: www.foodallergy.org

Juvenile Diabetes Research Foundation International
120 Wall Street
New York, NY 10005-4001
Phone: 800-533-CURE (2873)
Fax: 212-785-9595
E-mail: info@jdrf.org
Website: www.jdrf.org

National Institute of Allergy and Infectious Diseases
NIAID Office of Communications
and Public Liaison
6610 Rockledge Drive, MSC 6612
Bethesda, MD 20892-6612
Phone: 301-496-5717
TDD: 800-877-8339
Fax: 301-402-3573
E-mail: www3.niaid.nih.gov/
links_policies/contact.htm
Website: www3.niaid.nih.gov

National Institute of Diabetes and Digestive and Kidney Diseases
Office of Communications and Public
Liaison, NIDDK, NIH
Building 31, Room 9A04
Center Drive, MSC 2560
Bethesda, MD 20892-2560
Website: www.niddk.nih.gov

CANADIAN

Canadian Allergy, Asthma, and Immunology Foundation
774 Echo Drive
Ottawa, ON K1S 5N8
Phone: 613-730-6272
Fax: 613-730-1116
E-mail: caaif@rcpsc.edu
Website: www.allergyfoundation.ca

Canadian Diabetes Association National Life Building
522 University Avenue, Suite 1400
Toronto, ON M5G 2R5
Phone: 800-BANTING 416-226-8464
Fax: 416-408-7117
E-mail: info@diabetes.ca
Website: www.diabetes.ca

Appendix B:

Directory of On-line Resources

YOU'LL FIND A smorgasbord of fabulous on-line links to explore in this directory—all carefully handpicked with the idea of taking the worry and the guilt out of feeding your child. Just a reminder: You'll also find other helpful on-line resources listed in Appendix A, Food Tool 5, and scattered throughout the book. For link updates, please visit Motherofallsolutions.com.

Breast-feeding

American Academy of Pediatrics: Breast-feeding Resources
www.aap.org/healthtopics/breastfeeding.cfm

Baylor College of Medicine: USDA/Agricultural Research Services Children's Nutrition Research Center: Breastfeeding
www.kidsnutrition.org/consumer/archives/#breastfeeding

Breast-feeding Basics
www.breastfeedingbasics.com

Bright Future Lactation Resource Centre Ltd.: Jack Newman's Breast-feeding Resource Handouts
www.bflrc.com/newman/articles.htm

International Lactation Consultant Association
www.ilac.org

Kellymom Breast-feeding and Parenting
www.kellymom.com

La Leche League
www.lalecheleague.org

La Leche League Canada
www.lalecheleaguecanada.ca

Medline Plus: Breast-feeding
www.nlm.nih.gov/medlineplus/breastfeeding.html

Motherisk
www.motherisk.org

ProMom: Promoting the Awareness and Acceptance of Breast-feeding
www.promom.org

USDA Team Nutrition: Feeding Infants: A Guide for Use in the Child Nutrition Programs
teamnutrition.usda.gov/Resources/feeding_infants.html

World Health Organization
www.who.int

Infant Formula

Napnap.org: Successful Bottle-feeding
napnap.org/Docs/bottle_eng.pdf

USDA Team Nutrition: Feeding Infants: A Guide for Use in the Child Nutrition Programs
teamnutrition.usda.gov/Resources/feeding_infants.html

WHO: International Food Safety Authorities Network: Enterobacter sakazakii in Powdered Infant Formula
www.who.int/foodsafety/fs_management/No_01_Esakazakii_Jan05_en.pdf

Food and Nutrition

3-a-Day of Dairy
www.3aday.org/3aDay/

5to10aday.com
www.5to10aday.com

American Dietetic Association
www.eatright.org

American Dietetic Association: Starting Solid Foods
www.eatright.org/ada/files/infant_book.pdf

American Dietetic Association: Transitioning to Toddlerhood
www.eatright.org/ada/files/toddler.pdf

Baylor College of Medicine: Children's Nutrition Research Center
www.kidsnutrition.org

Canada's Food Guide to Healthy Eating: Focus on Preschoolers
www.hc-sc.gc.ca/fn-an/food-guide-aliment/res/
fg_preschoolers-prescolaire_ga_e.html#4

Canadian Council of Food and Nutrition: Reliable Links
Canadian and International Sources of Nutrition Information
www.ccfn.ca/in_action/links.asp

CDC.gov: 5 A Day
www.cdc.gov/nccdphp/dnpa/5aday/

Dietitians of Canada
www.dietitians.ca

Food and Drug Administration
www.fda.gov/

Food and Nutrition Information Center
www.nal.usda.gov/fnic/

Food and Nutrition Information Center: Food Composition
www.nal.usda.gov/fnic/etext/000020.html

Georgetown University: Bright Futures Nutrition Family Fact Sheets
www.brightfutures.org/nutritionfamfact/index.html

Georgetown University: Bright Futures in Practice: Nutrition (2nd Edition)
www.brightfutures.org/nutrition/pdf/index.html

Health Canada: Children and Healthy Eating
www.hc-sc.gc.ca/fn-an/nutrition/child-enfant/index_e.html

Healthy People 2010: Portion Size Tool
hp2010.nhlbihin.net/portion/servingcard7.pdf

Institute of Medicine of the National Academies: Food and Nutrition
www.iom.edu/CMS/3708.aspx

International Food Information Council
www.ific.org/

Iowa State University: Food for Fitness and Fun
www.extension.iastate.edu/food/

KidsNutrition.org: Culinary Tips—Dress Up Vegetables
www.kidsnutrition.org/consumer/nyc/vol_2004_4/page4.htm

Maternal and Child Health Library: Child and Adolescent Nutrition
www.mchlibrary.info/KnowledgePaths/kp_childnutr.html

Medline Plus: Child Nutrition
www.nlm.nih.gov/medlineplus/childnutrition.html

Medline Plus: Infant and Toddler Nutrition
www.nlm.nih.gov/medlineplus/infantandtoddlernutrition.html

MyPyramid.gov
www.mypyramid.gov

National Food Information Center
www.nal.usda.gov/fnic/

Nick Jr. Kids: Portions Chart for Ages 2 to 6
www.nickjr.com/parenting/health_fitness/nutrition/kids_portions_chart.jhtml

Nutrition for Kids
www.nutritionforkids.com

Nutrition.gov
www.nutrition.gov

University of Nebraska Food Website
lancaster.unl.edu/food/

USDA Team Nutrition: Building Blocks for Fun and Healthy Meals
teamnutrition.usda.gov/Resources/buildingblocks.html

USDA Team Nutrition: Feeding Infants: A Guide for Use in the Child Nutrition Programs
teamnutrition.usda.gov/Resources/feeding_infants.html

Vegetarian Resource Group
www.vrg.org

We Can: Go, Slow, and Whoa Foods
www.nhlbi.nih.gov/health/public/heart/obesity/wecan/downloads/gswtips.pdf

Wellpoint.com: Healthy Habits, Healthy Kids
www.wellpoint.com/healthy_parenting/docs/Healthy_Habits.pdf

Food Labels

Health Canada: Food Labeling
www.hc-sc.gc.ca/fn-an/label-etiquet/index_e.html

Healthy Eating Is in Store
www.healthyeatingisinstore.ca

IFIC.org: Food Ingredients and Colors
www.ific.org/publications/brochures/foodingredandcolorsbroch.cfm

National Institute of Health: Reading the Food Label
www.nhlbi.nih.gov/chd/Tipsheets/readthelabel.htm

Food Safety

Canadian Food Inspection Agency
www.inspection.gc.ca/english/toce.shtml

FDA: What You Need to Know about Mercury in Fish and Shellfish
www.cfsan.fda.gov/~dms/admehg3.html

FoodSafety.gov
www.foodsafety.gov

Health Canada: Food and Nutrition Surveillance
www.hc-sc.gc.ca/fn-an/surveill/index_e.html

Health Canada: Food Safety
www.hc-sc.gc.ca/fn-an/securit/index_e.html

Cooking Reference Charts

Colorado State University: Ingredient Substitutions
www.ext.colostate.edu/pubs/foodnut/09329.pdf

Health.com: A Cook's Reference
www.health.com/health/pdf/cook.pdf

University of Georgia: Cooking Basics—Kitchen Equipment
www.fcs.uga.edu/pubs/PDF/FDNS-NE-102a.pdf

University of Georgia: Ingredient Substitutions
www.fcs.uga.edu/pubs/PDF/FDNS-NE-109a.pdf

University of Georgia: Weight and Measures Conversion Chart
www.fcs.uga.edu/pubs/PDF/FDNS-NE-107a.pdf

USDA: How to Buy Various Types of Food
www.ams.usda.gov/howtobuy/

Recipes—Baby Food

CanadianParents.com: Baby Food Recipes
www.canadianparents.ca/CPO/CanadaCooks/BabyFood/

Iowa State University: Making Baby Food
www.extension.iastate.edu/Publications/PM793.pdf

utrition Service—Team Nutrition:
aby Food
ɔv/tn/Resources/feedinginfants-ch12.pdf

aby Food
ɔmebabyfood.com

Recipes—Meals for Toddlers and Preschoolers

dmoz: Cooking for Children: Recipes
dmoz.org/Home/Cooking/For_Children/

FamilyFun: Recipes
familyfun.go.com/recipes/

Fresh Baby: Fresh Ideas Archive
www.freshbaby.com/healthy_eating/archive.cfm

KidsHealth.org: Recipes for Kids
www.kidshealth.org/kid/recipes

Nick Jr. Meal Finder
www.nickjr.com/food/meal_finder/index.jhtml

Today's Parent Food: Cooking With Kids
www.todaysparent.com/food/cookingwithkids

**USDA: Food and Nutrition Service—Team Nutrition:
Child Care Recipes—Food for Health and Fun**
teamnutrition.usda.gov/Resources/childcare_recipes.html

Wholesome Toddler Food
www.wholesometoddlerfood.com

Recipes—Special Diets

Celiac Sprue Association: Gluten-Free Recipes
www.csaceliacs.org/recipes.php

KidsHealth: Recipes for Kids on Special Diets
kidshealth.org/parent/recipes/

Misc. Kids: Allergy and Asthma Recipes
www.cs.unc.edu/~kupstas/FAQ_recipes.html

General Recipe Sites

All Recipes
www.allrecipes.com

Cooking Smart Magazine
www.cookingsmartmagazine.com

DairyGoodness.ca
www.dairygoodness.ca

Epicurious.com
www.epicurious.com

Foodnetwork.com
www.foodnetwork.com

Food Network Canada
www.foodtv.ca/

Kraft Canada
www.kraftcanada.com

Kraft Foods
www.kraftfoods.com

MealMakeoverMoms.com: Recipes and Tips
www.mealmakeovermoms.com/recipes/

Meals Matter
www.mealsmatter.org

Mealtime.org: The Global Pantry
www.mealtime.org/files/ethnicpantryfinal.pdf

National Heart, Lung, and Blood Institute: Heart Healthy Home Cooking: African American Style
www.nhlbi.nih.gov/health/public/heart/other/chdblack/cooking.htm

National Institutes of Health: Delicious Heart-Healthy Latino Recipes
www.nhlbi.nih.gov/health/public/heart/other/sp_recip.pdf

National Pasta Association
www.ilovepasta.org

The New Homemaker: Home Cooking
www.thenewhomemaker.com/homecooking

Reluctant Gourmet
www.reluctantgourmet.com

USA Rice Federation
www.usarice.com

Whole Grains Council: Whole Grains from A to Z
www.wholegrainscouncil.org/WGAtoZ.html

Recipe Management Software

Big Oven
www.bigoven.com

Busy Cooks
www.busycooks.com

Living Cookbook
www.livingcookbook.com

MacGourmet
www.advenio.com/macgourmet/

Food Co-ops and Batch Cooking

The Dinner Co-op Page
dinnercoop.cs.cmu.edu/dinnercoop/

Easy Meal Preparation Association
www.easymealprep.com

Eatgrub.org: Grub Parties
www.eatgrub.org/parties.htm

OrganizedHome.com: Feed the Freezer
www.organizedhome.com/content-85.html

Squidoo: Once a Month Cooking
www.squidoo.com/onceamonthcooking/

Encouraging Kids to Be Physically Active

American Heart Association: Choose to Move
www.s2mw.com/choosetomove/

Canada's Physical Activity Guide for Children
www.phac-aspc.gc.ca/pau-uap/paguide/child_youth/children/index.html

Georgetown University: Bright Futures in Practice: Physical Activity
www.brightfutures.org/physicalactivity/pdf/index.html

Healthy Start for Life Activity Planner
www.dietitians.ca/healthystart/Active_Living_Planner.pdf

Mothers in Motion
www.caaws.ca/mothersinmotion/home_e.html

National Association for Sport & Physical Education
www.aahperd.org/naspe/

Public Health Agency of Canada: Canada's Physical Activity Guide for Children
www.phac-aspc.gc.ca/pau-uap/paguide/

We Can: Ways to Enhance Children's Activity and Nutrition
www.nhlbi.nih.gov/health/public/heart/obesity/wecan/

Growth Charts and Weight Issues

Dietitians of Canada: Speaking of Food and Healthy Living: Children and Weight—Parents' Perspectives
www.dietitians.ca/news/downloads/SFHL_Report_English_2005.pdf

Growth Charts and Body Mass Index for Age Charts (Age Two to 20)
www.cdc.gov/growthcharts/

Medline Plus: Obesity in Children
www.nlm.nih.gov/medlineplus/obesityinchildren.html

Feeding Problems and Special Health Concerns

American Academy of Asthma, Allergy and Immunology
www.aaaai.org

American Cleft Palate-Craniofacial Association/Cleft Palate Foundation
www.cleftline.org

American Diabetes Association: Diabetes in Infants and Toddlers
www.diabetes.org/uedocuments/DiabetesInfantsToddlers.pdf

American Speech-Language-Hearing Association
Feeding and Swallowing Disorders in Infants and Children
www.asha.org/public/speech/disorders/feeding_swallowing.htm

Auckland Allergy Clinic: Allergy Library
www.allergylibrary.co.nz/physician.html

Canadian Allergy, Asthma, and Immunology Foundation
www.allergyfoundation.ca

Canadian Diabetes Association
www.diabetes.ca

Canadian Food Inspection Agency: Allergy Alerts and Food Recalls
www.inspection.gc.ca/english/corpaffr/educ/alerte.shtml

CeliacHealth.org: Gluten-Free Diet Guide for Families
celiachealth.org/pdf/GlutenFreeDietGuideWeb.pdf

Children with Diabetes
www.childrenwithdiabetes.com

Exceptional Parent
www.eparent.com

Food Allergy and Anaphylaxis Network
www.foodallergy.org

Juvenile Diabetes Foundation International
www.jdrf.org/

KidsHealth: Recipes for Kids on Special Diets
kidshealth.org/parent/recipes/

March of Dimes
www.marchofdimes.org

Medline Plus: Diabetes
www.nlm.nih.gov/medlineplus/diabetes.html

Medline Plus: Food Allergies
www.nlm.nih.gov/medlineplus/foodallergy.html

Medline Plus: Gastroesophageal Reflux
www.nlm.nih.gov/medlineplus/gastroesophagealrefluxhiatalhernia.html

National Digestive Diseases Information Clearinghouse: Gastroesophageal Reflux in Infants
digestive.niddk.nih.gov/ddiseases/pubs/gerdinfant/

National Institute of Diabetes and Digestive and Kidney Diseases
www.niddk.nih.gov

North American Society for Pediatric Gastroenterology, Hepatology and Nutrition
www.naspghan.org

Kitchen Tools, Timesavers, and Organizers

The Baker's Catalogue
www.bakerscatalogue.com

ChefTools.com
www.cheftools.com

Cuisinart
www.cuisinart.com

D*I*Y Planner
www.diyplanner.com

Golda's Kitchen
www.goldaskitchen.com

Harold's Kitchen
www.haroldskitchen.com

IKEA
www.Ikea.com

Life Hacker: Life Hacks
www.lifehacker.com/software/life-hacks

Oxo.com
www.oxo.com

Remember the Milk
rememberthemilk.com

Rubbermaid
www.rubbermaid.com

Stain Shield
www.stainshield.com

University of Nebraska: 30+ Time-Saving Kitchen Tools
lancaster.unl.edu/food/ciql.htm

Zyliss
www.zyliss.com

Mealtime and Feeding Gear for Babies, Toddlers, and Preschoolers

Avent
www.avent.com

Babystyle
www.babystyle.com

Bumkins: Super Bib
www.bumkins.com

Cheftools.com: Alphabet Cookie Cutter Set
www.cheftools.com

Cocoacrayon: Bob's Your Uncle Placemats
www.cocoacrayon.com

Dex Products: Baby Food Processor
www.dexproducts.com

The First Years: On-the-Go Booster Seat
www.thefirstyears.com

FreshBaby.com: Food Trays (for freezing baby food)
www.freshbaby.com

Gerber.com: Spill-Proof Cups and Feeding Products
www.gerber.com

Kidalog.net
www.kidalog.net

Mabel's Labels: Labels
www.mabel.ca

Magic Bullet
www.buythebullet.com

Medela
www.medela.com

Monstermarketplace.com: Trebimbi Cutlery Puppets
www.monstermarketplace.com

Pampered Chef: Crinkle Cutter
www.pamperedchef.com

Pop Art Toaster
www.poparttoaster.com

Prince Lionheart: Dishwasher Basket and Spill Proof Cup Valve Cleaner
www.princelionheart.com

Sassybaby.com: On-the-Go Feeding Set, Crumb Catcher Feeding Bib, and Extra Gentle Soft Tip Spoons
www.sassybaby.com

Frozen Organic Baby Food

Bobo Baby
www.bobobaby.com

Healthy Sprouts
www.healthysprouts.ca

Sweetpea Baby Food
www.sweetpeababyfood.com

Child Health and Development

American Academy of Pediatrics
www.aap.org

Canadian Institute of Child Health
www.eparentingnetwork.ca

Canadian Paediatric Society
www.cps.ca

Centre of Excellence for Early Childhood Development
www.excellence-earlychildhood.ca

Hospital for Sick Children: AboutKidsHealth
www.aboutkidshealth.ca

Invest in Kids
www.investinkids.ca

National Association of Pediatric Nurse Practitioners
www.napnap.org

National Health Information Center: Healthfinder
www.healthfinder.gov

Tufts University Child and Family WebGuide
www.cfw.tufts.edu

Zero to Three: National Center for Infants, Toddlers, and Families
www.zerotothree.org

Kitchen Culture

American Frozen Food Institute: History of Frozen Food
www.affi.com/factstat-history.asp

Cornell University: Hearth—Home Economics Archive
hearth.library.cornell.edu

The Food Museum On-line: Food-Related Toys and Advertising Characters
www.foodmuseum.com/funplay.html

Food Timeline: History Notes—Baby Food
www.foodtimeline.org/foodbaby.html

The Grocery List Collection
www.grocerylists.org

History of the Feeding Bottle
www.babybottle-museum.co.uk

Oldways: Food Issues Think Tank
oldwayspt.org

PBS: The Meaning of Food
www.pbs.org/opb/meaningoffood

Sally's Place: Cookbook Stores
www.sallys-place.com/food/chefs-corner/cookbook_stores.htm

Slowfood.com
www.slowfood.com

Society for Neuroscience Brain Briefings: Taste Intensity
web.sfn.org/content/Publications/BrainBriefings/taste.html

Further Reading

I FOUND THE following books helpful while researching this book. In some cases, the entire book was invaluable. In other cases, one section of the book—or the author's take on one particular subject—was particularly useful. For mini-reviews of many of these books, please visit the book reviews area of Motherofallsolutions.com.

Albert-Ratchford, Theresa. *Cook Once a Week, Eat Well Every Day.* Toronto: HarperCollins Publishers Ltd., 2005.

Barber, Marianne S. *The Parent's Guide to Food Allergies: Clear and Complete Advice on Raising Your Food-Allergic Child.* New York: Owl Books, 2001.

Bissex, Janice Newell, MS, RD, and Liz Weiss, MS, RD. *The Moms' Guide to Meal Makeovers: Improving the Way Your Family Eats, One Meal at a Time!* New York: Broadway Books, 2004.

Bradshaw, Brenda, and Lauren Donaldson Bramley, MD. *The Baby's Table.* Toronto: Random House Canada, 2004.

Collins, Lia Cipriano, MA, MFT. *Caring for Your Child with Severe Food Allergies: Emotional Support and Practical Advice from a Parent Who's Been There.* New York: Wiley Publishing Inc., 2000.

Coss, Linda Marien. *How to Manage Your Child's Life-Threatening Food Allergies.* Lake Forest, CA: Plumtree Press, 2004.

Douglas, Ann. *The Mother of All Baby Books.* New York: Wiley Publishing Inc., 2002.

_____. *The Mother of All Toddler Books.* New York: Wiley Publishing Inc., 2004.

_____. *The Mother of All Parenting Books.* New York: Wiley Publishing Inc., 2004.

_____. *Sleep Solutions for Your Baby, Toddler and Preschooler: The Ultimate No-Worry Approach for Each Age and Stage.* New York: Wiley Publishing Inc., 2006.

Ely, Leanne. *Healthy Foods: An Irreverent Guide to Understanding Nutrition and Feeding Your Family Well.* Belgium, WI: Champion Press, 2001.

Ernsperger, Lori, PhD and Tania Stegen-Hanson, OTRIL. *Just Take a Bite: Easy, Effective Answers to Food Aversions and Eating Challenges!* Arlington, TX: Future Horizons, 2004.

Fish, Donna. *Take the Fight Out of Food: How to Prevent and Solve Your Child's Eating Problems.* New York: Atria Books, 2005.

Giles, Fiona. *Fresh Milk: The Secret Life of Breasts.* New York: Simon & Schuster, 2003.

Givot, Scott. *Kitchen Genius: 500 Tips to Cook Like a Pro.* London: MQ Publications Ltd., 2004.

Gold, Dr. Milton, ed. *The Complete Kid's Allergy and Asthma Guide: The Parent's Handbook for Children of All Ages.* Toronto: Robert Rose Inc., 2003.

Goldfarb, Aviva. *The Six O'Clock Scramble: Quick, Healthy, and Delicious Dinner Recipes for Busy Families.* New York: St. Martin's Griffin, 2006.

Hill, Rachael Anne. *Healthy Food for Kids: Quick Recipes for Busy Parents.* New York: Ryland, Peters, and Small, 2005.

Joachim, David, et al. *Brilliant Food Tips and Cooking Tricks: 5,000 Ingenious Kitchen Hints, Secrets, Shortcuts, and Solutions.* New York: Rodale Inc., 2001.

Kalnins, Daina, RD, and Joanne Saab, RD. *The Hospital for Sick Children Better Baby Food: Your Essential Guide to Nutrition, Feeding & Cooking for All Babies & Toddlers.* Toronto: Robert Rose Inc., 2001.

Karmel, Annabel. *First Meals: Fast, Healthy, and Fun Foods for Infants and Toddlers.* New expanded edition. New York: Dorling Kindersley, 2004.

Lambert-Lagacé, Louise. *Feeding Your Preschooler: Tasty Nutrition for Kids Two to Six.* Reprint. Toronto: Stoddart Publishing Co. Limited, 1999.

Legere, Henry, MD. *Raising Healthy Eaters: 100 Tips for Parents.* Cambridge, MA: Da Capo Press, 2004.

Linardakis, Connie. *Homemade Baby Food Pure and Simple: Your Complete Guide to Preparing Easy, Nutritious, and Delicious Meals for Your Baby and Toddler.* New York: Three Rivers Press, 2001.

McClendonn, M. Ed, Marie, and Cristy Shauck. *The Healthy Lunchbox: How to Plan, Prepare, and Pack Stress-Free Meals Kids Will Love.* Alexandria, VA: Small Steps Press, 2005.

Mendelson, Cheryl. *Home Comforts: The Art & Science of Keeping House.* New York: Scribner, 1999.

Mendelson, Susan, and Rena Mendelson. *Food to Grow on: Give Your Kids a Healthy Lifestyle for Keeps.* Revised. Toronto: HarperCollins Publishers Ltd., 2005.

Miller, Jan. *Kid Favorites Made Healthy: 150 Delicious Recipes Kids Can't Resist!* New York: Meredith Books, 2003.

Mohrbacher, Nancy, IBCLC, and Kathleen Kendall-Tackett, PhD, IBCLC. *Breastfeeding Made Simple: Seven Natural Laws for Nursing Mothers.* Oakland, CA: New Harbinger, 2005.

Moll, Lucy. *The Vegetarian Child: A Complete Guide for Parents.* New York: Perigee Books, 1997.

Newman, Dr. Jack, and Edith Kernerman. *Dr. Jack Newman's Visual Guide to Breastfeeding: The Best Visual Guide for Mothers and Health-Care Professionals.* Toronto: Planting Seeds Productions, 2005. (DVD)

Newman, Dr. Jack, and Teresa Pitman. *Dr. Jack Newman's Guide to Breastfeeding*. Toronto: HarperCollins Publishers Ltd., 2003.

Olivier, Suzannah. *What Should I Feed My Baby?: The Complete Nutrition Guide from Birth to Two Years*. London: The Orion Publishing Group, 2003.

Olson, Cathe. *Simply Natural Baby Food: Easy Recipes for Delicious Meals Your Infant and Toddler Will Love*. Arroyo Grande, CA: Goco Publishing, 2003.

Omichinski, Linda, RD, and Heather Wiebe Hildebrand, RN. *Tailoring Your Tastes*. Winnipeg: Tamos Books Inc., 1995.

Parsons, Russ. *How to Read a French Fry and Other Stories of Intriguing Kitchen Science*. New York: Houghton Mifflin Company, 2001.

Pearson, Liz, RD, and Mairlyn Smith. *The Ultimate Healthy Eating Plan That Still Leaves Room for Chocolate*. Vancouver: Whitecap Books Ltd., 2002.

Peel, Kathy. *The Family Manager Takes Charge: Getting on the Fast Track to a Happy, Organized Home*. New York: Perigee Books, 2003.

Physicians Committee for Responsible Medicine. *Healthy Eating for Life for Children*. New York: John Wiley & Sons, Inc., 2002.

Pica, Rae. *Your Active Child: How to Boost Physical, Emotional, and Cognitive Development through Age-Appropriate Activity*. New York: McGraw-Hill Companies, Inc., 2003.

Pruess, Joanna. *Supermarket Confidential: The Secrets of One-Stop Shopping for Delicious Meals*. Guilford: The Lyons Press, 2004.

Ray, Rachael. *Rachael Ray's 30-Minute Meals for Kids: Cooking Rocks!* New York: Lake Isle Press, 2004.

Roblin, Lynn, RD, and Bev Callaghan, RD. *Suppertime Survival*. Toronto: Suppertime Survival, 2005.

Satter, Ellyn. *How to Get Your Kid to Eat...But Not Too Much.* Boulder: Bull Publishing Company, 1987.

_____. *Secrets of Feeding a Healthy Family.* Madison, WI: Kelcy Press, 1999.

_____. *Child of Mine: Feeding with Love and Good Sense.* Palo Alto, CA: Bull Publishing Company, 2000.

Shield, Jodie, RD, and Mary Catherine Mullen, RD. *American Dietetic Association Guide to Healthy Eating for Kids: How Your Children Can Eat Smart from 5 to 12.* Hoboken, NJ: John Wiley & Sons, Inc., 2002.

Tamaro, Janet. *So That's What They're for: The Definitive Breastfeeding Guide.* 3rd edition. Avon, MA: Adams Media, 2005.

Tamborlane, William V., MD, ed. *The Yale Guide to Children's Nutrition.* New Haven: Yale University Press, 1997.

Walker, W. Allan. *Eat, Play, and Be Healthy: The Harvard Medical School Guide to Healthy Eating for Kids.* New York: McGraw-Hill, 2005.

Welch, Michael J., MD, ed. *American Academy of Pediatrics Guide to Your Child's Allergies and Asthma.* Toronto: Random House of Canada Limited, 2000.

Yaron, Ruth. *Super Baby Food.* 2nd edition, revised. Peckville, PA: F.J. Roberts Publishing Company, 1998.

Young, Nicole, and Nadine Day, RD. *Blender Baby Food: Over 125 Recipes for Healthy Homemade Meals.* Toronto: Robert Rose, Inc., 2005.

Yummy in My Tummy: 6–12 Months Good Eating Habits for Life. Montréal: The Liandrea Company Inc., 2006. (DVD)

Index

K

kangaroo care, 19, 24, 32
Kendall-Tackett, Kathleen, 17, 19
kidney beans, 220, 224
kitchens, 75, 168–169, 171
kites, 156
kiwi fruits, 216
knives, 101

L

labels, ingredient, 239–240
lactation aids, 24, 31, 39
lactose intolerance
  cause of, 209
  diarrhea causing, 206
  formula feeding and, 49
  preschoolers and, 139
  toddlers and, 111
lasagna, 229
latch
  flat or inverted nipples and, 27
  inadequate milk supply and, 25
  position and, 18–19, 27
  refusing to eat and, 24
laxative effect of juices, 119
legumes. *See* beans and legumes
lentils
  adding tastes and textures, 85, 91
  iron in, 122
  meal ideas, 228
  purée preparation, 220, 224
lethargy, 206, 210
lettuce, 230
lima beans, 218
limits, setting, 103, 104
lips, 209, 211
liver paté, 112
low-fat foods, 83, 111, 139, 149
lox, 72
lunch, 136–137, 228, 232
luncheon meats, 72, 85, 117
lymphoma, 13

M

macaroni and cheese, 228
macaroni salad, 187
mangoes, 67, 216, 223
manners, 132
mashed foods, 81, 87, 225
massages, 69

mastitis, 28
meals
  atmosphere of, 129, 145
  distractions, 107–108
  eating at table, 119
  family dinners, 179–181
  involving children in preparation, 189
  planning, 161–165
  predictable times of, 102
  preparation of, 171–178
  rules, 198–199
  size of, 136–137
  snacks and, 120
  special meals, 197
  time limits, 109
  See also breakfast; dinner; lunch; snacks
meat
  adding tastes and textures, 85, 86, 91
  creative presentations, 195
  as finger food, 87
  as first food, 55
  handling, 168
  importance of, 122
  preschooler serving sizes, 140
  purée preparation, 220, 224
  rejection of, 112
  risk of, 72
  toddler serving sizes, 114–115
meatballs, 229
meatloaf, 112, 229
medical conditions, 50, 193, 200
MedicAlert bracelets, 69
medications, 16, 26
medicine droppers, 24
melons, 67
Mendelson, Susan and Rena, 129
meningitis, 13
menstrual cycle, 14
menu planning, 161–165
metabolism problems, 50
microwave ovens, 51, 79
milestones, eating
  for babies, 54, 62–63, 67, 90–91, 93
  for preschoolers, 132–134
  for toddlers, 101–104
milk. *See* breast milk; cow's milk
milk, raw, 72, 117